TR 9814825 7

Trafford C

W9-CKA-383

THE
UNFORGIVEN

LIBRARY & IT CENTRE - TRAFFORD COLLEGE			
Date Received			5.6.14
Order Number			Donation
Price			£5.00
Tagged	✓	Tutor	
Section	Fiction	Classmark	796.334
Extension/Spine			BAG
Loan Type	S	Barcode	9801482S7
Catalogued by & Date		FH	12-8-14
Date completed			28.8.14

In May 1972 Paul Rogerson, aged five, was a Liverpool supporter when Leeds United won the FA Cup for the one and only time. He switched allegiance just in time to see Leeds lose to Sunderland the following year. An award-winning business journalist, he is currently Editor-in-Chief of the weekly legal magazine the *Law Society Gazette*.

Rob Bagchi lasted almost as long at Sportspages bookshop as Don Revie spent at Elland Road. He works for the *Guardian*, for whom he writes a weekly sports column, and is the author of four books.

THE STORY OF
DON REVIE'S LEEDS UNITED

ROB BAGCHI AND
PAUL ROGERSON

First published in Great Britain
2002 by Aurum Press Ltd
7 Greenland Street
London NW1 0ND
www.aurumpress.co.uk

This updated edition published in 2009 by Aurum Press Ltd

Copyright © 2002 and 2009 Rob Bagchi and Paul Rogerson

Rob Bagchi and Paul Rogerson have asserted their moral right to be identified as
the Authors of this Work in accordance with the Copyright Designs and Patents
Act 1988.

All rights reserved. No part of this book may be reproduced or utilised in any form
or by any means, electronic or mechanical, including photocopying, recording or
by any information storage and retrieval system, without permission in writing
from Aurum Press Ltd.

A catalogue record for this book is available from the British Library.

ISBN 978 1 84513 470 9

7 9 10 8 6
2011 2013 2012

Designed in Swift Light 10/14pt by Geoff Green
Printed by CPI Bookmarque, Croydon

CONTENTS

FOREWORD TO THE 2009 EDITION

'Don Revie made Leeds United, plank by careful plank, ushering boys towards greatness, buying with brilliant judgment and always building to last – welding talent to talent, spirit to spirit, to attain tremendous collective strength.' Hugh McIlvanney, 1975

Don Revie OBE, the first Footballer of the Year to graduate as Manager of the Year, is the black sheep in the game's hall of fame. No manager of his calibre and record has a smaller constituency of advocates and yet the evidence in this book stakes out a claim for greatness on his and his team's behalf that stands in the face of thirty years of muck-raking and innuendo about their venality.

The role he played in engendering the modern game is also largely forgotten. He boiled down his approach to being the father of the Leeds United family, saying time and again that 'I look on every one of them at this club as my own son'. But there was more to him than this modest job description. He turned a provincial Second Division side from what was then still a parochial city into arguably the best team in England for a decade from 1965. For a time he even made the city synonymous with his football club. He achieved this by training the players, devising the on-field strategy, scouting the best prospects in Britain, persuading them to join his crusade, designing the kit they played in, sorting out their finances and vetting their girlfriends. On any given day he was consigliere, masseur, dietician, transport manager and coach.

In essence he was the alpha and omega of Leeds United. He built a great team but he may be said to have failed to create a great club because the system and structure he developed depended entirely on him. United's rise as England's finest squad could not have happened without him. Great teams, however, grow old. Great clubs have stronger foundations. By doing almost everything himself, Revie had become indispensable – as the Leeds board found to their cost when they repaid his service by giving his job to the man in football who hated him most.

These authors' first encounter with Brian Clough was fleeting but instructive. It came on 11 September 1974, outside Leeds Road, the then home of Huddersfield Town. It was Paul Rogerson's first away match – a League Cup tie. He was just seven years old.

Four months earlier Leeds United, under Don Revie, had ascended a peak of excellence then unprecedented in English football, remaining unbeaten for twenty-nine consecutive league matches on the way to the First Division Championship. But even then the team had appeared uneasily conscious of what was already a cliché – that when it really mattered, when the summit was in sight, Leeds would stumble and fall. Reverting to type, a string of late-season defeats saw Leeds come close to handing the title to Bill Shankly's Liverpool, who would soon assume the mantle of the nation's best team.

Not that this was apparent to the young Paul Rogerson on that particular day. The Elland Road board, renowned even in Leeds for their provincial circumspection, had acted completely out of character by recruiting as Revie's replacement a man who avowedly loathed both Revie and United. But that man was also brilliant, precocious and careless of reputations; the mirror image of the team he had taken over. If anyone could replace a group of players who were growing old together, it was surely he: Brian Howard Clough.

That it was not to be should have been apparent even to a seven-year-old, poised as he was with his autograph book by the door of the Wallace Arnold coach (it had to be Wallace Arnold), from which Clough disembarked. *Private Eye* coined the ever-present appendage 'ashen-faced' for its managerial stereotype Ron Knee and it would be an apt description of Clough at that moment. He appeared so out of sorts he might have been ill. Pallid and tight-lipped, he swept into the stadium without looking anyone in the eye. Not what we had been led to expect at all. Revie's players trooped in behind him, equally sullen and impassive. There was clearly trouble at t'mill.

Paul recalls the moment so clearly now only because of what came later. In the early evening of 30 May 1979, the authors of this book, both now twelve, were crouched in a chilly caravan on the East Yorkshire coast watching a small black-and-white television with mounting alarm. Nottingham Forest, even less fashionable than United had been (though never so hated), were about to become only the third English club to win the European Cup.

It was the bitterest moment of their lives as football supporters. Four years earlier a performance of scandalous refereeing had stolen that same trophy from Leeds, as surely as if Franz Beckenbauer had slipped it into his Adidas holdall before the whistle went at the Parc des Princes in Paris. But this time we only had ourselves to blame. It really should have been us.

David Peace's recent novel, *The Damned United*, which re-imagines Clough's infamous forty-four day debacle at Elland Road, essentially taps into the same vein of anger, blame and recrimination that this book did when it was first published. To this day Leeds United are indeed 'damned'; unforgiven by the footballing fates for the sins of Don Revie and his team, whether real or imagined. The image that adorns the original cover of Peace's book, that of Clough leading out Revie's team before the 1974 Charity Shield, seems in retrospect to presage so much that was to come: hands clasped behind his back, Clough looks like the chief undertaker at the head of a funeral cortege.

Before you dismiss this contention as fanciful, even pretentious, consider the facts. Howard Wilkinson's first act on becoming manager in 1988, when the club was foundering at the wrong end of the Second Division, was to order the removal of all pictures of Revie and his players from Elland Road. What was this but a public exorcism? Three decades before Gypsy Rose Lee, a promenade fortune teller who had appropriated the famous stripper's name, came to Elland Road at Revie's invitation. She asked everyone apart from the manager to leave the ground, stood in the centre circle and scratched the grass, scattered some seeds and visited all four corners of the pitch before informing Revie over a cup of tea that the jinx he felt had caused his team's bad luck had been lifted. In the same office that Revie talked of hoodoos and hexes that had to be banished, Wilkinson clearly saw his predecessor's legacy and the club's tendency to seek solace in nostalgia as the curse he himself had to purge.

What's more it seemed to work, at least for a while, as Wilkinson delivered promotion and then the First Division Championship. To some it no doubt seemed fitting that he had replaced Revie's beloved captain, Billy Bremner – that coiled and crabby personification of his managerial style on the field of play.

It was a false dawn. The 1992 title remains Leeds United's sole meaningful achievement of the last 35 years, an extraordinary record of failure for a club with such a large and diffuse support. If you doubt the latter, consider that even today leedsunited.com is the third most-visited club website in English football, after those of Manchester United and Liverpool. Even in Division Three, a lot of people still care.

It is not so much that those same footballing fates put in the knife, but also that they twist it. Forest won the European Cup with two players at the heart of the team who Brian Clough had previously signed for Leeds – only for them to be derided as markedly inferior to Bremner and Mick Jones. Those players were John McGovern and John O'Hare. How sweet it must have been for them.

Even during the club's rare moments of triumph, Nemesis was never far away. Eric Cantona became an adored talisman as his irresistible cameos helped propel Leeds to their third title. He went on to score a hat-trick at Wembley as Leeds beat Liverpool in the 1992 Charity Shield. And then – what? 'Wait a minute,' someone must have said: 'Aren't Leeds supposed to be dour and utilitarian?' So Leeds sold him. For next to nothing – to Manchester United. Who immediately won their first title for twenty-six years, thereby establishing a domestic hegemony that endures to this day. The worst transfer decision in British football history? You be the judge.

Wilkinson was sacked in 1996 following a humiliating 4-0 home drubbing by . . . Manchester United. And yes, Cantona scored. Of course he did.

The present volume is too slim to describe in any detail the torturous decline of the Peter Ridsdale era and its aftermath, when Leeds United's capacity for self-harm moved from the changing room to the boardroom. Suffice to say that two members of that side were Lee Bowyer and Jonathan Woodgate and its manager was the aspiring author David O'Leary. Oh, and the executive chairman was the kind of guy who rents goldfish.

And so, two relegations later, with the stadium and training ground sold off to relieve debts, Leeds tread water in a division to which they had never previously sunk. And ignominy continues to be piled on ignominy. Histon, a village which most Leeds fans could not place on a map, recently bundled United out of the FA Cup. No one but an excitable ITV commentator was at all surprised.

Today the chairman is Ken Bates, whose comically abrasive nature somehow suits the club's reputation for put-upon bellicosity. Approaching 80 and resident in Monaco, one wonders whether Bates truly knew what he was letting himself in for. He found out soon enough, with play-off final defeats against Watford (Championship) and Doncaster Rovers (League One) that were so one-sided as to be embarrassing. Over 50,000 Leeds supporters showed up for the latter Wembley showpiece, thousands of them accommodated in the Doncaster end. When tickets ran out at Elland Road amid chaotic scenes, Rovers had to close their own ticket office after it was inundated by opposition fans.

If anything leavens what is not a particularly uplifting story, it is this. Still they come, and in large numbers, seemingly inured to failure. Half a century after Don Revie arrived at Leeds, initially as a player, he would have been perplexed by this. One of his great bugbears was the complacency with which the Leeds public appeared to regard his team's success; crowds for lower-profile games were often disappointing, even when the club was chasing the title.

He, however, would have been the first to see the essential difference between the Second Division club with no history he took on and the one marooned in the third tier with unrealised, possibly unrealisable, potential that bears its name. It is only because of what he built, and what was long since dismantled, that the club's support is so substantial. Unforgiven still, we know that only renewed success will bring redemption.

Rob Bagchi and Paul Rogerson
January 2009

THE LEEDS UNITED FAMILY

Barry Davies is not a man to condone violence. But on 17 April 1971 the normally polished *Match of the Day* commentator came dangerously close.

Needing a win against West Bromwich Albion to draw away from the nagging challenge of Bertie Mee's Arsenal side, Don Revie's Leeds United are already 1–0 down. Then, a poor ball from Norman Hunter cannons off Tony Brown into the Leeds half, where Albion's Colin Suggett is loitering at least 15 yards offside. More in hope than expectation, Brown continues his charge towards goal, and linesman Bill Troupe duly raises his flag. So transparent is the offence that there is a moment of suspended animation while players on both sides wait for referee Ray Tinkler to blow his whistle. He does not. An almost apologetic Brown continues on towards the Leeds goal before squaring for Jeff Astle to execute a simple tap-in. Astle, smirking and still half-expecting the referee to see sense, jogs back to the halfway line. A decision of almost baroque incompetence has cost Don Revie and Leeds United the championship.

As the truth dawns that Tinkler has given the goal, Elland Road explodes with rage. There follows one of English football's most bizarre pitch invasions. A handful of spectators, many of them advancing in years, emerge from the packed stands to remonstrate with Tinkler, who is now surrounded by burly policemen. One bewhiskered invader is nattily attired in what is surely a Burton's blazer. This is Leeds after all. A breathless Davies is as incredulous as the players: 'Leeds will go mad,' he shouts, 'and they have every justification for going mad!' If only momentarily, Tinkler's personal safety appears to be in jeopardy. Twenty years later, Johnny Giles is still indignant: 'They weren't hooligans, they were grown men. How he could give the goal there, I just don't know.' Don Revie, stunned that a season's graft has been undone by one single individual, walks on to protest but appears to think better of it. Hunched in a blue gabardine raincoat and chewing fiercely, he gazes skywards in disbelief. He has seen it all before. Davies, screaming now to be heard above the crowd, sympathizes. 'Don Revie, a sickened man,' he yells. 'Just look at him, looking at the heavens in disgust!'

Utter the words 'that bastard Tinkler' to any Leeds fan over a certain age and you'll meet with instant recognition. That infamous afternoon has come to encapsulate the Revie era, when one of the greatest club sides English football has ever produced ran the gauntlet of official obduracy, media disapprobation and ill fortune of some-times grotesque proportions.

Barry Davies, mindful of the displays of genius he was lucky enough to be paid to watch, was normally an honourable exception. Just two months earlier he had looked on enraptured as Leeds had demolished Southampton. They hadn't merely won 7–0: they had finished up playing a humiliating game of keep-ball with their cowed opponents. 'Leeds are putting on a show, and poor old Southampton just don't know what day it is,' Davies enthuses. 'It's almost cruel.' The television sequence is one of the most famous in the history of British football.

These days the stadium junkie Simon Inglis can justifiably – and memorably – describe Leeds' Elland Road stadium as '(looming) into vision like a giant industrial combine'. This dramatic if absurdly symmetrical complex is a monument as much to that simple decision to appoint Don Revie as manager of Leeds United, as to the influx of TV cash into the elite football clubs in the 1990s. Indeed, since the death of John Charles, who used to attend most home matches and could usually be spotted in the unpretentious concourse bar conceived to honour him, there is no evidence of anything pre-Revie at Elland Road except for a bust of the Gentle Giant that adorns a banqueting suite in a stand which now bears his name.

Revie, quite simply, did not save Leeds United, for when he took over there was not much worth saving. He made them. Not in the way that Shankly and Busby spectacularly revived the fortunes of temporarily moribund institutions, nor in the way that Kevin Keegan effectively rebranded Newcastle United in the early 1990s. He built Leeds from scratch, systematically, and with no history, culture or real constituency to fall back on.

The forty years since the establishment of the club in 1919 was one long false start, a kind of 'phoney war'. If its one-year apprenticeship in non-league football had come in the mid-1950s rather than in 1919, it is debatable whether it would have made any significant difference to the club's future success. While it is ironic that John Charles, still United's most celebrated player, was the star of this pre-Revie respite, those first forty years have had no impact on the club nor its sense of itself. It was Revie and Revie alone who made the club, its profile and, most importantly, the self-image that continues to predominate to this day.

But Don Revie was also a remarkably idiosyncratic individual. That he should appeal to the gods for succour when Tinkler sabotaged his season was entirely in character. Deeply superstitious, he wore a 'lucky blue suit' for important matches and carried a rabbit's foot with him into the dugout. On home match days he would stroll to a particular set of traffic lights near the ground and then exactly retrace his steps, convinced that this odd ritual would swing the game his way. In the early 1960s Revie arranged for the exorcism of a mythical 'gipsy's curse' from Elland Road, apparently imposed when a Romany community were evicted from the South Leeds scrubland where the stadium would stand. Later he would betray his fear of all feathered creatures by banishing the club's emblem, a peacock, from shirt badges.

By the po-faced 1990s eccentricities of this nature could get you the sack, at least if you were the England manager. However, this was a more colourful era, when English football was still primarily a sport arousing animal passions and not a conduit for flogging overpriced nylon to south-east Asia. Everyone thinks fondly of Bill Shankly and his gnomic philosophizing, or Malcolm Allison – an acquaintance of the Kray twins – and his Cup-tie fedoras. Yet to characterize Revie as a fanciful man would be spectacularly inaccurate. He was, in fact, an arch-pragmatist, for whom devoted acolytes would compose extensive 'dossiers' on the club's opponents ahead of match day. Whether that pragmatism was, in truth, cynicism in another guise is partly what this book is about.

As far as his players were concerned, Revie was deeply conventional, searching out men with stable family lives who wouldn't give him trouble. His nickname, 'The Don', was entirely appropriate, as he set to create a clannish, collegiate atmosphere within the club itself. Pre-match stresses were eased by sessions of bingo and carpet bowls, among men who would play and socialize alongside each other year after year. None of Revie's protégés, one could safely say – unlike the sainted Becks and his fragrant wife – would have considered receiving guests on a gold throne after taking their marriage vows.

When Revie arrived, Leeds were unfashionable and provincial in outlook, and had spent forty years skipping between the top two divisions to little effect. The club was to provide the perfect environment for Revie's brand of bellicose introversion. On the wall in the Home dressing room he hung up a sign that read: 'Keep Fighting'. The club's directors, meanwhile, persisted in playing the part of rag-and-bone men who'd been made a free gift of a thoroughbred. Their gaucheness was to cost Leeds dear once the talisman had gone.

Eight years ago, on the death of the legendary Manchester United manager Matt Busby, a minute's silence was held, and impeccably observed, at league grounds across the country. But not at Ewood Park, Blackburn. There, hundreds of away supporters from Leeds disrupted the tribute by chanting 'There's only one Don Revie' throughout. Only four years had passed since Italia '90, when Gazza and Pavarotti made watching football a respectable leisure activity. No one wanted to be reminded of the tribal loathing that had turned watching the game in the 1980s into a form of social leprosy.

A leader in the *Independent* summed up the national mood: 'The failure of Leeds fans to honour football's dead properly should be seen for what it symbolises: a nastiness that has in the past besmirched football's reputation and remains latent.' The club was hugely embarrassed. Manager Howard Wilkinson declared himself 'numb'; the perpetrators were 'out of touch with the rest of football'. Chairman Leslie Silver vowed to ban them for life. And Revie's widow, Elsie, said Don would have been 'horrified' by the fans' behaviour had he still been alive.

Those supporters deserved their comeuppance, and not only for their lack of respect for Busby. Revie's name was dragged through the mud, along with that of Leeds United. But much of the criticism was disingenuous. No one who truly understands what it has meant to be a Leeds supporter over the age of thirty should have been remotely surprised by the episode.

Ask the supporters of other clubs to name the great British managers of the game's 'golden age' and they recite a familiar list: Busby, Shankly, Stein, Clough, Nicholson, Catterick. Revie's name will be mentioned grudgingly, if at all. So why did those 'morons' (Joe Lovejoy) step so far beyond the pale? Because Leeds fans loath Manchester United? Not really. They did it because outside West Yorkshire, Revie's own achievements, though they stand comparison with those of any English manager, have been largely forgotten. Only Brian Clough can also claim to have turned an unfashionable, provincial club into a European colossus. But Revie and Leeds United just weren't liked. They may have been gifted, but they were also rough, cynical and utilitarian; even today they remain unforgiven.

It is a truism among journalists softened by the passage of years that Don Revie's team did not gain the plaudits it deserved. The same, it is more rarely acknowledged, is true of the man himself. Revie's abandonment of the England job in 1977 sharpened the pen of scribes already ill-disposed towards him, and many remain unsympathetic even now. One renowned football writer, in a recent encomium to Bill Shankly, added as an aside that his principal adversary Don

Revie was 'forgotten everywhere outside Leeds'. Paeans to late 1960s and early 70s football in the lads' magazines routinely talk of Clough, Busby, Stein and Shankly, with barely a nod to Leeds. Yet to talk about this era without devoting a large chunk of the narrative to Don Revie is like trying to talk about the Bodyline series without mentioning Douglas Jardine. For such observers the mantra that must be repeated, with scant consideration of the era in which the team played, is still 'dirty Leeds'. Yes, Leeds had Norman 'Bite yer Legs' Hunter; but Chelsea had Ron 'Chopper' Harris, and Liverpool had Tommy Smith. You didn't get sent off for kicking the ball away back then and Leeds weren't the only team who took note. As Barry Davies recognized, there was cruelty, but there was much beauty, too.

As this book recounts, Revie's achievements were phenomenal, even though his team so often stumbled at the final hurdle. Ironically, perhaps only Brian Clough, Revie's successor and his most outspoken detractor, can be said to have surpassed them. While at Nottingham Forest, he too turned a formerly insignificant club into a European powerhouse, winning the European Cup that Revie had craved. Revie's team did make it to the final of that competition when their mentor had gone, but again they were to be unjustly denied by eccentric refereeing.

Since Revie left Leeds almost thirty-five years ago, the club has almost bankrupted itself trying to emulate his success. Fourteen managers have come and gone, ex-players among them, but the club has managed only one major honour, the 1992 Division One title. It is not a coincidence that the man who broke the cycle of failure, Howard Wilkinson, made it a priority to banish all pictures of cup-toting players from the Revie era. He recognized a club living on past glories, and for that every Leeds supporter should be grateful.

Even now, Leeds United remains a modern enigma: there is still something manufactured about them – the club from nowhere. How a team from this rugby league city, deep in the heart of a cricket-mad county with no discernible football tradition, managed to propel itself to the very pinnacle of the European game is not simply the story of one man and his peculiar obsessions.

Revie, as 'Svengali', was intrinsic to Leeds' emergence, but like Sir Alex Ferguson after him, he was fortunate to prosper from an extraordinary crop of young talent at his disposal. Yet the virtuosity of these players tends to be neglected. Even Leeds fans tend to focus on the retro-kitsch of the Revie era – the Scratching Shed, the Kids' Pen, the sock tags and the 'smiley' badge – rather than the men behind it. Others focus on less benign images: the popular perception of Leeds in the 1960s and 70s has been formed not least by one single game, the 1970 FA Cup Final Replay against Chelsea, probably the most notoriously violent game in English football history, in which for two hours a recklessly indulgent referee permitted foul after foul to go unpunished and long-standing personal vendettas to be fought out. Though both sides were equally culpable, Leeds were to elicit little sympathy after their extra-time defeat. Here was proof of the rumours that had circulated for years: that they were a particularly cynical and lawless team. It would take three more years, with a team in its dotage playing fluent attacking football, for them finally to be appreciated.

The Cup Final song has become a tawdry annual custom but Leeds' 1972 version, 'Leeds United', at least attempted to publicize the remarkable skill and character of Revie's players. Set to a bizarre brass and piccolo accompaniment, the Leeds squad overcame their initial embarrassment to belt out this eulogy to themselves.

Each player is spotlighted for at least a line, most notably Billy Bremner, who is characterized as a 'red-headed tiger... who goes like a human dynamo', and Paul Madeley, famous for his versatility, who is portrayed as 'the eleven Pauls'. Although the other side of this single, 'Leeds, Leeds, Leeds', has long been adopted by Leeds fans as their official anthem, it is this obscure composition that first promoted the players as individuals and not as Revie's well drilled, efficient and merciless machine.

It is true, on the whole, that they were like-minded souls, and with one or two exceptions their camaraderie has endured. But first and foremost they were a group of individuals with diverse temperaments, opinions and ambitions. There was Jack Charlton, the garrulous senior pro with his fabled 'black book', supposedly for recording the names of those players who merited physical retribution. Formerly an ill-disciplined journeyman stopper, both irascible and argumentative, he flourished under Revie's coaxing to become the defensive lynchpin of England's 1966 World Cup triumph. However, his fundamental nature hardly changed. He remains the same engaging, implacably single-minded soul he was in the 1950s.

His conspicuous self-confidence is in marked contrast with Gary Sprake, the mythically error-prone goalkeeper. Only months before his death, Revie was to concede that Leeds would undoubtedly have won more if he had replaced the insouciant Welshman earlier. This is harsh. While Sprake lacked confidence and had made several blatantly ghastly mistakes, his agility and ability were never in question. Indeed, he played over 500 games for the club, picking up five medals along the way. Not a bad return for the man who was habitually taunted by the Liverpool Kop with their rendition of 'Careless Hands'.

The emotional fulcrum of the team was its midfield pairing of Billy Bremner and Johnny Giles. The late Billy Bremner was seen to personify Revie's Leeds, yet his aggression and pronounced unwillingness to admit defeat masked a fine football brain and a prodigious array of skills. Though quick in the tackle, he was so much more than a spoiler. Bremner could dictate the game with his sophisticated and accurate passing, and, with his seemingly boundless energy, he often linked up with the attack to score spectacular and crucial goals. As Revie's captain, he was thought to enjoy a 'father and son' relationship with his manager, but he, too, remained his own man. A heavy smoker, he often went boozing with Jack Charlton contrary to Revie's wishes, and thought little of rowing with his boss over discipline and tactics.

Johnny Giles was more worldly and, having been brought up at

Old Trafford, less susceptible to Revie's paternalistic methods. Yet it was to prove the ideal match as he channelled his grievances with Manchester United, where he felt under-utilized and mistrusted, into becoming a formidable, if sometimes ruthless, professional. His ingenious style and lithe grace helped him become a world-class player, while his current status as one of the most respected journalists in Britain and Ireland confirms his articulate savvy. In Hilton's homage he was simply 'The Brains'. But he also had a sly and malicious side. When a young Frank Worthington, playing for Leicester City in the early 1970s, attempted to nutmeg Giles, he was assailed with, 'Take the piss out of me or Leeds United ever again and I'll break your fucking leg for you!' Worthington later claimed that this was the most disgraceful thing ever to have been said to him on a football field.

Others, too, could show this malevolent streak. Paul Reaney is often cited by George Best as the toughest and dirtiest opponent he ever faced. On the television footage of Leeds' 1972 FA Cup Final victory, as Arsenal line up a free kick, Allan Clarke's hand disappears behind Charlie George's back and delivers a ferocious tug to his flowing locks. Was this a blow on behalf of short-back-and-sides Yorkshire anti-fashion, or just another spot of gamesmanship?

All this has been dwelt upon at tiresome length by Leeds' numerous detractors. The plain truth has to be faced: if the opposition wanted to fight, Leeds would fight. If they wanted to play, then Leeds would play. To say they were simply too gifted to have to resort to such tactics disregards the prevailing football climate and Leeds' vehement will to win.

What this book attempts to do is to redress the balance: to acknowledge Leeds' faults and examine them in the light of 1970s football, as well as from the rosy perspective of thirty-five years' hindsight. But we will also bring the individual players themselves out of the hoary hinterland to which they have been condemned for their supposed villainy, while footballers of the so-called 'maverick' era who could execute pointless trick after pointless trick but never won anything are hailed as lost English heroes. So 'Here we go with Leeds United', as Les Reed put it, to reassess 'Top Cat' Cooper, 'Lasher' Lorimer, Eddie 'The Last Waltz' Gray *et al*, and see what made them tick and what made their turbulent journey so memorable.

ONE

YORKSHIRE'S
REPUBLICAN ARMY

o English provincial city has changed in recent years as much as Leeds. In the years following the millennium the self-styled 'fastest growing city in the UK' became a financial services powerhouse second only to London. Smart, premium-priced loft apartments replaced the derelict mills that once overlooked the Leeds-Liverpool canal. Chic restaurants and expensive themed bars supplanted the down-at-heel boozers where it was frowned upon to ask for lager on draught.

Alan Bennett's bittersweet tableaux of Leeds life in the 1940s – where tight-knit communities lived in back-to-back streets with identikit names – now seem like curious museum pieces. Poverty remains, of course, as, in some places, do the back-to-backs. But to the city's burghers they are redolent of the past and no longer central to the city's perception of itself. This groundshift in the structure of the local economy has only recently reached its apogee in the last few years, with the high-profile opening of Harvey Nichols' department store – the first outside London – the success of hip hotels like Hotel 24 and the White Rose rail service to London with its sleek Eurostar trains. Yet the process actually began before World War II. The share of the local labour force employed by the three largest industries in 1911 – tailoring, engineering and textiles – had fallen from 45 per cent to 30 per cent by 1951, and although half the workforce remained in manufacturing, over two-fifths were by then in service jobs.

Manufacturing continued to decline rapidly, slowing growth in total employment. However, the city was remarkably prosperous before the recession of the mid-1970s. Unemployment stood at less than 1 per cent in the boom years of 1955, 1961 and 1965, and job vacancies exceeded numbers employed. This relative affluence greatly increased leisure opportunities, but the fact that these were increasingly home-centred had its downside. By the year of Revie's appointment as manager, over three-quarters of Leeds households had television sets. But TV rang the death knell for the Theatre Royal (which closed in 1957) and the Leeds Empire (shut down in 1961). Cinema after cinema also gave up the ghost, though many of these arresting buildings remain, housing carpet warehouses and bingo halls.

Eating out, too, had become more diverse, with more exotic fare to be found alongside that great Leeds institution, Nash's Elizabethan Fish and Chip Restaurant. One guide to the city published in 1961 noted that the best cuisine in town was to be found at the Queen's, Metropole and Parkway hotels. (This advice was not lost on Don Revie, who was once spied by Alan Bennett waiting by the door to the Queen's' kitchens. 'He uses the Queen's Hotel as a takeaway,' the dramatist breathlessly noted in his diary.) Though the city was thriving economically, architecturally it was at its nadir. Many of the great Victorian and Edwardian buildings were being torn up along with the tramlines as the vulgarians in the city's Planning Department knelt down before the god of poured concrete.

The journalist Don Watson grew up in Leeds during the 1960s and 70s and sees the changing urban landscape of his home town as the quintessential city of the era. 'Leeds was the apotheosis of the seventies,' he wrote in *My Favourite Year*. 'After all it was here that the outdoor scenes of *A Clockwork Orange*, the film whose aesthetic defined the decade, were shot. The concrete stanchions and flyovers of the self-styled Motorway City of the seventies were breaking through the shell of the Victorian textile city like the skeleton of some grotesquely beautiful insect in a futuristic horror movie.' Much had been achieved in the name of progress. The startling Quarry Hill Flats, housing 3000 people on a 23-acre site only ten minutes walk from Leeds' most fashionable streets, dominated the city skyline.

When completed in 1938, they had taken hundreds of families out of the squalid tenements that bordered the city centre. By 1961 they were already obsolete, the Council having to fork out £500,000 to bolster the corroded steel infrastructure in the hope of eking out just another ten years' life. The lesson of this doomed project did not stop the philistinism flourishing for the next two decades, with the planners' beloved boxy, concrete structures completely overshadowing the sorry, soot-encrusted Victorian monuments that, once saved from the demolition derby and sandblasted clean, would form the heart of the city's shopping theme park thirty years later.

In the 1970s Leeds United's slump on the football field was mirrored in a decline in the quality of the city's nightlife. Leeds acquired a reputation as a late-night haunt of tramps and alcoholics as the dance halls and all-night coffee bars faded away. Until the late 1980s it was common for coach-loads of revellers to travel to nearby Wakefield, which at that time had a far more vibrant pub-and-club scene. In 1961, though, Leeds was already the '24-hour city' that the City Council has bragged about so much in recent years. Jimmy Savile cut his teeth as one of the country's first disc jockeys at the Mecca Ballroom in the County Arcade in the late 1950s and early 60s. The doormen back then were just as belligerent, the only difference being that 'no fucking trainers' seems to have replaced 'Piss off, Elvis' as their war cry. Even Teddy Boys shrank before them. They used to pay 6d to have their sideburns shaved to the regulation length lest they breached the Mecca's strict sartorial code.

If anyone had said in 1961 that the city's football club would soon become the most famous thing about Leeds, they would surely have left themselves open to ridicule. With three Rugby League clubs – Bramley, Leeds and Hunslet – and the domineering presence of Yorkshire County Cricket Club at Headingley, Leeds United had never managed to make inroads into the fan base of the two traditionally popular sports, thought to be more 'Yorkshire' in spirit than namby-pamby 'soccer'. Football in Leeds was regarded as a bit of a joke, a handful of decent players here – Willis Edwards, Bert Sproston,

Wilbur Cush – the odd famous manager there – Dick Ray, Major Frank Buckley, Raich Carter – but absolutely bugger-all to show for it. The archetypal yo-yo club, Leeds United had lurched from promotion material to relegation fodder throughout their forty-year history.

Things might have been different if their precursors, Leeds City, had not been thrown out of the League in 1919, having been singled out for making payments to players during World War I, a practice so widespread it's hard not to think that as relative newcomers, they were the easiest target for the Football Association to victimize. Leeds City's manager Herbert Chapman, 'Football's Emperor', went on to become the architect of Huddersfield Town's Championships in the 1920s before making an even bigger contribution to Arsenal's dominance of the game in the 1930s. It's difficult to speculate what might have occurred had he stayed, but there can be little doubt that the club itself, tied to the ambitions and fortunes of football's first great innovator, would at least have had a higher profile than the one it enjoyed in the dismal forty years since his departure. If anyone could ever have built a nothing club into something, that person was Herbert Chapman. Doubtless he would have been lured away long before he had time to erect his marble halls at Elland Road, but Leeds City were deprived the dividends of their foresight in appointing such a remarkably talented manager.

There is evidence that United's transformation from Second Division also-rans to European giants was achieved in spite of the Elland Road Board. Much of the credit for Revie's appointment must go instead to Ronald Crowther, the sports editor of the long defunct *Yorkshire Evening News*. Leeds had continued to cultivate their pre-war mediocrity in the late 1940s and 50s. Revie's predecessor, Jack Taylor, poached from Queens Park Rangers in May 1959, was the club's sixth manager since 1945. He took the club down in his first full season.

Exhibiting rather more ambition than his fellow fans, Crowther was irked by the club's underachievement. Even before joining the *Daily Mail* in the 1960s, he had acquired a national reputation as a crusader for truth and justice in the murky environment of post-war football.

At the *News* he repeatedly challenged the Leeds directors, outraged that the club seemed to be dying of neglect. Like a character from a bad kitchen-sink novel of the early 1960s, the tenacious reporter kitted out in full porkpie hat garb, he was not a man to be intimidated. 'Banned from the ground, he paid at the turnstile, balanced his type-writer on a crash barrier and carried on attacking, until revolution and Don Revie arrived,' his obituary recalled. 'Having stood on an invasion beach, firing his captain's revolver at German dive-bombers – "it was supposed to inspire the men," he chuckled – he was hardly likely to be bullied.'

Don Revie was born into a working-class family in Middlesborough in 1927. His mother died while he was still an infant – an early bereavement from which the amateur psychologists among his critics inferred a quest for security inspiring all his subsequent actions.

He certainly found some security at Leicester City, his first of five professional clubs. There he married the Leicester manager's niece, Elsie Duncan. Clocking up four different clubs in seven years gave him the title for his autobiography, *Soccer's Happy Wanderer*, the major part of which is devoted to his spell at Manchester City from 1952–1956. It was at Maine Road that he enjoyed his greatest success, picking up six England caps and a reputation as an incisive and intelligent player.

The game that made him famous, the 1956 FA Cup Final, was an early indication of his tactical ingenuity when, together with the Manchester City coaching staff and senior players, he adapted the deep-lying centre-forward's role played by Nandor Hidegkuti to devastating effect in Hungary's 6–3 and 7–1 thrashings of England in 1953 and 1954. His stormy relationship with the City manager, Les McDowall, meant that he did not hang around for long after his celebrated performance in the Final, moving on to Sunderland in 1956 and, his career winding down even though he was still only twenty-nine, Leeds two years later.

The prospect of Revie quitting Leeds United in the early months of 1961 was not a matter of great concern to the club. At thirty-one the former England international was past his best when he joined from

Sunderland in November 1958, though he did not retire from playing for another five years. Anxious to secure a player-manager's job as his on-field career drew to a close, it was cursorily reported that he had applied for just such a post at Bournemouth in February 1961. But Revie's reputation as one of the game's more cerebral individuals had spread much further afield. Chester City and Tranmere Rovers also entered the running for Revie's services. Then, three weeks before he took over at Elland Road, Revie was invited to become player-coach of the semi-professional Australian club Adamanstown, near Sydney, on a five-year contract. The New South Wales club offered to fly Revie, Elsie and their two children out to Australia, provide them with a house and find Revie work outside football. He would also receive a salary as part-time coach. The offer was declined, however. A more unlikely 'cobber' could not be imagined. Barbecues and Bondi Beach would never have appealed to the home- and hearth-loving Don.

Revealing that streak of insecurity that was a key facet of his character, Revie asked Crowther to draft his letter of application for the Bournemouth post. But on 13 March, Jack Taylor quit the Leeds job with twelve months remaining on his three-year contract. A Barnsley man who made his name as a full-back at Wolves, he had been a disastrous appointment; but the Board preferred to keep him on rather than pay out the £2,500 due to him if they took the initiative and terminated his contract. Fortunately, Taylor eventually solved their dilemma for them. The United Board's fiercest critic, Ronald Crowther, told his disciple Don Revie to pitch for the Leeds job instead of Bournemouth.

As Jack Taylor left to clear his desk, with the players' farewell gift of a 'fitted dressing case' clamped under his arm, the Leeds directors faced a pretty bleak outlook. In 1959, even though they were then at least in the First Division, they had found it almost impossible to attract a manager. Indeed, Taylor had been their sixth choice. It seems astonishing, if not ludicrous, that before Taylor had finally conquered his misgivings and agreed to move from Queens Park Rangers, Sam Bolton, Leeds' haulage contractor chairman, had offered the job to

Charlie Mitten of Newcastle United, Archie Macauley of Norwich City, Bob Brocklebank of Hull City, Willie Thornton of Dundee and, most astoundingly, to Arthur Turner of non-league Headington. If Mitten's rejection was understandable, the next four degenerated from the embarrassing to the humiliating.

In the aftermath of Taylor's departure, speculation over his successor conspicuously failed to rage. This reflected the city's limited expectations of the football club. No talk then of a 'sleeping giant', a description that would be over-employed when United re-entered Second Division purdah two decades later. The following day's headlines were dominated instead by Floyd Patterson's sixth-round knockout of the Swede Ingemar Johansson in Miami. The *News* was no exception, with United travails relegated to a downpage item reporting that club secretary Cyril Williamson would assume managerial responsibilities pending the appointment of a successor. Sam Bolton admitted to being preoccupied with arrangements for that week's FA Cup Semi-Final between Leicester City and Sheffield United, to be staged at Elland Road. Given their indebtedness, cash came first, the appointment could wait. 'We have not yet had time to consider an official appointment,' a stressed Bolton said. 'We shall give the matter plenty of thought in the near future.'

'It will not surprise me,' wrote Ronald Crowther, ever the pessimist, 'if United carry on with a secretary-manager – Mr Williamson – at the helm, with chief coach Syd Owen responsible to him for team affairs.' Williamson's qualifications for this early forerunner of the 'director of football' position were less than compelling. A former Grade One referee, he was the archetypal 'blazer'. Former roles included a stint as Chairman of the FA Youth International selection committee and Secretary of the Leicestershire and Rutland FA. His reluctance to take on the responsibility probably saved the club from the inevitable consequences of its suicidal incompetence.

It has become part of Leeds' folklore that Harry Reynolds, soon to succeed Bolton as chairman but then still only a junior director, was moved to consider Revie only while writing him a reference to support his application to become player-manager of AFC Bournemouth. It has been interpreted as the moment the club's destiny changed, while emphasizing how close United were to losing their own particular 'messiah'. For once, however, the legendary parsimony of the Leeds directors – and particularly Reynolds, an eccentric self-made millionaire who continued to live in a two-up, two-down terraced house – served them well. When Bournemouth asked Leeds to name a fee for Revie, their chairman baulked at the £6,000 quoted.

In reality, therefore, the Leeds Board had little choice but to take the radical option and appoint Revie. Mired in the lower half of the Second Division, they were palpably less marketable to the ambitious or established manager than they had been two years previously. After such a variety of managers and methods since the war, it was little wonder that Eric Stanger in the *Yorkshire Evening Post* concluded: 'Nothing would benefit Leeds Utd more than a long stable period of sound management. In fact, in their financial position, it is their only hope for the future.'

Not only was Revie available, affordable and impressively full of ideas, he was also, ideally, aware of the staff's shortcomings and the precariousness of the club's standing at the bank. Crucially, he was far more likely to accept the offer than any other candidate suited to the job.

Three days after Crowther's erroneous prediction, the die was cast. The thirty-three-year-old Revie was appointed on a three-year contract – on terms markedly inferior to those that Taylor had enjoyed. His pay was pegged at the £20 maximum, which had until recently been the maximum wage. The contractual dispute between Chelsea's then chairman Ken Bates and the flamboyant Ruud Gullit in the late 1990s reportedly hinged on the player-manager's insistence on keeping the 'playing' part of his salary long after he ceased to play an effective on-field role. In contrast here, the Leeds Board were insistent that Revie should keep his 'playing' contract for as long as possible. It was far cheaper that way. Desperate to stay in football and singularly unsuited for the stock career route of the ex-professional running a pub, Revie knew he had little option but to agree. He never forgot their initial caution, hardly a brilliant tactic to adopt with one so temperamentally vulnerable. In future, even if their compromised position at the bank had given them little choice, they would pay a heavy price for their attempt to screw him.

TWO

WHEN YOU'RE YOUNG

evie described his new job as a 'real challenge'. 'I am very pleased with my contract,' he went on, confirming it gave him 'full power on selection, transfers in and out, training – all aspects of the work necessary to get a good playing staff'. Cyril Williamson was left to handle purely administrative matters. And the new manager also offered an immediate insight into his philosophy: the attention to detail for which he was to become notorious. The team would build up a series of 'set moves', he announced, from goal-kicks, thrown-ins, free-kicks and corners. 'I shall try to get defensive systems and attacking systems that will operate throughout all our teams,' he told the *Yorkshire Evening Press* on the eve of his first game in charge. 'Any players moving up from one team to another will know just what is wanted.'

And from the outset Revie also set out to foster the *esprit de corps* that would later be interpreted as bloody-minded insularity. 'If everybody pulls together, from the directors right down to the women who do the cleaning and the washing, and is Leeds United-minded, then we shall get somewhere,' he added. This was no idle word. The referee, Jack Taylor, who would later take charge of the 1974 World Cup Final, recalled turning up at Elland Road in the 1960s to witness Revie giving the cleaning staff cash to put on the horses. 'If they won, they were twice as happy; if they lost, they were still happy,' Taylor remembered. The Elland Road washerwomen were similarly indulged. Lugubrious Tykes to a woman, it is fitting that they should feature on the BBC's video tribute to the Revie era at Leeds, *The Glory Years*, pulling the team's shirts out of the wash.

Revie took as his inspiration the achievements of Manchester United under Matt Busby, though his team would never be granted the same unquestioning media adulation. A week after his appointment he took himself to Old Trafford to learn from the master. Great minds clearly thought alike, as Busby endorsed the young pretender's determination to establish a consistent coaching pattern throughout the club, so that junior players promoted to the first team would be familiar with the style of play.

Revie's inheritance, however, was meagre. The players were largely mediocre, with one or two exceptions journeymen pros or poorly motivated tyros with genuine potential but desperate to leave the resolutely retrograde environment. The 'relegation hangover', which frequently infiltrates the minds of players, has been seen to affect numerous clubs in the first season following the trauma of demotion. One way of relieving its symptoms is through major surgery. Yet since their relegation the previous summer, Leeds' average attendance had slumped from the barely respectable 22,000 to the positively spartan figure of 13,500. Limited funds had been released in the spring of 1960 to enable Taylor to buy Freddie Goodwin from Manchester United in an attempt to shore up a defence that had leaked 78 goals in 32 games in the slide to the bottom of the First Division. There had been some improvement after his arrival: Leeds won four of their remaining ten fixtures – but it was far too late to stave off the inevitable.

By the beginning of the 1960/61 season, the bank's apprehension had become palpable, and Taylor's request to recruit a few reliable, experienced professionals had understandably been rejected by the Board. After protracted negotiations he had been allowed to buy Eric Smith from Celtic, but that hardly amounted to the root and branch modification that was necessary after such a feeble season.

The other alternative, to generate funds by selling one or two players, was also denied him. Of the relegated squad, only three players had any significant monetary value: Billy Bremner, who was just seventeen and had only recently broken into the first team; John McCole, scorer of 22 goals that season but widely perceived as a functional penalty-box predator and little else, and who, anyway, would be vital to Leeds' attempt to achieve promotion; and Jack Charlton, whose inconsistency on the park and militancy off it put off a whole host of suitors. There was to be no quick fix.

With cash and confidence ebbing away after every setback, Leeds' 1960/61 campaign lurched towards disaster. It was this same inadequate squad, drained of all purpose and with no set game plan, that would assemble before Revie on a fateful March morning for his first training session. With no prospect of funds becoming available until the summer, if at all, he was stuck with them.

Nonetheless, Revie was fortunate to benefit from Jack Taylor's only notable legacy: two innovative if irascible coaches – Les Cocker and Syd Owen.

Today there is no real distinction between the terms 'trainer' and 'coach'. In those days they were two separate trades. Les Cocker, the former Stockport County and Accrington Stanley forward, had learnt, like so many of his contemporaries, the fundamentals of fitness in his wartime service with the Reconnaissance Regiment in France after D-Day. He was temperamentally and professionally qualified for the position of 'trainer'.

One of the first generation to take the FA Coaching Certificate, he supplemented his tactical acumen with exploratory studies in physiology and, more unusually, also dabbled in the avant-garde sports sciences of kinesiology and biomechanics. He had a stormy start with his new charges, who were contemptuous of his dedication to their development, and had many a run-in with that self-styled 'one man awkward squad', Jack Charlton. Yet barely a year after joining Leeds, he was summoned to Lancaster Gate and offered the prestigious job of putting England squads through his revolutionary sequence of sadistic drills, a position he was to occupy from 1966 right through to 1977.

For all his ructions with Charlton and the initial scepticism of the other 'seen it all' seasoned pros, it was obvious that he was doing something right. Fanatical and often abrasive, there was a touch of zealotry in his soul. Indeed, in Brian Clough's characteristically brusque judgement he was an 'aggressive, nasty little bugger'. 'Pots' and 'kettles' spring to mind, but it was just these qualities that made Cocker so valuable to Revie. His loyalty was unreserved and he brought structure, obstinacy and a certain impassive relentlessness to his task, which was to become the cornerstone of Leeds' physical authority.

Cocker was rather more than the stereotypical 'sergeant-major' coach, but there is little doubt that, more often than not, he played that role to perfection. However, it was the more cerebral Owen who actually conducted the technical sessions. A full England international, from 1941–46, he had served in the RAF with distinction, on active service in Egypt, Austria and Italy. Along with Cocker, he had joined Leeds from Luton Town in the summer of 1960 to help Taylor's beleaguered team achieve promotion in their first season back in the Second Division.

Unlike Cocker, he had a distinguished pedigree both as a player and a coach, and had actually, briefly, been a manager himself. Having been sacked by Luton Town after less than a year in charge, he was impatient in his desire to prove that the progressive methods he had discovered at Lilleshall could be a success as much on the field as on the blackboard. He, too, had problems imposing his more modern philosophy on the conspicuously cynical Charlton, but eventually, after one episode when Jack 'offered to take my coat off to him', Charlton realized that he was rapidly beginning to unleash his dormant potential under Owen's shrewd instruction.

It was, perhaps, inevitable that their war service so markedly shaped their personalities, and many of those clichés concerning 'regimentation' and 'military precision' administered later to depict Leeds as little more than a troop of bellicose automatons can be traced back to their influence. Similarly, Les and Syd bolstered Revie's more non-conformist tendencies and were happy to play up their team's truculent outsider status. But what made them so integral to Revie's crusade was their fervent enthusiasm and simple flair for teaching young players. As Billy Bremner recalled to Bernard Bale in his posthumously published official biography:

> They spent hours in analysing a youngster's abilities, finding out how to improve his strong points, and even how to eradicate or at least remedy his weaknesses... I still shudder when I think of all the hours of hard graft that I spent under those two taskmasters. They made me lose buckets of sweat, but everything that they told me was for my own good, and any improvement that I ever made was thanks to their constant attention to detail.

The majority of managers take years to assemble the right blend of character in their backroom staff. Those fabled partnerships of Matt Busby and Jimmy Murphy or Bill Shankly and his boot room boys – Bob Paisley, Joe Fagin and Reuben Bennett – were not ad hoc creations. From day one Revie had his team in place. Additionally, his assistant Maurice Lindley had also worked for Jack Taylor and was to flourish as Revie's chief scout and, more notoriously, as the principal compiler of those infamous dossiers.

Therefore, despite his own lack of experience, and however dire the immediate situation appeared to the Leeds public – a less than auspicious league position, the £40,000 hole in the overdraft and dwindling attendances – the small crumb of comfort available to him on his appointment was that he had some foundations to build on. At his first press conference he had already mastered the art of manager-speak: 'I fully understand that I have a difficult job,' he said soberly, 'but it can be done if we all pull together. My aim is to be firm but fair.'

Now it was on to the traditional 'Call me "Boss"' rendezvous with the first team squad. For a new player-manager the hardest task is that first meeting with the players, tinged as it is with embarrassment and the necessity of underlining one's new status. Kenny Dalglish, for one, found it difficult to adjust, as former team-mates like Phil Neal were blatantly unwilling to acknowledge his advancement. All the banter, gossip and day-to-day gripes of dressing-room life now have to be exchanged for a detached gravitas. At least Revie could out-trump the 'show us your medals' brigade with his England caps and FA Cup Winners medal from 1956. But it would be anachronistic to expect much prima-donnaish posturing from the squad that hung on Revie's introductory words. National service graduates all, players then were closer in style to Harry Enfield's splendid caricature of Charles 'Charlie' Charles (though obviously of rougher stock) than to today's temperamental Premiership poppets. They listened as he delivered his up-beat common-sense monologue, welcomed him with no explicit reservations and, pulling on their heavy cable-knit sweaters, trudged across the West Stand concourse to Fullerton Park for his first training session.

The best player in Revie's first squad, Grenville Hair, the popular left-back, was different. Good enough to have been selected to represent the Football League, if not quite of sufficient quality to merit an England cap, he was a solid, efficient footballer with nearly ten years' experience as a first team regular. His rugged consistency and composed demeanour was the one element of stability in Leeds' continuing defensive crisis. His record of one goal in 443 games, however, makes the famously shot-shy David Batty's record look like Gabriel Batistuta's in comparison. Although he was only twenty-nine when Revie took over, his best years were behind him. In the short-term, he remained Leeds' best player, and there can be little doubt that Revie came to rely on his steady professionalism as he tackled the brittleness of his defence.

Of the rest, there's no telling how they may have fared in a better team. Until very recently, if one was to ask a Leeds fan to compile the club's best ever XI, the only addition to Revie's vintage 1970s side would have been John Charles, possibly selected ahead of Mick Jones at centre-forward. No other players from Leeds pre-history would even come close. Few were to make any mark on the club or its subsequent salvation. All had shown some promise at one time or another and most had at least turned out at a higher level. But the blend was all wrong.

For example, the goalkeeper, Alan Humphreys, was far too inexperienced for the task assigned to him. On occasion he proved himself to be a strong and nimble shot-stopper, but he singularly failed to dominate his chaotic defence. All too often as his team-mates retreated in front of him, he was left exposed, and by the time of Revie's appointment had conceded 57 goals in just twenty-six appearances. As an anxious young keeper who had lost the respect of his equally culpable colleagues, it is hard not to feel some sympathy for him. He went on to rebuild his career, albeit at a less demanding level, with Mansfield and Chesterfield, but by 1961 he was already, in the game's callous terminology, 'shot'.

His suffering had not been eased by the lack of organization among his colleagues. Unusually for this period when vast squads were considered exorbitant luxuries, especially in Yorkshire, Taylor had already selected twenty-four different players as he endeavoured to achieve some harmony. This constant chopping and changing is the hallmark of the perpetually struggling side and was to be a feature at Leeds United until late 1962. This was not squad rotation as we know it today: it was evidence of a manager who did not have a clue as to his best permutation.

Of the regulars, few had much future under Revie, though he was to persist with some of them until they were finally jettisoned two years later in favour of the precocious teenagers in the youth team. Most have since vanished into obscurity, but they do not necessarily deserve to be denigrated. They were not veterans, happy to prolong unfulfilled careers. Most were under twenty-five. The club failed them just as much as they failed the club, as their promising talents were ruined, ruling out forever all ambition of following John Charles to success and auspicious transfers. Not one of their careers was to recover from the nerve-shredding experiences at Elland Road. It was downhill all the way afterwards, into the Third Division, at best, for all of them. Their misfortune is often forgotten. They weren't lazy or overpaid or individually inept, however poorly they performed collectively. They were simply the wrong players, too young for the Second Division maelstrom, badly coached and led by men bereft of any tactical ingenuity.

Among those stationed in front of the novice goalkeeper, Freddie Goodwin, the Brian Epstein lookalike, had joined Leeds to reignite a stalled career over the Pennines at Manchester United. A former 'Busby Babe', he had shone intermittently at Old Trafford after graduating into the first team in the aftermath of the Munich disaster but could never quite convince Matt Busby that he had sufficient class to prosper at the highest level. Originally a midfielder, he was converted to centre-half in the hope of capitalizing on his perceived versatility.

Chronically one-paced and over-reliant on his brute strength, he nevertheless had much to offer a struggling side. Good in the air and blessed with natural authority, he succeeded Revie as captain at the nadir of the 1960/61 season. Unfortunately, in contradiction to all his other admirable leadership qualities, he lacked composure. His method was redolent of the 'get some blood on your boots' approach loved by fans, but it failed to mask his technical flaws.

Managers love forceful characters and are willing to excuse many defects if effort is always shown – but it can have its downsides. Goodwin managed to persuade Taylor (and Revie too, initially) that Leeds should adopt a man-to-man marking system. It enabled Goodwin to exploit his powerful tackling style, but other players were run ragged tracking attackers all over the park. Charlton hated it but reluctantly deferred to his senior colleague. Revie evidently felt that Goodwin's value to the team outweighed his limitations and persevered with their skipper's illogical system for another year simply because it was felt it suited him best.

Goodwin battled on as captain until the following season, when Bobby Collins, a man who exhibited grit to an almost psychopathic degree, won the arm-band through sheer force of personality.

The only other defenders at Revie's disposal were John Kilford, a future clergyman, who had oscillated between the first XI and the reserves for the past three seasons, and Willie Bell, who was ultimately to thrive at full-back but was then regarded primarily as a midfielder. Jack Charlton would have been the obvious choice to cement some cohesion, but he had yet to be accepted as responsible enough, so prone was he to outbreaks of petulant indiscipline. In any case, Revie had another role for him.

So much for Leeds' inconsiderable defensive resources; the midfield was in even worse shape. Here, the purist would probably insist that only 'wing-halves' should be referred to as midfielders according to the accepted wisdom of the age, but strict adherence to the 2–3–5 (WM) formation had long been abandoned even in the unenlightened environs of Elland Road.

In stark contrast to the cumbersome rearguard, Leeds' midfield was largely populated by deft, languid players with attacking inclinations but without the guile to unlock defences. Revie's options were, as they say, limited. His predecessor had left a comically lightweight roster of diminutive inside-forwards, tackle-shy wing-halves and, in one case, a singing winger now more famous for his variety act than for the prowess that had led him to score twice for England v Brazil on his debut some years previously.

Bobby Cameron, Peter McConnell and Colin Grainger (the crooner) were all comfortable with the ball at their feet but far less proficient at winning it back from the opposition. All were 'form' players who enjoyed intermittent 'hot streaks' but were rather more noticeable for their infuriating timidity. The one orthodox wing-half, Eric Smith, was more typical of the kind of hard Scottish professional that had dominated the English game for much of the century. He was a bright, bubbly individual, always ready to get stuck in and who refused to get too depressed over the gulf in class and facilities between his former club, Celtic, and Leeds United. Often injured and slow, even by Leeds' standards, Smith was nevertheless always capable of digging in when necessary.

A couple of extraordinary signings from South Africa completed the squad of British players. In his meticulous survey 'Colouring Over the White Line', Phil Vasili rights the common misconception that the emergence of black footballers in England was a 1970s phenomenon, rehabilitating scores of forgotten pioneers such as Arthur Wharton, Walter Tull and Roy Brown, and movingly recreating their quiet heroism in the face of the country's prevailing xenophobia. Ever since the 1920s, casual racism had consigned generations of black players to the peripheries of the game. There had been some significant breakthroughs, but after 1945 the pre-war trickle of black talent into football had almost died out. In a society under the pressure of persistent discrimination, which still generally regarded black people as, at best, intriguing curiosities, the widescale acceptance of black footballers was still some way off. The boom in Commonwealth immigration had certainly not made much impact in Leeds by the time Gerry Francis arrived from Johannesburg in 1957.

As Leeds United's first-ever black player, Francis's place in the social and cultural history of the club is assured, but his fitful displays on the right wing are far less likely to be remembered. There is no evidence that his career was hampered by prejudice. In common with most other Leeds players, his spell at Elland Road was one long depressing cycle of dazzling display followed by stagnation, dropping down into the reserves, improvement and recall, before the sequence started all over again. His appearances became more regular in the 1960/61 season, his last with the club, but he only managed forty-six league games in his four years there before Revie offloaded him to York City in the summer.

In comparison, Francis's compatriot, Albert Johanneson, was to become an integral part of the revolution. Like all people who die in horrific circumstances, Johanneson tends to be defined by the manner of his death. An all-pervasive sense of waste and tragedy tinged with guilt overshadows his friends' recollections. Few recall the levity or the joy or the skill. They are displaced by the images of the lonely dislocated alcoholic, forever scrounging cash, and the miserable last years in a council tower block where his body ultimately lay undiscovered for days. To understand this sense of grief, it is important to remember why the 'Black Flash' shone so brightly in Revie's first successful Leeds team.

He made his debut four games into Revie's reign and for the next six years was to provide the only element of glamour in a drab Leeds side, wrapped up in a brand of energetic pressing football designed to restrict the opposition's time on the ball and force errors. It must have seemed like a godsend to Revie when he first received the report from a South African schoolteacher recommending the twenty-year-old. Johanneson's fare from Johannesburg was chicken-feed compared to a transfer fee, and after only a couple of training sessions, Revie felt that he was ready for a contract and for first team football.

In the future he would succumb to big match nerves and bouts of self-doubt, and he would continue to torment his team-mates with outbreaks of the winger's disease – conceding possession and momentum at crucial moments. But for the majority of the time he was a quick, strong runner and a clinical finisher. He ended up with a strike rate of more than one goal in three appearances, a ratio most out and out centre-forwards would consider as satisfactory. For a winger it was sensational. For all the flaws in his game, which became more explicit as the quality of the players around him gradually improved, and the feelings of inadequacy that sabotaged his personal happiness, Albert Johanneson was taken to the Leeds fans' hearts because he lit up Elland Road in its age of austerity and his displays offered a tantalizing glimpse of what lay ahead once all the tedious hard work had been done.

Finally, alongside all these players that only older Leeds fans have ever heard of, were the two stars – Jack Charlton and Billy Bremner. Not that prone to petulance and unfocused aggression, as both were, their future renown would have been easily discernible amongst all the other dross on show.

Charlton, as we have seen, was mouthy, often unprofessional and felt under-appreciated. Was it because his younger brother had so comprehensively overshadowed him, or was it his anger at squandering his career at Leeds? Whatever, in 1961, at twenty-five, he was a complete pain in the arse. He objected to everything, from the 'stupid' rulebook to the idiocy of the coaching staff. If chastised in the dressing-room after a game, he wasn't averse to throwing the odd teacup, and his astounding surliness had alienated just about everyone at the club, Revie included. In his autobiography, published in 1996, Charlton recalls a typical argument with Revie from the 1960/61 season when they were both still players: 'I'd gone charging up the field with the ball and Don said to me afterwards, "If I was the manager, I wouldn't play you. You're always messing about."

'"Well you're not the manager," I said, "So what the hell?"'

As Jack's colleague, Revie was already fed up with him. As his manager, no one expected this tempestuous relationship to last very long. What seems certain is that he never lost his intolerance of criticism or his know-it-all subversive tendencies, only that he eventually came to listen to two people, Revie and Sir Alf Ramsey, when they had patiently won his respect.

Bremner, on the other hand, had good reason to trust Revie right from the start. From the moment he'd been called up to the first team in January 1960, Revie had taken it upon himself to be the youngster's mentor. Before his debut at Chelsea, the two men had roomed together. There was a fifteen-year age gap between the senior pro and his seventeen-year-old protégé, but Revie helped to settle his nerves, coaxed him through his first games and constantly made himself available for advice and reassurance.

By 1961 Bremner was a first team regular, albeit in the unfamiliar role of outside-right, but being only eighteen he had not yet conquered the abiding homesickness for Stirling and his girlfriend Vicky. Willing to give everything for Revie until the end of the season, he still wanted to leave the club in the summer, preferably for Celtic, who had already expressed their tentative interest. It took countless discussions over the next two years, and even a summit meeting

between the manager and the future Mrs Bremner, to persuade Billy
that his future lay in Leeds.

It is hardly surprising that with nine games of the season left and just
these players to choose from, there was no miraculous upsurge in
form. In fact it was an extreme disappointment, as Leeds won just one
game, drew four and lost four of the remaining fixtures. Neither were
they recognizably Leeds United, playing out their last games in their
traditional blue and gold kit. Though the training sessions had now
become shorter, with the coaches paying more attention to detail
than the monotonous physical jerks the players had grown used to,
there weren't many signs that the ailing company was under new
management.

The Revie epoch commenced at Fratton Park with a pitiful 3-1
defeat to Portsmouth and limped on through April without ever
really capturing the imagination of the Leeds public. The one high
spot was a 7-0 thrashing of soon to be relegated Lincoln City, but it
was played out in front of a paltry crowd of 8,342. The four draws
may have secured their survival but there was very little enthusiasm
in the city, as Leeds recorded their lowest league attendance since
1934 in their last home game, another workmanlike draw against
Scunthorpe.

The one trick Revie pulled in these first games, however, was
straight out of the Leeds history books. Back in 1951 Major Buckley,
on a whim, had decided to try John Charles at centre-forward after an
outstanding season at centre-half. Over the next few years Nat
Lofthouse acclaimed him as the best defender he had ever played
against; simultaneously, Billy Wright hailed him as the finest centre-
forward he had ever seen. For several seasons after Charles's transfer
to Italy, Juventus exploited his versatility by playing him up front
until he had scored before withdrawing him to shore up their defence
to ensure maximum points.

Could lightning strike twice? For the remaining games of the
season Revie tried to do the same with Jack Charlton. It was a

plausible gamble, one that the bare statistics deem a success. Twelve goals for Charlton in twenty games as a striker would suggest that Revie was on to something. But all the same, by Christmas 1961 Charlton had failed to emulate the multifaceted Charles. He didn't really know what he was doing, and though the goals came, they came mainly from set pieces. Revie's first foray into alchemy was abandoned within the year.

It wasn't much of a honeymoon period for the rookie manager. He later conceded that he had half expected to be sacked at the season's end. At least, he felt, it could not get much worse. Yet rather as a quack's radical cure makes the patient deteriorate further before he revives, so the next few months would see Leeds plunge even lower, and Revie's capability would be open to question.

THREE

T he summer of 1961 saw Yorkshire seeking a hat-trick of County Championships and England attempting to regain the Ashes from Richie Benaud's formidable Australian tourists. The Eichmann trial dominated the front pages of even the provincial press, and on the back pages Leeds United were marginalized within their own city, as the Yorkshire public's abiding love of cricket was well served with the sort of in-depth news, reports and analysis that football in the city had never attracted. United were almost invisible against the backdrop of Brian Close's benefit season and Fred Trueman's match-winning perform-ance in the second innings of the Headingley Test, which squared the Ashes series.

Unhappily, the high hopes of mid-July had subsided by the summer's end. At Old Trafford, Benaud bowled Australia to an impregnable lead, Close's test recall ended in ignominy as he was scapegoated for England's defeat, and Yorkshire grudgingly conceded the Championship to the blue bloods of Hampshire. A prevailing sense of optimism dashed was to prove an apposite augury for Revie's first full season in charge.

Not that there was much hype to begin with. The remarkably pre-scient pseudonymous fan 'Still Hopeful' captured the mood in a letter to the *Yorkshire Evening Post*: 'If progress is to be made in the coming season, far better judgement will have to be displayed in the choice of players. Falling gates will not be arrested if we are to suffer a repetition of the mediocrity served up last season. Expecting a lukewarm public to roll up at increased prices is a ticklish business. Progress can only be made by judicious purchasing of the right kind of player.'

Without the wherewithal for a spot of immediate 'judicious purchasing', Revie had to resort to other means to engineer a more positive team spirit. Always thought of as a 'player's manager', in that he was always perceived to back his players in their wage claims, his first move was to recommend the abolition of differentials among his first-team squad. For a club in Leeds' predicament the package of up to £43 10s per player per week was enormous, but the fine print, as so often, revealed that the Board retained the upper hand.

The basic wage was increased to £20 per week, to be supplemented by a £5 appearance fee, a £4 win bonus and a complex sliding scale of incentives aligned to attendances above 20,000. To qualify for the full bonus of £14 10s, Leeds would have to draw a crowd of more than 31,000 – a gate of 18,000 above the previous year's average. It's hardly surprising that it was the ever obstreperous Charlton who saw through this scheme and asked to be transfer listed. Convinced that senior players naturally deserved a greater salary than the juniors, he was only persuaded to sign the new contract (which ensured him £14 in the close season) in early July on the proviso that Leeds would release him if an acceptable bid was received.

Having refused Revie's offer of the captaincy because of his wage dilemma, Charlton arrived for pre-season training still bearing a grudge, telling reporters, 'I still want to get to a club where I can get more money.' If that seems a little mercenary, he was obviously well aware that several clubs, including Manchester United and promotion favourites Liverpool, were considering strengthening their defensive options for the new season, even though neither Busby nor Shankly was subsequently to become famous for their largesse during contractual negotiations. Revie's 'subversive' notion of equality seemed disrespectful to someone as touchy as Charlton, and could be pejoratively and hilariously portrayed as smacking of highly dubious communist practices. Typically, no one else bothered to complain.

Revie's other noticeable pre-season innovation was the abandonment of the club's traditional blue and gold strip. Though the
decision effectively jettisoned forty years of United's history, astonishingly little was made of it at the time. The replacement colours
were to be all white, in quite deliberate imitation of the famous all
white of the finest team in the world, Real Madrid. To re-profile a
club so efficiently on such a whim demonstrated the man's flair
and vision, drawing a line under the failures of the past. That
nobody remonstrated with him for it – there was none of the usual
campaigns or petitions to save Leeds' heritage – is an early sign of
the Board's growing willingness to indulge him and of the inter-
minable apathy of the majority of Leeds fans.

Such a flagrant psychological gimmick – in the hope that some
part of Real's aura of invincibility would rub off on his own players –
was risky. If he pulled it off, it would be interpreted as a masterstroke.
If 'New Leeds' continued to founder, however, it could look like hubris
and finish his career. To invite comparisons with Gento, Di Stefano
and Puskas when all he had was McConnell, Peyton and Cameron...
one has to admire Revie's nerve.

Motivational stunts aside, Revie knew that the talent at his disposal needed organization and technical improvement if Leeds were
to perform with more consistency in the coming season. First he
scrapped the unpopular 'Rule Book' which dictated what a player
could and could not get up to in his personal life in favour of a more
common-sense approach. Then he returned from a short break having
devised a training programme to keep the players stimulated during
all the necessary but laborious fitness work. It was a sort of team version of 'Superstars', dividing the first-team squad into four groups of
six to compete against each other for prizes in everything from cross-
country running and sprint sequences to physical jerks and five-a-
side, not to mention rounders, cricket and golf.

As Cocker and Owen kicked off the programme in Farnley Park in
mid-July, Revie told the press: 'My one aim is to make them Leeds
United-minded. Get that, and much else falls into place.' A fortnight

of intense competition ensued, with a gratifyingly high level of enthusiasm evident from even the most lacklustre team members. Given something interesting to do instead of the usual treadmill approach, the revival of morale was palpable. Many photographs of Revie that summer show him constantly smiling, glowing even, as he leaves another session. Perhaps he felt that he'd cracked it. After years of stagnation, this more sophisticated strategy, it appeared, was convincing even the sceptical journeymen that Leeds were finally beginning to take positive strides forward. Few were more impressed than Charlton, who withdrew his transfer request in early August and let it be known that he was a candidate for the captaincy once more. Revie was not slow to claim this as a ringing endorsement of himself and his new methods: 'Both he and I are very happy at his change of mind. He has been enjoying the training – indeed his team won my training competition. He thinks, like I do, that United are going places and he will be very happy with us.' Not for the first time with Big Jack and Leeds United, it was to be a false dawn.

The culmination of Revie's scheme to foster team spirit was a party in 'Ringways', the mid-market, city-centre restaurant. For the first time directors, staff, players and their wives were brought together to commemorate the success of pre-season training. His belief that a club should act more like a family than a community of individuals was prominent from this point onwards. Reflecting on his own feelings of isolation whenever he joined a new club, and drawing on the experience of his wife Elsie who had dutifully followed him from city to city, he understood the importance of domestic harmony to a footballer's form. He resolved never to leave anything to chance with his boys. His welcoming address set out to convince the wives that they, too, had a critical role to play in his long-term plan. In later years this would extend to visits, cards, flowers and presents for all the wives and children as he positioned himself as not only a father figure to his players, but also as head of the whole Leeds United community. For the time being the families were grateful to be treated as part of the club and relieved that someone had recognized their significance. Their growing devotion to him should not be underestimated.

After a spirited evening full of conviviality, awards and speeches, Revie issued a plea to the fans asking for tolerance and encouragement. All very well: actually getting them to turn up in unprecedented numbers to stave off the threat of bankruptcy was going to be harder.

It is a maxim of the football manager's fevered code that Boards inevitably only release resources when it's almost too late. Such brinkmanship then allows them to don the mantle of the 'saviour', which is why most provincial bigwigs get involved in football in the first place. With wholesale changes impossible, Revie purchased just one player, the less than legendary Derek Mayers, a winger from Preston North End. Though by Christmas this policy appeared to have undermined Leeds' ability to compete with Liverpool, Sunderland and the season's improbable dark horses Leyton Orient, Revie later maintained that it was only fair to give his squad the opportunity to impress him.

Leeds' alarming lack of credit was to be Revie's undoing that season, but in early August he vehemently refused to ameliorate the situation by selling Billy Bremner to Arsenal.

After such a restorative pre-season, the season began just as promisingly, with victories over Charlton and Brighton, featuring two goals from Bremner and a debut strike from the new boy Derek Mayers. The public, however, remained unconvinced. The opening-day attendance of 12,916 was less than half the breakeven point for the club, notwithstanding the increased price structure. A slump in attendance was probably caused, the club tried to argue, by 'nagging wives'. Sympathetic journalists, happy to portray the typical Leeds male as some sort of browbeaten Andy Capp caricature, warmed to the theme. Struggling to come to terms with a more liberal notion of working-class Leeds womenfolk than the strident harridan it had relied on in the past, the *Yorkshire Evening Post* commissioned a poll.

The survey, however, revealed that it was the supporters themselves who chose to stay away. They claimed that tickets were 'too dear', there was 'poor accommodation for spectators' and Leeds were a team of 'no stars'. In a local economy where a Saturday morning shift was still commonplace, the rival attraction of Saturday afternoon television persuaded many to stay at home. It was depressing reading for the Board.

Beating two such perennial makeweights as Brighton and Charlton showed signs of form, but to prove that it wasn't just an early season spurt, Leeds' next game against Liverpool, who had finished third in the two preceding seasons, offered a more realistic trial. Liverpool had been relegated in 1954 and had struggled for years, but after two years of careful nurturing by Bill Shankly, this was their breakthrough season. In front of a massive 42,000 Anfield crowd they duly handed out a comprehensive 5–0 drubbing. The gulf in class between the two sides was never more marked; lightweight and far too slow, Leeds never really got into the game as the clever movement of Ian St John pulled their defence to pieces.

With their confidence shattered and clearly rattled, they could pick up only one point from the next four games. In the midst of this dismal run it seems that Revie had a flash of inspiration. Suddenly he remembered he had one hitherto overlooked player on his books, the Footballer of the Year for 1955, no less: reluctantly he picked himself. At the age of thirty-four, playing in an even more withdrawn position than the one that had made him famous, he was unable to compensate for the general paucity of talent around him. If truth were told, injuries and age had eroded his ability to make much of a difference. Revie's bold but futile gesture couldn't arrest Leeds' slide.

The team lacked bustle, drive and punch. One disgruntled fan was provoked to write a comical lament: 'What about the poor nippers? For goodness sake, United, give them something to cheer! Wake up!' Failing to attract the 'nippers' and playing a brand of wishy-washy football without the rugged passion that would have compensated for their dire results, Leeds now saw their attendances drop below 10,000.

In mid-September, Revie sold John McCole to Bradford City. This at least bought the club some time with the bank, but by sacrificing the team's most prolific goalscorer he left himself open to the charge of accelerating the downward spiral, as poor results bred poor attendances which bled United dry. In fact, though, in these early years this man, whose powers of motivation and tactical wizardry would later make him famous, had far more impact as a true manager than as a coach. He took responsibility for everyone, from the youngest apprentice to the tea ladies. He, not the Board, made the crucial decisions, constantly cajoling and persuading them, fretting his way through the gate receipts, allocating his meagre resources, tirelessly scouting for new talent, nervously plotting for the big breakthrough. It was this energy that saved him.

At the end of September, with only 7 points from ten games and panic spreading, Revie and the Board faced the AGM of the Supporters' Club. Anywhere else it would have been a pretty explosive occasion. Here, the fans, perhaps still drowsy from their steaming pie and pea suppers, remained as phlegmatic as ever. Maybe they were mollified by director Sam Bolton's revelation that he and four others had each made interest-free loans of £3,500 to the club over the summer simply to keep United afloat. The Board, he admitted, had presumed on good attendances in the autumn to sustain the club through the winter weather that habitually decimated their revenue – a clear illustration of how marginal football clubs muddled through in the early 1960s.

But Bolton's gloomy tone soon turned apocalyptic: 'I know you are doing well, but you must do better if we want to keep soccer in Leeds.' His concluding vote of confidence in Revie's team was hardly a ringing endorsement: 'We shall back Mr Revie to the fullest extent, and his team, which is better than a lot of people think.'

The Supporter's Club Chairman, Mr Dixon, thanked Bolton for his candour and sought to sum up the feelings of his members. Mr Revie, he opined, 'had a terrible and Herculean task. We know his plans but a youth policy takes time and, looking at the league table, that is something that we haven't got. It is up to us as supporters to rally people through the turnstiles.' But apart from a tokenistic pledge to redouble fundraising efforts (even more 'beetle drives'), no one present had any idea how to save the club. With some cash flow to postpone the Board's concerns about insolvency, Leeds hobbled on into winter.

Yorkshire society was not particularly impressed by the ostentatious display of wealth. Those at the top tended to be self-made men, unashamedly proud of it and conspicuous only by their willingness to accept the kudos of civic responsibility. Leeds United would not be saved, therefore, by the generosity of a single benefactor. Salvation would lie, if at all, with the milieu in which the Board already felt most comfortable: with those who had 'got on' – businessmen, aldermen, magistrates and their ilk.

After years of fatalistic inertia, one week of belated action at the end of November 1961 can still be described as the defining week in United's history. Without it, it's arguable whether there would be a professional football club in the city today. With no further borrowing facilities on offer from the bank, Sam Bolton's strategy had been two pronged: vigorous appeals to the business community's sense of duty and vanity, combined with a touch of self-sacrifice – half Lord McAlpine, half Captain Oates.

It must have been a pretty hard sell, but Bolton's skilful and tenacious flattery paid dividends. Albert Morris ran Morris Wallpapers and Manny Cussins managed the John Peters Furnishing Group. Both men lived in the city's affluent Alwoodley district, were prominent figures in various Jewish charitable organizations, and were fans of the club. Bolton now persuaded them that a successful football club could be a distinct asset not only to their portfolios, but also to the community itself. Within days, Morris and Cussins joined the Board and each immediately made interest-free loans of £10,000 to help loosen the bank's stranglehold. Bolton's grand design had been to increase Board membership to a quorum of ten, notionally backing the club to the tune of £100,000, but he soon had to settle for just the two new recruits. Within five years they would be turning away

would-be directors by the dozen with the disdain of those who had
dared and won.

 At an eventful company AGM on 8 December came Bolton's own
resignation as Chairman. 'I have taken a lot of kicks,' he said, 'and I'm
afraid I'm getting to the point where I can't stand up to kicks like I
used to.' It was a tacit acknowledgement that good intentions were no
longer enough. He had put the building blocks in place; now the club
needed a man who could drive Leeds on to prosperity.

 Harry Reynolds' most important asset was time. As a retired millionaire, the new chairman would be able to devote increasingly large
chunks of his day to the club, all the time strengthening his relationship with Revie. During this same AGM he invited Revie to outline his
difficulties to the Board. The club's only way forward, responded Revie,
lay in the production of its own players (advice almost certainly given
to him by Matt Busby earlier in the year). A lot of his time, Revie went
on, was spent 'sitting on doorsteps in company with other clubs but
we will go on searching for the best boy players'. Reynolds told the
meeting he had 'never heard such ideas better put. He will have all the
backing the new Board and I can give him.' Revie finally bought a new
centre-forward, his former team-mate Bill McAdams from Bolton, and
Leeds managed to beat Champions-elect Liverpool in their pre-
Christmas rematch. But then another dismal run accumulated only
three points from the next nine fixtures. By the end of February, Leeds
had hit the bottom of the division. Some messiah! Some revolution!

 In transfer deadline week, as the Third Division beckoned, with all
its glamour ties – Halifax, Northampton, Peterborough – Revie suddenly sprang into action with the desperation of a drowning man.
Certainly he'd identified many transfer targets in the past, often
taking Reynolds with him on the long car journeys to chew over the
fat, but the selling clubs tended to stall while they sought replacements. In the early 1960s the only way to convince solvent clubs to
part with players who didn't enjoy freedom of contract was to pay
over the odds – anathema to the Yorkshire psyche.

 By the beginning of March, however, it was the only option left.

Reynolds released £55,000 from the kitty and the only question was how many players Revie could get. He wanted six but ended up with three, one of whom proved to be the most important signing in the club's history. More than setting the tone for the next thirteen years, he constructed the DNA pattern that has subsequently defined it – the myth of 'dirty Leeds'. There are so many stories about Bobby Collins that it is surprising no full biography of him has ever been written. For now we have to make do with the countless anecdotes in more famous players' autobiographies.

The best tribute came from Bremner in *You Get Nowt for Coming Second* (a Harry Reynolds motto if ever there was one): 'If one man doesn't make a team, Bobby Collins came nearer to doing it than anyone else I have ever seen on a football field.' He was like a force of nature. 'Bobby was a strange person in some ways,' writes Eddie Gray. 'He was very aggressive and confrontational – even to his team-mates or those who professed to be close to him... In recent years I have played a few charity matches with him for Leeds United's former players team, and even in his sixties, he still had the propensity for getting into fights.'

This geriatric timebomb, still causing mayhem on the field despite pushing seventy, instilled such a formidable appetite for winning through his leadership and outrageous competitiveness that it blew away the indifference that had stunted the club's development for forty years.

It helped that he felt he had something to prove. Although many Goodison Park regulars were upset, no one was more piqued that Everton had accepted Revie's offer than Collins himself. As a celebrated Scottish international enjoying a successful spell on Merseyside after hitting so many peaks with Celtic, why on earth would Everton want to farm him out to another club? And not just any club, but one propping up the Second Division? The only inference which could be drawn was that at thirty-one, Harry Catterick, Everton's avuncular manager, thought him 'past it'. Collins turned the rancour he felt at this rejection into a one-man crusade to embarrass Everton's folly.

In paying £25,000 for the 5ft 4in inside-forward (the *Yorkshire Post* priced him at £390 per inch, more expensive than gold), Revie quickly harnessed Collins' violent emotions by giving him the responsibility he had craved, making him captain in all but name. Revie was never a control freak when it came to his lieutenants. If it wasn't carte blanche, it was close to it, as Revie delegated all on-field authority to the diminutive firebrand. Although he had appeared intermittently himself throughout the season, and even the week prior to Collins' signing, he never played again. In conjunction with United's two other deadline week captures – Ian Lawson and Cliff Mason – Collins' Leeds lost only once in March before they faced their last seven fixtures crammed into a twenty-one-day period in April.

Their season hinged on the ludicrously gruelling traditional Easter weekend that encompassed games on Good Friday, Easter Saturday and 'Easter Tuesday'. All three matches were superficially dull draws, two against Bury, one versus Derby, which contained, according to reports, 'plenty of bodily impact' but 'precious little sustained football'.

At the time, that double-header with Bury was an instantly forgettable fixture. More than fifteen years later, however, it was to become mythicized as one of the most notorious matches of the Revie era. In the *Daily Mirror* Bob Stokoe, who had been the Bury manager back in 1962, alleged that Revie had offered him £500 to throw one of the games. These rumours, which have been well aired in football circles for many years, have yet to be proven. Innuendo of this nature has stuck to Revie since his death, but significantly it was only widely disseminated after his supposed apostasy in quitting the England manager's job in 1977.

One will never know, but the weight of evidence the *Sunday Times* used to undermine the *Mirror*'s story seems pretty convincing. How was Revie, on £38 a week, able to afford the substantial bung of Stokoe's claims? Is there any prior history of Revie's involvement in match fixing? Why did Stokoe wait fifteen years to tell his story and then only when paid £14,000 to do so? Leeds fans might add that if

Revie was trying to fix matches, why did he leave it so late? That there are no other witnesses than the profoundly embittered Stokoe argues against Revie's guilt.

United's penultimate game, the goal-less draw at Elland Road with Bury, still left them on a knife edge, even more so since their main relegation rivals Swansea Town had games in hand owing to postponements caused by the South Wales smallpox epidemic. Although the Collins-inspired run of eight games unbeaten had hauled Leeds out of the bottom two, they had only taken maximum points from two games, leaving them in a precarious position.

Needing a point to ensure survival, Leeds travelled to St James' Park to face Newcastle with a contingent of 3000 fans – nearly half their total attendance at some home games earlier in the season. Thanks to a mesmerizing display from the recently restored Johanneson, Leeds won 3–0. However, this match was the second of the three games in Revie's career said to have been fixed (the third was against Wolves in 1972). The *Daily Mirror* in its 'Revie File' quoted an anonymous source who claimed that he had been present when Revie had 'tapped up' Newcastle's captain, Stan Anderson. The informant went on to allege that the Newcastle players were offered £10 each to lie down for Leeds, and such was Anderson's ire at the suggestion that Revie had to apologize.

Again, the failure of anyone to go 'on the record' about this is revealing. There's never been any independent corroboration of this anonymous witness's 'evidence'. One would think that with Revie dead for over a decade and the threat of libel having receded, if anyone had firm evidence it would have come to light. What remains is gossip. How can one overlook the fact that Newcastle only finished three points above Leeds and had already lost seventeen games that season? That Newcastle's motivation since assuring themselves of safety was in question is fair comment, but pub talk that the match was fixed is way off the mark. What is certain is that by the inspired purchase of Collins, Revie's holding operation had saved the club from relegation. Now it was time to turn the whole thing around.

FOUR

Leeds United seems to suffer more than most clubs from transfer speculation. In straitened times it gives the fans hope that the club remains an enticing prospect for top-drawer talent. In the early 1990s not a summer would pass without the club's managing director, the bombastic Bill Fotherby, arriving back from some exotic location to announce that although no big name had actually *signed* for the club, negotiations were continuing. Throughout July and August one would read in the papers how close the two sides were and how ecstatic the star in question was at the thought of 'putting pen to paper'. Journalists were dispatched to Leeds/Bradford Airport to capture the first interview with the incoming player. Strangely enough, Thomas Skuhravy, Reuben Sosa and Faustino Asprilla all failed to arrive.

Journalists don't call the summer months 'the silly season' for nothing. No matter how unattainable the target might be, some hack will run with it. It's an arrangement that suits all sides: it excites the fans, keeps the club in the headlines and provides acres of easy copy for the local newspapers.

In 1987, for instance, they suddenly splashed on United's attempt to buy Diego Maradona from Napoli for £10 million. Why the best player in the world, only a year on from Mexico '86, would want to join a club once again firmly stuck in the Second Division was never sensibly debated. How Leeds were in a position to contemplate smashing the domestic transfer record by a firm £8 million wasn't even investigated. It seemed enough that a club official had tentatively hypothesized on its feasibility. Why, fans began to wonder as Maradona never materialized, were they felt to be so gullible as to believe that a superstar talent at the height of his career would leave Serie A to join a struggling Second Division club? Older fans could tell them why. Because it had happened before.

The punchline of the old joke runs: 'You call it Yorkshire, we call it paradise.' One can detect the pride underlying the self-deprecation. All the same, one doubts that living in the Broad Acres, even in today's yuppified Leeds, beats the Italian Riviera, being well paid, playing for the most famous football club in Italy, regularly winning major honours and the adulation of hundreds of thousands of fans throughout one's adopted nation. Back in 1962 it seemed preposterous. However, as early as April that year, news began to appear in the papers that John Charles still hadn't accepted a year's extension to his Juventus contract. It is true that after winning three scudettos in the past four years, 1961/62 had been a disaster for Juve, who had plummeted to twelfth; but it still seemed inconceivable that they would sell their talisman, a man who had scored 108 goals in five glorious seasons. After all, forty years on he's still gauged as the best overseas player in Italian football history. But homesickness is an odd thing, and Charles, after five years of luxurious exile, was pining for more familiar haunts. So began the most drawn out and damaging transfer saga Leeds United had ever undertaken, conducted using all the technology of the time: the telegram, the cable message and the pre-booked trans-continental telephone link.

In his last season at Elland Road, Charles had scored 38 goals in just forty appearances, but more significantly for the Board, he had drawn an average attendance of over 32,000 to each home game. Admittedly, this had been in the First Division, but it clearly played a part in the Board's thinking, as they freely admitted. Short of signing Pelé, Leeds couldn't have acquired a player more certain to attract a crowd than John Charles. 'Our aim is to get back into the top flight,' pronounced Harry Reynolds. 'If there is going to be a Super League, we want to be in it.' It was almost thirty years too early to start worrying about the Premiership, but there was a sense that the club was running out of time to establish itself among the elite.

Juventus didn't hesitate to hint that Arsenal and Tottenham were also interested in Charles. Leeds, who were basing their whole plan for financial recovery on Charles' return, couldn't afford to let him move elsewhere. 'Don't worry,' said Reynolds, 'We'll get the money somehow if Juventus will let him leave.' The *Yorkshire Evening Post* emphasized Charles' enthusiasm at the prospect of 'coming home'. In early July, Reynolds, Revie, Albert Morris and Percy Woodward, the Vice Chairman, resplendent in their summer-weight suits, took the BEA jet from Yeadon Airport to Turin to start the tortuous transfer dialogue. What would the hard-nosed Yorkshire businessmen, more Bradley Hardacre than Timothy West, make of the mercurial Umberto Agnelli?

United's team had asked to conduct the talks at Turin Airport so as to 'get it done quickly', but in intense heat they failed to nail down a deal. Agnelli refused to sell Charles before he had signed up replacements, and both his top targets were still resting after Brazil's June World Cup triumph.

Juventus, meanwhile, had invited Charles to be present for the talks – a telling contrast with the British view of players as, essentially, commodities like cattle. 'It is not known for that to happen in English football,' grumbled Reynolds. But in fact it was Juventus' respect for Charles, in keeping him posted on developments and allowing him to speak with Leeds, which pushed the deal through. While Reynolds and his co-directors took care of the money side, Don Revie outlined his plans for the club to Big John. This casual conversation sealed the day. Impressed by Revie's formulation of a game plan based largely on his aerial dominance, Charles issued an ultimatum. He wouldn't sign a new contract; he was going home and that was that.

Instead of conceding, however, Agnelli resigned his post, leaving the Leeds delegation 'pouring with sweat' (Woodward), to return to Leeds to claim that the deal was '99 per cent certain to go through'. It would be a further month of sleepless nights, frantic telegrams, daily bulletins in the press and constant panic at the rumours of being gazumped before Leeds pulled off what should have been the greatest public relations coup of all time – re-signing the best British footballer of the post-war era. Instead, badly handled from the start, it turned into a fiasco that almost bankrupted the club.

English clubs, in a spirit of co-operation, generally allow transfers to be paid in instalments. Indeed, Leeds still owed money for Collins, Lawson and their other summer signing, Jim Storrie, the payments falling due at regular intervals over the next two years. This was not the Juventus way. When United had sold Charles in 1957, they had demanded and received the £65,000 fee up-front. It made perfect sense, therefore, for Juventus to insist on reciprocal terms. The return fee, haggled down to £53,000, would have to be paid 'on the nail'.

Having already made hefty down-payments on five players since the previous Christmas, the directors had little choice but to stump up the cash themselves. With their personal liabilities beginning to mount, it was not long before they devised a scheme to recoup their outlay. Leeds fans, delighted by Charles' return and generous in their praise of the Board's philanthropy, were in for a shock.

Reynolds emerged from July's Board meeting to announce a 45 per cent hike in season ticket prices, rising from £7. 7s. to 10 guineas. The Board, he rather obtusely explained, were 'giving the public a chance to show the firmness of their promises to support the club if the Board embarked on a policy of team-building and bringing personalities to Elland Road...'.

Even Manchester United's top-price tickets were only £8.10s. Overnight, Leeds had become the most expensive Football League club to support outside London. 'The increase in prices,' wrote one season ticket holder in a letter to the *Yorkshire Evening Post*, 'is tantamount to repayment by ticket holders and others of directors' loans and not an extra paid for the pleasure of seeing John do his part in the recovery of Leeds Utd.' This mini mutiny didn't unduly trouble the Board. What were season ticket holders going to do? Switch to another team? Even if a few held out, enough would not be able to resist paying the increased price to make it worthwhile. Now the Board proceeded to dig themselves into a deeper hole. They waited until Charles had actually arrived in the city before divulging the result of their deliberations on standing prices. This time the boost was a prodigious 150 per cent, from 3s to 7/6. One wag noted that 'King John's shilling has turned into 4/6!' As a declaration of war on their own fans, the Board's parsimonious initiative could scarcely be bettered. They should have known better than anyone that it's always unwise to muck about with a Yorkshireman when it comes to brass. The city went mad.

No blame was attached to Charles as he disported himself around the city's social circuit. Garlanded wherever he went, he was welcomed like a conquering hero, opening nightclubs, even doling out the trophies at the Elland Road dog track. The fans' ire was directed solely at the Board. A fulminatory petition signed by more than seventy Corporation Depot workers ran as follows: 'Dear Mr Revie and Reynolds, You have again hit the jackpot. You have put the first nail in the coffin of Leeds United. We are afraid that you will get a very poor turn out for the funeral of Leeds United this season.' Others sent wreaths and sarcastic letters thanking the club for bringing Charles back but arguing that it was 'A pity we can't afford to watch him.'

More sympathetic observers, like the journalist Phil Brown, tried to put the Board's policy in perspective. One only had to look at the club's finances, he explained. On payment of Charles' £53,000 fee, the club's total borrowings would exceed £200,000, 'a record in the history of professional football in this country'. This was 'a terrible load for even the wealthy men who compose United's Board to shoulder for too long without substantial relief'. The problem was that when they had rallied to the club's rescue, no one had thought their loans would have to be repaid so quickly. What was supposed to be long-term investment, priming the pump for the club's expansion, was in reality nearer, in Brown's words, to 'the gambler's last throw'. Due perception is everything: the Board members were thought to have accepted the plaudits for rescuing Leeds, only to claw back their cash at the first opportunity. What else were people going to think? Far more cunning chairmen would have let the fair-weather fans in at the old prices for the opening games to gawp at Charles in the hope of hooking them first and diddling them later.

For a brief period, Harry Reynolds became the most loathed man in Leeds. Most people in this predicament would now stop digging, but Reynolds' pride was dented since his integrity had been questioned. He chose this moment to launch another ill-advised offensive. Reluctantly reversing the directors' decision to make the first two games of the season all-ticket (the idea of collecting the gate money for ticket sales more quickly than normal had spectacularly backfired, with less than 6000 pre-sales for each game), he couldn't resist taking a swipe at his paying public as 'these nigglers, people who haven't been interested before'. It was these 'summat for nowters', he went on, who were the guilty men in Leeds' decline. 'If they do not want football in Leeds, what's the use of trying?' Abusing one's customers is a singularly unorthodox approach to marketing.

While the local papers were receiving a record post bag on any issue in their history, Don Revie was attempting to assimilate a patently unfit John Charles into the new Leeds United set-up. The previous year he had given the Board two options. Either they wait three or four years for their policy of youth development to reach maturity, or they could go for broke sooner. For much of 1961 and 1962 the former had been the agreed way forward, and Revie had begun to offload the likes of McConnell, Cameron and Humphreys while signing coveted fifteen-year-old kids like Jimmy Greenhoff.

With the purchase of first Collins, then Charles, the blueprint had subtly changed. In the summer of 1962 promotion was back on the agenda. Having had to prop up the club in its relegation spell, the Board felt that they had compromised their original design anyway, so the signing of Charles was meant to reinforce their switch to the fast-track route back to the First Division. In economic and playing terms, they'd gone back to boom and bust. In his final press briefing before the first game of the new season, Revie was careful to rule out all talk of promotion. 'I do not build castles in the air,' he said. With less than two weeks of pre-season training to get Charles fit after months of inactivity, he was right to be circumspect.

On paper, Leeds looked to have a fair chance. Revie's ideal line-up was starting to come together: two pacy wingers in Johanneson and Bremner; steely guile at inside-forward with Collins and Storrie, and a world-class centre-forward in Charles. The rest of the team, from Younger in goal to Smith in midfield, was rather more prosaic, but as a whole, they were as good as anything else in the division. If the defence could gel and the individual players began to assert themselves more, United's attacking unit would intimidate most teams. Understandably, therefore, the game plan was pretty rudimentary. They would play to their strengths – get the ball wide, give it to Charles and trust that Collins and Storrie would exploit any uncertainty caused by Charles' metaphorical and physical stature. If Charles could unlock defences coached by Helenio Herrerra, what difficulties could Walsall pose?

The Board, moreover, had agreed to Revie's proposal to improve the player's conditions, if not their pay. No more apartheid on trains: they would travel in first class with the officials, and the standard of hotels for away fixtures was to be radically upgraded. Revie's whole outlook was, as Jack Charlton revealed, that 'Leeds United is a lump of ground. It's the team that matters.' Once again, he was proving to them that, for him, they were worth fighting for. Once again, pre-season training was rounded off in a restaurant; but this time the players, now furnished with swankier single-breasted club blazers and redesigned ties, treated their besieged Board to dinner at the Parkway Hotel, to 'thank them for the encouragement given when things looked blackest'. The 'club spirit' Revie had talked about so often was demonstrably thriving.

Contrary to all pessimistic expectations, thousands of extra fans poured through the turnstiles to witness John Charles' homecoming. The only problem was that they were Stoke City fans. Leeds kicked off the 1962/63 season at the Victoria Ground in front of 27,000 people with an impressive 1–0 victory, Jim Storrie scoring a debut goal.

Despite all the acrimony caused by the price hike, surely this start would help to swell the gate for Leeds' first home fixture? The club certainly thought so: kiosks adorned with John Charles posters were opened in the city centre. Rotherham United were hardly a big mid-week draw at Elland Road, but even so, the attendance of 14,119, barely 500 above the previous season's abysmal average, sent Reynolds into an apoplectic rage.

Still worse, though Charles scored, Leeds contrived to lose 3–4, with the defending particularly poor. Reynolds wondered if many 'genuine' fans were still on holiday: the next opponents, Sunderland, a fairly local rival, would, he said, present a better test of the new pricing structure. Thanks largely to travelling Wearsiders, Reynolds got his wish. The gate shot up to 17,753 and Leeds managed another 1–0 win, but it was obvious that the experiment had run its course. Immediately after the game the Board reversed the swinging price rises, Reynolds graciously apologized for all the offence he had caused and announced more modest prices for the rest of the season.

Yet if the fans who thought they had defeated a monumental injustice now refused to pay for John Charles, then Leeds United, with imminent payments due on Collins, Lawson, Storrie and even McAdams, couldn't afford the luxury of keeping him. After five months of expensive wooing and only three games, the word was discreetly put out, principally to the Italian media. When less than 15,000 people from a city of over half a million were prepared to stump up to see Charles play, it was time to cash in and revert to Plan B. Perversely, it always takes time to make a quick change. Leeds picked up only one point from their next three games, even though Charles scored twice. The attendance for Leeds' first home game after Reynold's volte-face was a healthy 28,312, their highest crowd for more than two years. It came too late, however, to justify the financial gamble the club had taken on Charles. By far the most noticeable thing about these games was Collins' performances as he stepped up to lead the team in the absence of Goodwin. The injured Goodwin also relinquished his place in the long-term future of the club, as Revie's progressive inclination replaced him with Willie Bell.

Although Collins, the 'Pocket Napoleon' of Goodison Park, probably wouldn't merit a place in Leeds' best ever XI, he was nonetheless the best captain Leeds have ever had. Even Bremner, his only real rival for that honour, deferred to Collins: 'I always felt confident that so long as Bobby was in the team, he would bully, coax, cajole, cool us down when we were in danger of losing our heads, encourage and praise us whenever we did anything good, and generally look after us like a father.'

Or, to put it another way, he was an intense little bugger who refused to let anyone intimidate him and demanded resilience from his colleagues, even if he had to petrify them into it.

Like Dave Mackay at Tottenham, Collins led by example; but it always helped that both men's team-mates were, in a sense, terrorized by the fear of falling short of their volcanic captain's standards. To Collins, nothing was sacrosanct. 'If you stepped out of line in training,' said Everton's Colin Harvey, 'then he would do you no danger, but having said that, you looked up to him because of his ability.' Eddie Gray recalls being smacked about the head for being duped in a running competition, and even Jack Charlton was a little apprehensive around the midget firebrand. 'I got on all right with Bobby, but I didn't like to play against him. Even when we were playing five-a-side, you never knew what he was liable to do because he wanted to win so much.' Collins, the cliché had it, would fight with his mother over a game of dominoes. Most important of all, he hectored the other players throughout the whole game; it taught them the value of communication he had so assiduously learned at a higher level. Had Revie persevered with his line-up of 'seen it all' professionals, their silent complacency would probably have diluted Collins' influence. Now, therefore, Revie gave his indomitable drill sergeant more impressionable minds to mould.

Though Revie had been in his post for nearly two years, and despite all the money he had recently spent, after six games Leeds had played six, won two, drawn one and lost three, a mirror image of their opening six fixtures of 1961/62. Then, his solution was to pick himself. This time he jettisoned half his team.

Hitherto, the *Yorkshire Evening Post* had only mentioned the Leeds reserve team in order to bemoan the cancellation of a scheduled bus service to its games owing to poor demand. Now, however, it was taking notice of a sequence of wins by a team that included eight players under the age of nineteen. Contrary to the accepted version, this first wave of young professionals had actually been signed by Jack Taylor as apprentices at the age of fifteen, but under the tutelage of Owen and Cocker and with Revie's motto – confidence, concentration, courage – guiding their education, several of them had started to exhibit the required maturity for first team conflict.

In the meantime, Revie was constantly adding to their ranks by signing up the best schoolboy talent, particularly from Scotland. Following any report of potential from his Scottish scout John Barr, Revie and Maurice Lindley would decamp in Revie's blue (lucky blue, of course!) Ford Zephyr to assess the players themselves. If they 'fancied' the player, a long courting process would be instigated involving many repeat trips, 'gifts' for the family, telephone calls and 'holidays' in Yorkshire, culminating in the boy signing apprenticeship forms on his fifteenth birthday. All clubs essentially have the same approach to convincing young talent that theirs is the ideal club, so Revie must have had something unique to entice so many to sign for Leeds in the face of offers from more famous clubs. Most of the Scottish lads and their families have admitted that until Revie appeared on their doorsteps, they'd never even heard of Leeds United. Once he was inside their home, they seldom went elsewhere.

The secret of his technique was his affable empathy with working-class families. He was prepared to chat away for hours, drinking endless cups of tea and charming the grannies with his confident yet unflashy manner. For someone perceived as insecure and prone to occasional bouts of John Prescott-like incomprehensibility, he was a master of this seduction process. He was always sincere with the parents, ready to outline his vision for Leeds and their son's role in it with a painstaking attention to detail. 'He continued to visit my parents in Scotland whenever he was up there,' says Eddie Gray, 'and did the same for Peter Lorimer's... He did a fantastic selling job.'

And if all this failed, he could always sort out a little extra cash for the player, which would naturally find its way home: sign the player on amateur terms and arrange an undemanding little job in the vicinity of Elland Road for quadruple the regular £7 per week maximum. All part of the service! Taking advantage of the amateur loophole was hardly an uncommon practice in the game, and though officially scorned, it was highly effective in securing kids from less well-off families. Leeds signed both Eddie Gray and Peter Lorimer as amateurs, even though they had apprenticeship offers from Celtic, Manchester United, Chelsea and over twenty other clubs. These two recruits at fifteen, straight from the Scotland schoolboy XI, were still a bit green for first-team action, even under the current circumstances. Their older colleagues in the reserves, with the assurance of youth and better footballing habits than many first teamers, were just about ready to graduate.

At the time, picking three seventeen-year-olds and one eighteen-year-old was seen by sympathetic commentators as Revie's attempt to 'do a Cullis' and emulate Wolverhampton Wanderers' successful youth policy; others saw it as a strange and potentially lethal gamble. It has subsequently been interpreted as the defining moment in the club's history. The four players in question – Gary Sprake, Rod Johnson, Paul Reaney and Norman Hunter – were all contemporaries of Bremner and had played in the same youth sides. Only Sprake had ever played for the first team, when he'd been flown to Southampton on the morning of the game the previous season and unhappily conceded four goals. On the Thursday before Leeds' seventh game of the 1962/63 season, the four players were called aside after training and told, 'underneath the main stand', as Hunter recalled, that they'd been picked for the first team. Hunter, Reaney and Sprake were selected in the positions they would hold for at least the next ten years, while Johnson, a quick, slight forward, deputized for the injured Charles up front.

Astonishingly, Leeds won 2–0 with, according to the *Yorkshire Post*, the youngsters 'bringing a zip the side has badly needed'. The most impressive debutant, Rod Johnson, scored one of the goals, but it was the other three who cemented regular first-team places. Hunter, incredibly, would not miss another league match until April 1965. Near the end of his life, in an interview with John Motson looking back on his career, Don Revie paid a highly emotional tribute to each of his lads. Hunter, he said, was so consistent that he got a level of 'about 85 per cent' from him each week. If this seems an unwitting damnation with faint praise, what Revie actually meant was that Hunter wasn't a 'form' player, that right from his debut he effortlessly reached a standard which kept him in the team for fifteen years. Back then, Hunter was a ball-playing midfielder with good stamina and a good range of passing with his consummate left foot. It was only later that the ferociousness of his tackling, celebrated in the famous 'Norman bites yer legs' banner, began to overshadow his more creative attributes.

What Revie appreciated in a young player was pretty simple. If they had ability, desire and a willingness to work, he tended to sign them without bothering about their size or where they would eventually play: it would work out somehow. Many players benefited from his unblinkered approach. Hunter was an inside-forward who became a midfielder and then an international centre-back; Terry Cooper a winger who mutated into the best left-back in the world; Eddie Gray a central midfielder converted into a winger; Bremner and Giles wingers turned central midfielders. This 'eye' for potential has been all the more underrated because it didn't work when Revie tried it with mature players for England, packing the midfield time and again with central defenders. But this alchemist's skill with younger players transformed Leeds United.

With the highest paid player in the country now recovered from injury and just about to move into an £8,000-house in the village of

Collingham the club had been obliged to purchase for him, John Charles naturally returned to first-team duty for the next match; Sprake, Reaney and Hunter all kept their places. Chelsea, who were to be promoted that season under Tommy Docherty, were thrashed at Elland Road by a Leeds team reduced to ten men after Eric Smith broke his leg in the 4th minute. The few match reports that exist of this unimportant fixture note the excellence of Johanneson's performance in scoring both goals and significantly point to 'a new atmosphere abroad at Elland Road', with the 27,500 in the stands staying behind after the game to applaud the players in 'a constant fever of excitement'.

Once again the optimism proved premature. Of the next five games Leeds drew three and lost two, and despite home attendances in excess of 25,000, the on-field experiment with Charles, the one thing everyone had been confident of, was just not working. As a centre-forward at least, his capacity for Second Division football was exhausted. If he had scored regularly, he could have justified the transfer even though Leeds could no longer afford to retain him. But with his rickety confidence reflected in his slow and uncharacteristically hesitant contributions, the overtures from Italy were becoming increasingly difficult for club and player alike to resist.

The most trigger-happy element at a football club is usually its fans. It's even more common at Elland Road, where scores of players over the years have been subjected to withering criticism for not meeting the required standard. Even homegrown kids have been canned off after a couple of games; in recent years a succession of over-priced imports have also suffered virulent abuse. Leeds fans think it's healthy to do so. They've paid their money, and it's their right, they would maintain, as the true guardians of the club's spirit, to let the world know that Leeds United expects better. With Charles they made an exception, orchestrating a campaign for the club to show patience in the face of all the rumours concerning his impending departure: the Board should let him reacclimatize to English football, he remained a priceless asset and only needed, as

Phil Brown put it, 'a chance to hoist himself back on his own high pedestal'.

It was a complete misreading of the situation. The reasons for John Charles' second spell 'not working out' are complex. He was actually a thoroughbred centre-half who for many years had masqueraded as a centre-forward – with unparalleled success – but that experiment had reached its sell-by date. Leeds couldn't really afford him in the first place and they certainly couldn't afford a £53,000 centre-half even if he was still one of the best around. Their investment was meant to score goals. Most importantly, the Board had gambled on the transfer essentially paying for itself, but the supporters had proved reluctant to bear financially the 'Charles premium' and, given Charles' form, the Board were reluctant to underwrite the deal. Honourable as ever, Charles gave them a way out: 'I have reached the stage now where I can't sleep at nights,' Charles exploded after another poor performance in the 0–0 draw with Derby County, when he had continually drifted behind his support striker Jim Storrie. 'This is the first time my football has left me so long and I feel shattered. It was a mistake for me to come back.' Days later Leeds accepted AS Roma's £65,000 bid and put his still vacant house on the market. In hindsight this was, at last, the turning point. 'Let him go and cheer on Bobby Collins,' suggested a lone supportive letter in the *Yorkshire Evening Post*. 'A team built around Collins will surely go places.' Within three years they were in Europe. Roma's gamble on Charles would be just as short-lived as Leeds' had been: after only six months he went to Second Division Cardiff, and ended up four years later as player-manager of non-league Hereford.

Without Charles, most people feared the worst. Fortunately, Revie now stumbled by accident, as he freely admitted at the club's next AGM, on a more penetrative formula. He switched Jim Storrie to centre-forward, the former Airdrie man proving himself a revelation, scoring with the frequency that had been expected of the illustrious Charles. This rich streak saw him score 20 goals in his remaining twenty-seven appearances that season, and was the main reason that

Leeds entered December in a robust shape. For the first time in his managerial career, results had given Revie the breathing space to keep a settled side. From Charles' departure onwards he essentially stuck to a team based on nine regular starters – Sprake, Reaney, Bell, Charlton, Hunter, Bremner, Collins, Storrie and Johanneson – with the other two places open to youth players like Addy, Johnson and even Lorimer, or veterans like Hair and Mason. All nine kept their places for four years.

Following Charles' return to Italy, Leeds lost only once in nine games. It was slowly beginning to dawn on most fans that the messiah they were looking for was not Charles but their manager. The club itself, however, was in terrible shape. At the December AGM the accounts showed a loss of over £70,000 and debts amounting to £140,000. The club was only solvent thanks to the book value of the ground and the directors' guarantees to the bank. But no one seemed to care as a gregarious Reynolds urged everyone to toast the new optimism around the club and give 'thanks to our nursery policy'. 'With a continued free hand and the backing of supporters,' Revie enthused, 'We're on the way to having a good side.' The 'free hand' had been there from day one; the backing of supporters was still some way off, as attendances initially returned to their pre-Charles average of around 15,000. At least with regular gate income to bank, however disappointing, the Board was confident that the financial situation would improve as rapidly as the team.

Like most clubs, Leeds United's cash-flow came from gate receipts. It was the lifeblood of the club, paying for the maintenance of the ground and everyone's wages. In 1961/62 the annual running costs were £83,000, of which £70,000 was covered on the turnstiles, with the shortfall made up by gifts from the various supporters' clubs. The purchase of players was only made possible through the directors' largesse but tellingly in the form of secured loans to the club. It was made perfectly clear that the club's day-to-day costs were solely the supporters' preserve. Paying for John Charles allowed the business magnate to indulge himself in a romantic dream; paying the canteen staff's wages was a different matter altogether. The 'I pay my own way, I say, I pay my own way' stereotype of Yorkshiremen does hold some truth. If Leeds wanted a football team, the least the fans could do was fund its ordinary expenses.

Extraordinary circumstances then intervened. The winter of 1963, though not quite as severe, lasted even longer than the hard winter of 1947, hitting football far harder as a consequence. The whole of the north of England was frozen to a standstill under a blanket of ice. United's FA Cup third round tie with Stoke City, scheduled for January, was postponed twelve times. From 22 December to 1 March the club was in hiatus, unable to fulfil any of its fixtures. The loss of seventy days' trading would affect any business. Crucially, for a football club with large wage bills to sustain even though its income stream had dried up, there was only one solution. The directors had to shoulder the burden themselves. The Board reluctantly increased their personal guarantees to the bank, thus permitting a bigger overdraft. In addition, further loans were made by Reynolds, Cussins and Morris.

Leeds United emerged after its hibernation in early March, the team carrying on where it had left off, catapulting itself into the thick of a promotion race. It was a year too early, and with nineteen games to play, they were far off the pace. Moreover, the two points for a win system was prejudiced against the late surge; it was how a team started that counted. But they gave it a hell of a shot. In the remaining games Collins led from the front, often playing like a puppet-master on speed as he orchestrated attacks and co-ordinated his defenders with his dynamic passing, subtle use of space and ready courage to receive the ball from a team-mate, even when under intense opposition pressure. For football fans the definition of bravery is simple: a willingness to get hurt in the tackle. Leeds certainly had this in abundance, but players themselves have a more sophisticated concept: that a player should never hide – should be hungry for the ball however tight the situation, and have the technique and temperament to deal with it without panic. That was the major lesson Collins taught the youngsters. This, more than anything else, taught them the responsibility they had to the team. It made the club what it was to become in the decade to follow.

Of course, Leeds players were all too prepared to back each other up physically – they were notorious for it. But, more importantly, they backed each other up on the ball, which helped to eradicate the fear factor from possession and retention. It also gave the intelligent player far more options and the intelligent team far more attacking verve. In March 1963 Leeds finally began to play in the recognizable style of the 'Glory Years'. Though the personnel would subsequently change, the first glimpses are certainly evident in Eric Stanger's match reports from April. 'Their football at times, imaginative, fast and crowned by hard shooting was better than much that has been seen even in the 1st Division this season. Leeds are blending in a harmony of purpose which comes from every player being prepared to put team needs before personal achievement.' Bremner's famous adage 'Side before self every time' was inspired by this notion of collective responsibility that emerged that spring, and though it was Revie who constantly preached its benefits, it was Collins who showed them how to do it. This is a microcosm of the Leeds way. Revie did the theory; Owen, Cocker and Collins took the practicals.

Of the six teams still in the promotion shake-up – the others were Stoke, Chelsea, Sunderland, Middlesbrough and Huddersfield – United had the most games in hand, and by winning seven of their first ten games after the thaw, rapidly gained ground. The gangling Ian Lawson and the recently signed, fleet-footed Don Weston proved able foils for the rumbustious Storrie, who had developed into a tenacious centre-forward successfully encouraged to shoot on sight. In winning three games in four days over Easter, the unthinkable became a remote possibility. One man dissented from the consensus that such an inexperienced side could hardly hope to narrow the gap: Richard Ulyatt of the *Yorkshire Post*. With the 'pertinacious Storrie' and the 'presiding genius Collins', Leeds 'finally have a team good enough to go up'.

It was not to be. In this most abnormal of seasons, with so many games crammed into April and May to compensate for the two-month shutdown, mental rather than physical fatigue was always likely to hamper such a young team. With nine games to play, Chelsea were in second place but United had three games in hand on their flashy rivals; Leeds were six points behind them with the two teams still to meet at Stamford Bridge. If Chelsea were to be overhauled – still technically possible – Leeds had to win all their games in hand and then inflict defeat on the Blues. They achieved a creditable 2–2 draw in that game but promptly lost three of their next four, consigning them to fifth place. Don Revie learned the superiority of points in the bag to games in hand the hard way. All Leeds' subsequent success in the league came as front-runners. They were never happy in the chase.

It had been the slimmest of chances but Revie didn't seem so perturbed they hadn't made it. If they weren't ready, they weren't ready. Confident in the knowledge of 'even more young players up his capricious sleeve' (Stanger), he knew the breakthrough was imminent. Always looking for greater personal security, in May he asked for and was offered an improved three-year contract, which made him the best-paid manager outside the First Division.

He would remain touchingly grateful to the older players who had tried to bring stability to the club. Indeed, he would always make a fuss of them when they visited Elland Road and tell his team with a touch of hyperbole that if it were not for people like Cliff Mason, for example, there wouldn't even be a Leeds United. In two seasons he had tried and failed to construct a capable team around the players from his own era. In nineteen games he had seen what could be achieved with players from his own mould. After two years of unbridled mediocrity, the Revie Plan Mk II stood on the threshold of success.

FIVE

ANYTHING GOES

I n the summer of 1963 the nation was preoccupied with the twin attractions of the Stephen Ward vice trial and the Great Train Robbery. There was little room for the ephemeral football gossip concerning transfers and prospects. Even England's test cricket annihilation at the hands of Frank Worrell's West Indians received relatively scant coverage. In an age where we're used to football's unrelenting stream of speculation and all manner of unsought-for trivia, it can be disconcerting to discover that, as recently as the mid-1960s, once a season finished, there was no real news about a club or its players for more than six weeks.

Strangely little, however, was made at the time of another of Don Revie's superstitions. In 1963, in the belief that Elland Road was haunted by a 'gipsy's curse', he arranged for the ground to be exorcized. The transformation of his image from lovable 'eccentric' to 'nutter' was to happen much later. One has to remember that this sort of nonsense is not unusual in football. As late as the 1990s, Barry Fry, then manager of Birmingham City, would cheerfully recount how he had urinated in the four corners of St Andrew's to ward off the evil spirits affecting his club. Revie, too, was never self-conscious about his superstitiousness, and in 1970 allowed Yorkshire TV to film his pre-match routine, expounding on his habits in the commentary. 'I have the same blue suit on that I've had since the first match of the season,' he said, 'the same lucky blue tie, one or two lucky charms in my pocket – I have a spot up here, I walk up to the traffic lights every time, I turn around and walk back to the hotel.'

This bizarre promenade and all his other little foibles have been held up to ridicule, but essentially they were no more than harmless little rituals that comforted him. It's discernible from his droll voice-over that he, more than anyone, was aware of how silly it appeared. However, he continued to see his little ceremonies as a principal part of his match preparation, refusing to leave anything he might be able to control, however illogical, to chance.

The close season activities of the Leeds staff were as unpretentious as the men themselves. Fred Goodwin, for instance, was coaching in Rhodesia; Jack Charlton whetted his entrepreneurial skills in the Bradford cloth trade; Billy Bremner and his young bride visited friends and family; and Don Revie was on his usual golfing break in Scotland. All the previous season's exotic activity was replaced by a calmly confident sense of expectation. This time the priority was not consolidation, that dread word which depresses all football fans, but consistency; as the manager put it in full cliché mode, 'A good start is half the battle.'

The players' fitness had reached new levels, too. During the three-month mid-winter lay-off, Les Cocker had been able to take the players to the gym every day for his merciless stamina-building sessions. For those players who habitually liked nothing more strenuous than five-a-sides, it had been hard work, but they were quick to note its efficacy. In the fixtures that followed the break, they found they could intimidate teams with a hard-running 'pressing' game without running out of steam after an hour and conceding critical goals in the later stages, a practice that had plagued them all season. 'Considerable determination in a rugged style,' was one observer's description. They could still be outplayed on occasion, but they were never again to be outrun or outfought.

So much for the improvement in the players' bodies. What happened to their minds? In recent years the application of sports psychology has made great strides – many football teams striving to build 'team spirit' have come to rely on principles largely derived from the pithy aphorisms of the American Football coach Vince Lombardi. Back then expediency – subsequently and erroneously tarted up as a kind of modernist masterplan – was the keynote. Don Revie's players speak of him as a genius at man-management, often citing the fact that by 1970 he had eighteen internationals on his books and contrived to keep them all happy. This wasn't psychology, though: it was more of a technical skill – juggling players' egos, mollycoddling some, kicking others, as their personalities required. Pure common sense, in other words. Revie was always available for morale-boosting one-to-one chats, but the whole science of developing the individual's focus through self-analysis or visualization would have been anathema to him.

Revie's was a more practical goal: 'club spirit' rather than 'team spirit'. This demanded an institutional focus, not one exclusive to the players – forging a broader coalition throughout the club from the boardroom down, which included its entire staff and other diverse elements, from the stringers at the local papers to local businessmen in the executive supporters club, and most of its fans. How he achieved this was very similar to the methods used by Matt Busby and Bill Shankly: common courtesy, charisma and, most important of all, conviction.

There was soon evidence of this grand club spirit. Two members of Revie's backroom staff declined senior positions at other clubs. Maurice Lindley, the Assistant Manager and Chief Scout, could have gone to Hull City as manager in the summer of 1963, a job that guaranteed much greater income and prestige. But he opted to stay, telling the *Yorkshire Evening Post*, 'Things are better here now almost to a degree you would have not thought possible.' Similarly, Syd Owen, rumoured to be joining Bill Nicholson's staff at Tottenham, reflected that no headhunter could have persuaded him to desert a project that had been built on his sweat. He was very happy at Elland Road, he announced, 'And I want to see our present young players grow on into the first-class players I am sure they will become.' Most remarkably of all, even Jack Charlton's obsessive grumbling had slightly diminished.

Revie still had a couple of problem areas to deal with, however. His first dilemma was what to do with Billy Bremner, who had experienced such a loss of form towards the end of the previous year that he had been dropped. Bremner never took this sort of treatment lightly and resolved once again to return to Scotland for good. 'I was playing at inside-right,' he remembered in his autobiography, 'and nothing, it seemed, would go right for me. In fact I got the bird from the crowd. Well, what with being fed up anyway, and getting the bird from the crowd at Elland Road, I was really browned off.' Dismayed by the fickleness of the fans, he was transfer-listed at his own request. Unbeknown to him, though, Revie kept up a subtle, manipulative game with his asking price to deter suitors like Celtic and Hibernian while he figured out Bremner's ideal role in the team.

Revie had maintained for years that Bremner was the brightest talent at the club, and in a team that had long had trouble scoring, using him in the forward-line was pretty obvious. But though it had worked – 30 goals in three seasons – Revie recognized that it wasn't the best use of the player's talents. In August 1963 he decided to move Bremner permanently into midfield, a decision based on the Scotsman's grittiness as much as anything. The ploy paid off handsomely. His performance in a pre-season friendly against Roma (another part of the Charles severance package) showed real glimpses of maturity and commitment. The old impetuosity still simmered beneath the surface, but Revie was persuaded that Bremner's energy and ability, allied to the tricks learned from Collins, made him, despite his lack of inches, the perfect candidate at right-half.

Bremner's switch now left a gap in the attack, in the one area Revie had always struggled to fill: the number 7 shirt. In the past three years he had operated a revolving selection policy, calling on Bremner, Francis, Mayers, Hawksby, Weston and Henderson as makeshift outside-rights. None of them had made the position his own, and it left Leeds alarmingly lop-sided, as the midfield was instinctively inclined to distribute the majority of possession to the more consistently penetrative Johanneson on the left. Revie had long since been targeting one player as his long-term solution for the right flank, but he was faced with two difficulties: wringing more money out of the Board and pris-ing the player away from a club that footballers seldom voluntarily abandoned. Drunk on debt, the directors released another £30,000 without hesitation. As for the second problem, Matt Busby was about to make the greatest misjudgement of his career.

The object of Revie's interest was Johnny Giles. When he learned that, despite a decent contribution in the FA Cup Final only weeks before, Busby would not be picking him for Manchester United's open-ing fixture of the 1963/64 season, Giles had had enough. He'd been dropped before but had hitherto remained convinced that Busby would ultimately have to recognize his ability. By the Tuesday after the opening fixture he was transfer listed, and moments after the news had broken, Revie was joyfully speeding over the Pennines. It took less than a day to wrap up the whirlwind £33,000 deal. A year before, it had taken four months to sign John Charles. In 1963 it took a mere four days to sign a player that Revie had coveted for just as long.

Ironically, the other reason why Giles was itching to leave Old Trafford his conviction that he was better suited to play as an inside-forward than as a winger. He was not alone in being margin-alized out by the touchline – Bobby Charlton was stuck out on the opposite wing for much of the early 1960s. Yet so frustrated was he by Manchester United dressing-room politics and what Eamon Dunphy, a club apprentice at the time, called 'the anarchic atmos-phere' there, he was willing to drop a division to join Leeds, even if it meant another stint at outside-right. Revie, as ever, did a great selling job.

Twenty-five years after signing for the club, Giles recalled for John Motson, in an interview for the BBC documentary *The Glory Years*, his first impressions of Elland Road. 'I found the first day I went to Leeds an atmosphere I hadn't known at Manchester United. There was a buzz about the place, a keenness, a will and an attention to detail that wasn't at Manchester United. Manchester United wasn't run like that in those days, there it was more off the cuff. [Leeds] were in the Second

Division but there was an ambition and drive that I noted straight away.' In *A Strange Kind of Glory* he returns to that first day with Eamonn Dunphy: 'People were consciously thinking about the game, small things like throw-ins, free-kicks and corner-kicks were discussed and planned. People were intent on doing *something*. It wasn't all left to chance.' It's part of the Manchester United myth that no one ever prospers by leaving Old Trafford. Giles gives the lie to that.

Most accounts of the 1963/64 season portray Leeds' promotion campaign as a bit of a cakewalk. Once the trio of Giles, Bremner and Collins was established, it is assumed, United glided inexorably to the top of the division – Revie, the sorcerer, finally having got all the ingredients together to cast his spell. This rather underrates its significance. This was the season that established the prototypical Leeds United characteristics that would become so notorious. The football itself certainly lacked the champagne touch. It was all attritional efficiency and dour hard work. Leeds scored fewer goals than they had the previous year but functionally accumulated points along the way. Yet the season was never boring: it was littered with fouls, gamesmanship and running battles with the opposition.

The team dutifully obeyed Revie's new first commandment, 'Thou shall start well', losing only once in their first eight games before winning five in succession, a run that took them to the top of the table in mid-October. Crowds, always suckers for success, were also up, edging towards an average of 30,000, and for the first time in five dark years the directors could contemplate the nirvana of profitability. With only 2200 season tickets sold at the beginning of the season, it meant that Albert Morris could normally bank more than 25,000 entrance fees per fortnight. Add in the receipts from away fixtures, and the Board could even make inroads into the overdraft and recoup some of their personal loans to the club. The directors had been dominant figures in the club's salvation in spite of numerous mistakes, but at this point they effectively recede from the story.

It was unfortunate that Leeds should lose Jim Storrie to injury after only nine games of the season, since his absence tended to make their game one-dimensional. They became over-reliant on Albert Johanneson, who had his finest ever season, even with all the physical and racial abuse meted out by neanderthal full-backs terrified by his turn of foot. Don Weston deputized for Storrie for most of the first half of the season but, like Johanneson, his game was based on speed. He matched Albert's strike rate, but these two sprinters, often playing at breakneck pace, at the very edge of their capability, were as liable to make elementary blunders as torment the opposing team. Thirteen goals apiece were perfectly satisfactory for support players but hardly compensated for the loss of Storrie's productiveness. Similarly, their styles necessitated a higher tempo; they would receive the ball, dribble with it, pass, cross or shoot it in a matter of seconds, whereas Storrie had the strength and canniness to lead the line in the conventional way, playing with his back to goal, holding the ball up and inviting the midfield to influence the shape of the attack. Without him, goals from Bremner and Collins dried to a trickle.

Like much else, it was Collins who primarily ordained the pace of the game. 'Bobby would shut up the game and tell us when to break,' Bremner subsequently recalled. 'He made us go like bombs for a ten-minute spell. Then he would tell us to tighten up again before making us go again.' Storrie's loss made for a pinball-type attack, which in turn precipitated the more frenetic approach and a glut of fouls. By the time he returned, perhaps because they enjoyed it or simply because it worked, physical intimidation had become an ineradicable feature of the team's approach.

Did Don Revie actually tell his team to go out on the pitch and kick people? Or was it merely his old pragmatic thinking again? It certainly wasn't a ploy Leeds had originated. If anything, it had come out of all the friendlies against Italian opposition they had endured as part of the assorted Charles transfer sagas. The 'kill or be killed' attitude of some Italian defenders had made a huge impression on the players and they swiftly developed some of that ruthlessness – 'professionalism' was the euphemism they preferred themselves. Johnny Giles explained the reasoning behind it: 'You had to establish a reputation,' he wrote in *Forward with Leeds*, 'that would make people think twice about messing with you... I have certainly done things on the football field then that I am embarrassed about now, but one has to put them into the football climate that existed then.'

Giles' book was published in 1970 at the height of the 'dirty Leeds' uproar, so his 'no regrets' tone is not hard to understand. 'You had to get respect,' he went on to add, 'in the sense that people could not clog you without knowing that they would be clogged back.' In the early 1960s roughhouse tactics were accepted practice, and there was a thin line between standing up for oneself on the pitch and getting your retaliation in first. What Leeds set out to do was not nihilistic: it was a hyper-aggressive game plan destined to flourish by pushing the very limits of the laws. The suspicion that Revie directed all this is the fundamental impediment when football aesthetes discuss his credentials for 'greatness'.

It's important to recognize that the team was not unaware of their growing infamy – but neither did they glory in it. Indeed, the reputation did some of the hard work, as teams would already be apprehensive about meeting them weeks before a match. Nor was their confidence undermined by the hostility and scorn of opposing players and fans: they were getting results. 'The game's about glory, it's about doing things in style,' said Danny Blanchflower after his team had won the Double. 'It's about doing things in a style, with a flourish. It's about going out and beating the other lot, not waiting for them to die of boredom.' His words are often misinterpreted as an avowal that football is more about glory than winning. Well, Revie's team was 'beating the other lot', as per his win-at-all-costs attitude, but the thing about flair would have to wait. Blanchflower's Corinthian values could never apply to a provincial club weary after forty years of hard tack.

Not one of Revie's players will admit that their manager ordered them to use violence to get their way. The strongest hint is Jack Charlton's memory of Revie 'murmuring approvingly' as Jimmy Lumsden, a young apprentice, told how he'd dished out a 'real beauty' in a recent match. The truth is that Revie didn't need to tell them. He encouraged ultra-competitiveness on the training ground, saw that his own players were uncomfortable on the receiving end of hard tackling and let them draw their own conclusions. It was more moral ambivalence than depravity: he didn't tell them to do it but he didn't stop them either.

No doubt some players revelled in the bullyboy swagger, but if the indiscipline ever threatened to harm the team's prospects, Revie was not negligent. Later that season Bremner became the first Leeds player under Revie to face an official suspension from the Football League. His crime? Persistent dissent. In public Revie defended his player, who had got a three-match ban, but in front of his colleagues Bremner was rewarded with such a caustic bollocking he felt humiliated.

Referees in the early 1960s gave players far more leeway in the tackle than was healthy. On the whole, however, Leeds went as far as legally permissible but rarely further. They weren't always 'hard but fair'; they were plain hard. Yet one would think from all that's been said about them that common assault was a weekly occurrence. Eddie Gray, one of the few players considered untainted by the general villainy, recalls watching the team from the terraces as a young apprentice and being shocked by much of what he saw. In *Marching on Together* he reveals that even Revie 'used to wince at our approach'. But Leeds felt they had to fight their way out of the Second Division, relying on organization, set-plays and closing down space, utilizing both their superior fitness and physical strength to batter the opposition into submission. Once they had 'earned the right to play', as professionals put it, then they would play.

For all the emerging talent, Collins remained the star of the show. Fortified by his customary tots of Scotch before a game, he pulverized the opposition with his resourcefulness, vision and low cunning. We have seen how his influence changed the club from the inside, but Eric Stanger's match reports show how closely he had come to symbolize the team to the opposition. '"Stop Collins and you stop Leeds," they say in the Seond Division,' he noted. 'But how? He gets in such out-of-the-way places that he must be just about the hardest forward in the game to mark.' To such a young side he was irreplaceable; the only game Leeds lost in their first twenty was the one match Collins missed all season.

Despite the setback of that defeat to Manchester City, Leeds recovered to stay unbeaten until Boxing Day, with Ian Lawson, who had been on the verge of joining Scunthorpe, drafted in to supplement the front line. He was a barnstorming Ian Baird-type forward, and responsible for keeping Leeds United's promotion challenge afloat by scoring eight goals in those first twenty games. The defence had found a new meanness – twelve clean sheets in twenty-two games before Christmas – and Revie pronounced himself relatively happy with the first half of the campaign.

This was the season when Jack Charlton matured as a footballer. He had been attending courses at Lilleshall for a number of years and now, with his new role as mentor to a juvenile defence – Sprake, Reaney, Bell and Hunter – was allowed by Revie to co-ordinate his own defensive system. The delegation of duty seemed to inspire Big Jack. His method involved a great deal of moaning and shouting, but his ability to explain his zonal design and teach his team-mates the positional awareness to cover each other, not to mention his own impeccable form, ensured Leeds' best defensive record to date. With Collins and Bremner buzzing about in front as a protective shield and Giles always ready to help out, Sprake's goal was breached on only thirty-four occasions in the whole season.

Privately, however, Revie was unnerved by Leeds' failure to beat their close rivals – Sunderland, Preston, Charlton and Manchester City – and realized that a better class of centre-forward was necessary to push them further ahead. Weston and Lawson, the über-journeymen, had performed heroically, but any team as dependent on its defensive excellence as Leeds would draw too many games to gain promotion with ease. All success is built from the back, maintains Alan Hansen. With the drought up-front, 'shutting up shop' after clawing a goal was a plausible gamble that often paid off, though it led to frayed nerves amongst the crowd and in the dugout. For Leeds, the foundations were in place, but after losing the second match in their Christmas double-header with Sunderland by spurning numerous chances, Revie knew fresh impetus was required if they were to avoid being lassooed by the chasing pack.

Experts are forever banging on about the 'spine' of a team being of paramount importance – a tough core of experienced players running through the middle of the team – centre-half, central midfield and centre-forward. Without Storrie, Leeds were suffering from lumbago. The Board was now forecasting a small profit on the season's trading, so Revie had little difficulty in persuading them to release funds. Unfortunately, his major problem was that other clubs knew Leeds' predicament. In a seller's market he wanted a player who could almost guarantee promotion, but he had only a modest amount to spend. His scouts reported on a number of candidates, few of whom were likely to be released in the middle of a season unless the bid exceeded their value. Fortunately, one intriguing target was available, but he came with conspicuous risks attached.

Alan 'Peachy' Peacock had enjoyed a prolific spell at Middles-brough, initially as Brian Clough's partner, later as his replacement. He had scored 126 goals in 218 league games and played twice for England in the 1962 World Cup Finals in Chile. His heading ability alone was of the highest class, and in normal circumstances he would have been far beyond Revie's resources. Memorably described by Brian Glanville as 'a tall, straight guardsman-like figure even to the short haircut', he was just over 6ft tall, yet his timing and vertical leap placed him up with Tommy Taylor, John Charles and Nat Lofthouse as the finest exponents of the aerial arts since the maestro Tommy Lawton. His pedigree did not augur well for the club's bank manager, especially since Peacock was only twenty-six. Eighteen months earlier, Denis Law had signed for Manchester United from Torino for £115,000, and while Peacock, splendid player though he was, was not quite in Law's class, he should still easily have been above Leeds' price bracket. Luckily for Leeds, the discount on 'damaged goods' also applied in football. Peacock's persistent knee problems and recent serious cartilage operation, a career-threatening procedure back in 1963, meant that Middlesbrough were resigned to cashing in on the player while they could. They were not so blind to Leeds' position that they forgot to add on a clause that would provide them with a further £5,000 if Leeds achieved promotion. The initial price of £53,000 equalled the club's record transfer fee, a sizeable gamble but one that relieved the pressure on United's beleaguered attack.

Revie's happy knack of signing strikers who made an immediate impact continued with Peacock. Like Storrie and Weston before him, the genial Tees-sider scored on his debut in a disappointing 2–2 draw away to Norwich. The result left them clinging to top spot with thirteen games to play, but both Preston and Sunderland had closed the gap during United's post-Christmas stutter. It took some time for Leeds to adapt to Peacock's strengths, to get used to crossing more balls into the box instead of looking for the lay-offs or passes over the heads of defenders, the sort of service that suited Johanneson, Weston and Storrie. After four games with him in the side, they had only managed one win, a 1–0 defeat of bottom-placed Scunthorpe, and had contrived to lose 2–0 away to Preston, their third defeat of the season.

The little wobble was threatening to turn into something more serious. Preston's win had consigned Leeds to second place. Moreover, they had lost ground to another of their closest rivals and faced the prospect of tough fixtures against Middlesbrough, Newcastle and free-scoring Southampton. All three defeats to date had come away from home, but it was Leeds' home form that was causing most concern. Of the sixteen home games so far, they had won nine and drawn seven, failing to overcome teams like Derby, Cardiff and Northampton, who though not relegation material, were all stuck in the bottom half of the table. Although remaining undefeated at home was still an impressive achievement, something was wrong.

In his autobiography Billy Bremner tried to put his finger on it in a rather complicated theory. 'Maybe it's a feeling of inferiority, so far as those stay-away fans are concerned. We cannot convince ourselves

that they *should* be there to cheer us on. Or maybe we're frightened
that we won't live up to their expectations.' The size of home crowds
was something Bremner would lament throughout his career, but,
whatever the reason for Leeds' inability to finish teams off at Elland
Road, for the first time in five months Leeds appeared vulnerable.

It proved to be only a temporary crisis, as they haltingly refound
their autumn form. Revie's favourite bit of kidology – if they weren't
up to it, he would threaten to get his chequebook out – restored the
team's equilibrium. Johanneson and particularly Giles began to get
the measure of Peacock, opening up a multitude of new attacking
options. Four successive wins, at home to Southampton and Grimsby,
away to Newcastle (where George Dalton had his leg broken in a tackle
from Johnny Giles) and Middlesbrough (where Peacock scored a dramatic if uncharitable winner in the 87th minute) banished the jitters.
On Easter Tuesday, in front of a crowd of 40,105, the highest attendance at Elland Road since 1958, Weston and Johanneson ensured a
frantic victory over Newcastle to recapture first place. It left them
four games in which to amass the four points that would secure
promotion.

Excitement should have been at an all-time high, but again Leeds
were rather ill served by the numbers forking out to watch them on
their run-in. With two home games left, one would have anticipated a
lock-out at the turnstiles. Sadly, for their penultimate match at Elland
Road the curmudgeons stayed away. The attendance of 30,920 was
9000 down on the Newcastle game and, even allowing for the passion
that compels Newcastle fans to follow their club in such numbers, it
was a remarkable downturn in just four days. In a nervy match Leeds
emerged with a 2–1 victory over Leyton Orient thanks to goals from
Weston and Giles. With Preston slipping up, United only had to draw
their next match at Swansea Town to clinch promotion.

It was a nice piece of symmetry; eighteen months earlier in the
corresponding fixture Revie had blooded the youngsters, won the
match and set the club on course for this grand adventure. As a
throwback to that audacious experiment, he gave Terry Cooper his

debut on the left wing; Cooper repaid Revie by setting up the opening goal for Alan Peacock. Within 35 minutes Leeds were 3-0 ahead and promotion was assured. In a jubilant dressing-room Harry Reynolds, openly weeping, uncorked the champagne he'd requisitioned from a nearby pub, composed a telegram to congratulate Sunderland on their promotion, lionized his manager – offering him an improved contract, the third in three years – and promised to buy the fish and chips on the trip home. The tortuous journey had begun in South Wales; fittingly, it also ended there.

Precisely forty years earlier the club had won the only cup in its history, the Second Division title of 1923/24. Three points from the last two games would enable them to emulate their forgotten predecessors but they could only manage an insipid 1-1 draw with Plymouth Argyle even after a pre-match lap of honour, another Revie innovation. It was like 'waiting for a hot soufflé and being served cold porridge,' according to the *Yorkshire Evening Post*. Some wags in the crowd amended the lyrics of the new anthem 'Leeds United Calypso' to 'collapso', but the sense of anti-climax didn't stop the players from accepting 'a substantial gift of money' from the executive 100 Club or, for that matter, dancing through the night at their promotion gala at the Astoria dance hall.

Peacock's two goals away at Charlton the following Saturday meant that they could finally unlock the dusty trophy cabinet after four dire decades. In a defiant nod to his critics, Don Revie, totally unabashed, praised his squad's spirit to the hilt. 'They have obeyed my orders perfectly on and off the field,' he said. 'We have not always played popular football and the players have been denied gaining the flattering headlines that they would have because of their style. They have never grumbled once.' They would never really change. In just over three years Revie had relentlessly driven his young team over numerous hurdles, but his ambition was far from satiated. The best was still to come.

SIX

A STONE'S THROW AWAY

T he joy of promotion can be absurdly brief. As soon as the bunting has come down from the town hall, journalists and bookmakers begin to intrude on the euphoria with the smug cynicism that too often passes for expertise. Would that managers could hold these soothsayers accountable for their arbitrary pre-season predictions. Don Revie, thinner-skinned than most of his colleagues, scoffed at suggestions that Leeds would flounder at a higher level without substantial additions to his playing staff. 'I intend to give the present team a run in the First Division,' he said, 'and am very confident about them in that division.'

And why shouldn't he be confident? Had any of those who had forecasted a season of adversity for Revie's feisty upstarts looked at the record books? If they had done their homework, they would have seen that since the war, only one team promoted as Second Division Champions had been relegated the following season. Furthermore, without the disparity in wealth between the two divisions that has polarized the game in recent years, promoted teams generally prospered in the First Division. Liverpool, the current League Champions in only their second season since promotion, debunked the notion that Leeds would inevitably struggle. The earlier examples of Tottenham Hotspur and Ipswich Town, both League Champions in their first seasons back, thoroughly demolished it.

As for the fate of clubs built on the ability of one man, however, Ipswich Town provided a salutary lesson. Alf Ramsey shared Revie's autocratic drive and had steered another unfashionable provincial club to the First Division title; sadly, little more than eighteen months after his departure to Lancaster Gate, Ipswich were back in the Second Division. Pertinently for Leeds United, the contract Harry Reynolds had thrust on Revie in the Vetch Field dressing-room in April 1964 still lay unsigned in the manager's desk long into the autumn. United's vulnerability was not illusory; both Sunderland and Sheffield Wednesday, unarguably bigger clubs, were formally on the prowl for the manager's services. Reynolds might have rebuffed their initial approaches with apparent unconcern by stating, 'It is not our policy to release vital first class assets. Only the best will do for United'; most other commentators couldn't share his optimism. Billy Bremner would subsequently recall that as late as September, everyone at Leeds was resigned to losing Revie to Sunderland, the manager apparently attracted by the greater prestige and potential of his former club.

In 1977 Don Revie resigned as England manager to take up a lucrative post in Dubai coaching the United Arab Emirates national side. He drew a storm of vilification for 'scuttling' off to Dubai in a 'tawdry get rich quick scheme'; the headlines read simply 'Don Readies'. In 1964, however, the man who would later be dubbed 'Don Readies' did not walk out but, in a pattern that was to repeat itself time and again in his career, had all but resigned before once again plumping for the greater security of Leeds United. Many of his summers were ruined by these protracted bouts of agonizing indecision. Yet the Don 'Readies' jibe misses the point. Revie was never shy when assessing his own worth, but it wasn't money *per se* that motivated him. In life it was security; in football it was control. Leeds United always offered both.

If Reynolds was nervous about Revie's prevarication, the manager himself exuded calm confidence. Nothing could guarantee success in the First Division, but Revie had enough experience, albeit as a player, to recognize that Leeds' brand of high-energy football should continue to disconcert the opposition at any level. Back then the 'national game' wasn't so national. Leeds United might have had a reputation in the northern press, but without exposure on television, few teams would know exactly what to expect. Reports from the opposition's scouts on United in their pre-season friendlies could only broadly outline the team's shape and style. Much else would remain a mystery until their competitive debut, and by then it would be too late.

In the simpler environment of football in the 1960s Revie's contemporaries' prime concern was getting their teams to play to a set plan. If that worked, it removed the opposition from the equation. Revie, in contrast, always worried about the opposition first. It's doubtful if any other manager made such systematic use of scouts' information as Revie did. Cocker, Owen and Lindley were meticulous: they would report whether, for example, the goalkeeper was a 'flapper' or a catcher, or whether the right-half could accurately pass the ball across his body to the left-wing while running right, and then they would drill the team to modify their tactics to counteract the opposition's strengths and capitalize on their weaknesses. The famous dossiers would usually be ready by Thursday, and on Friday morning the reserves, instructed by Owen, would copy the style of Saturday's opponents in a long practice session. By the end of it the first team had worked out their positions by rote to such an extent that if X habitually bypassed Y to pass to Z, every member of United's side knew specifically what to do. Leeds were the most heavily 'coached' team of the era. It was the cornerstone of their success, at least until Revie finally trusted his players' instinctive adaptability.

The pre-season tour of Northern Ireland had gone extremely well, but for two minor incidents – Bremner being taken into custody for allegedly being intoxicated while asleep in his car and Johanneson's late return from his first trip back to South Africa in three years. It had been quiet by the standards of Revie's first years in the job. The fans had by now become accustomed to summer signings, and that sense of anticipation was exploited by a hoaxer putting up dummy newspaper hoardings around the city claiming that United had signed Denis Law for £200,000. An afternoon of hysteria in Leeds City Square ensued. Had Law genuinely been available, Don Revie would have joined a long queue for his services. But this season none of the players Revie admired were realistically attainable. Moreover, he quite liked the fact that his team was inexperienced and not cowed by the task ahead. 'We have eight players who have never played in Division One,' he said, 'but if we get away to a good start, there should be some surprises.'

In early August the Football Association produced the kind of surprise he hadn't bargained for. In a move interpreted by Revie as the first shot in a long campaign to sabotage and discredit Leeds United, it published a table of English clubs' disciplinary records: Leeds had the worst. The reports provoked a furious denunciation in the city, and closer examination revealed that it was a bit of a stitch up. In the 1963/64 season not one Leeds player had been sent off and only one professional, Billy Bremner, had been suspended for repeated misdemeanours. Countless other clubs had players getting first dibs on the rubber duck: at United they all bathed together. It transpired that Leeds' status came from a survey of the whole club: it was the number of sending-offs in junior football that had hoisted Leeds to the top of the FA's infamy league. Revie openly pondered on the FA's motives. Even the most paranoid Leeds fan would accept that the FA's 'vendetta' couldn't have started so early; regardless, they stood prejudged before the season started. No wonder the slogan 'Dirty Leeds' caught on so quickly.

Rated at 33/1 for both the title and the FA Cup, Leeds began the season as outsiders in more senses than one: their players already mythologized as part cannon fodder part assassin. In their last pre-season friendly they had slaughtered Wrexham 8–2, but an injury to Peacock left them facing yet another season with their principal striker sidelined. Revie's initial plan had revolved around the fit-again Storrie partnering Peacock, greedily feeding off the England international's aerial dominance, but another cartilage operation put paid to that until late February. It led to a reprieve for Don Weston, the one player whose First Division potential Revie had qualms about.

This strike force would hardly have set the world alight, and by half-time in Leeds' opening fixture away to Aston Villa, after a lung-bursting but pretty ineffective 45 minutes, they were already 1–0 down. Those who had written Revie's team off would have congratulated themselves.

Aston Villa, fourth bottom the previous season, weren't much of a force, but so comprehensively had they outplayed Leeds that Bremner, for one, remembered thinking, 'We're not going to be good enough.' Revie, however, didn't panic, and in his half-time talk warned the players that in sapping heat their desire to prove themselves had led them to play at a suicidal pace. In the second half, following his instructions to the letter, they played at a slower tempo. As though only now realizing that Peacock was absent and that both Storrie and Weston were both a good six inches shorter than their missing centre-forward, the team finally began to play the ball on the ground. Goals from Johanneson and Charlton secured victory and a lesson was learned. In 45 minutes, as Phil Brown cryptically put it, they had worked out how to play against 'tall timber with [a] small-built forward line'. It stood them in good stead for the next six months.

While the team was learning its lesson, Harry Reynolds had not yet learned his from the Charles fiasco. He couldn't help getting carried away, and for Leeds' home debut against the Champions Liverpool, gleefully prepared for the first capacity crowd at Elland Road since the 1920s. The club had reverted to their 'premium' pricing policy, and this time the lack of protest seemed to indicate that the increases were thought justified. No one got rich, however, betting on the Leeds public's enthusiasm. In fact, 36,005 people turned up for the team's first game back in the First Division for five years, and a match against the current league Champions to boot. Another way of putting it is that the ground was 19,000, one-third short of capacity. Admittedly, it was a mid-week game, but three games the previous season had attracted bigger crowds. It was an unambiguous indication of the real strength of football in the city. This reluctance of the floating core of Leeds supporters to show up in numbers is the fundamental reason why the club's credibility as a 'big' club was so regularly questioned. For far too long, whatever roots the club had laboured to establish still lay in shallow soil.

Even so, Reynolds' misplaced optimism had potentially disastrous consequences for the fans that did bother to turn up. His expectation of at least a 50,000 attendance led to the paddock stands being crammed full while vast swathes of terracing behind the goals were left vacant for all the non-existent latecomers. One fan complained that the crush was so intense he feared for his life; conditions, others claimed, were 'like the black hole of Calcutta'. Luckily for a penitent Reynolds, there were no major casualties.

If the administration of the club continued to be amateurish, on the pitch United tore Liverpool apart. Goals came from Weston, Bremner and Giles in a compelling 4–2 victory. In a nod to Liverpool's four famous sons, the *Yorkshire Evening Post* maintained that Leeds had won with their 'from me to you' keepball: not only did they outplay the Champions, they also out-Beatled them. The following Saturday, in front of an even smaller crowd, Leeds made it three wins out of three by defeating Wolves 3–2, with Storrie scoring his first goals for six months. Against both Villa and Wolves, moreover, they had battled back from losing positions, an encouraging sign that their form couldn't altogether be put down to 'promoted club syndrome'. It was too soon to tell definitively, but even to the London media they looked well equipped to cope with the challenge. If they could only convince their own supporters, Harry Reynolds would be as ecstatic as Revie.

Leeds' general form over the season was symptomatic of the problems faced by all decent young teams: a series of winning sequences – one of seven matches, one of five, one of four, one of three – interspersed with the odd defeat by one of their stronger rivals. Among their seven losses, the only team to beat them from the bottom half of the table was Blackpool, who thrashed them at Bloomfield Road in early September. By the end of that month, United had already lost four times, but then embarked on a storming run that saw them beaten only once until mid-April. Midway through that run, Revie finally signed the new contract, belatedly convinced that his team really was going to be able to maintain the challenge. Their results were even more impressive in the light of Peacock's injury. In an otherwise settled team Revie was never entirely comfortable with the striking combination, constantly experimenting with Weston, Belfitt and Johnson as he attempted to find the best substitute partner for Storrie. None of them ideally fitted all Revie's criteria but each made important contributions along the way. In his pre-Christmas crack at filling in for Peacock the nineteen-year-old Rod Belfitt scored four goals in seven games. In the end it was the goals of Charlton, Bremner, Collins, Giles and Johanneson that kept Leeds in contention, the quick inter-passing and ability of Giles, Bremner and Hunter to pick out runners causing as much havoc in the First Division as it had in the Second.

Havoc of a different kind was never far from the surface. On 17 October, the day Harold Wilson's election victory was announced, Spurs were beaten 3–1 at Elland Road in a match where the opposition received four cautions to Leeds' none. This trend was becoming increasingly prevalent. In the next home game against Sheffield United, Len Badger became the second opposition player sent off at Elland Road in four weeks. Were all these referees 'homers'? It seems unlikely. A pensive Revie put it down rather to Leeds' reputation. 'Opposing teams,' he remarked, 'have gone on to the field keyed up, expecting a hard match. The number of opposition players sent off in our matches proves it.' It was a subtle trick, simultaneously shifting the blame on to the opposition while jubilantly reminding everyone of the FA's report. Richard Ulyatt's match report from the Sheffield United game puts the situation into perspective: 'With the marking as close as it was,' he wrote, 'with the tackles so determined, youngsters not entirely in control of their elbows and older players slyly using theirs, it was not surprising that the man who suffered most contumely was the poor old ref.' It takes two sides to have an on-pitch war, and while Leeds weren't always the ones to 'kick off' first, neither did they shy away from the battle. This refusal to be intimidated was gradually swelling attendances at Elland Road and earning the bitter respect of their peers, but at away grounds it provoked outrage and contempt. Indeed, in Leeds' very next game it caused a riot.

Goodison Park has never been the most welcoming place for opposition teams to visit. Even before it became notorious in the 1980s for its hostility and fruit-throwing episodes, Jack Charlton viewed the crowd there as 'the worst before which I have ever played... there always seems to be a threatening attitude, a vicious undertone to their remarks'. On this particular afternoon, when the remarks of the crowd, however vicious, were the least of their worries: the Leeds players genuinely feared for their safety. Jack Archer of *The People* called it a 'spine-chilling' game, one littered with a long procession of fouls, the type Charlton described as 'sneaky things – going in over the top, boots hanging in late'. In only the fourth minute Giles and Sandy Brown, the Everton left-back, had jumped into a tackle just outside the Everton penalty area. Brown, incensed by the vigour of Giles' challenge and subsequently complaining of 'stud marks in the chest', got up and threw a left-hander at Giles and was predictably sent off. From then on the frenzied atmosphere saw both sets of players flying into tackles with the crowd baying for retribution. Gary Sprake in the Leeds goal was pelted with coins throughout, and any of his colleagues who ventured near enough to the touchline was met with a volley of missiles. When Willie Bell clashed with Derek Temple in the 39th minute, there was a real danger of a pitch invasion. Ken Stokes, the referee, was then himself hit by a missile. Now he simply stopped the game and took the unusual step of ordering both teams back to the dressing-rooms to cool down. 'The pitch was bombarded with apple cores and orange peel,' Archer recounted, 'and the stands rocked with shouts of "Dirty Leeds, Dirty Leeds".' With no banana projectiles to hand this time, the Everton crowd consoled themselves by going bananas instead.

When the match resumed after a ten-minute break, the carnage continued with particularly bad tackles from Norman Hunter and Roy Vernon that were described by Ian Guild of the *Yorkshire Post* as 'a disgrace to the game of football'. The match eventually finished in a 1–0 victory for United. Fortunately, the crowd had responded to an ultimatum from the police and there was no invasion of the pitch, but after the game an angry booing crowd had to be dispersed by mounted police from the streets surrounding the stadium. Strangely, it was the referee who was most vilified for his indulgence of Leeds: while United made a relatively quick getaway, he had to be barricaded in his changing room for several hours after the game.

From the safety of their coach, which had to withstand another barrage of missiles, the Leeds players must have reflected on the ill feeling that had almost overwhelmed them. How far had they been responsible for provoking it? There has never been a satisfactory answer. Had the atmosphere been especially ugly from the kick-off, Bremner's assertion that 'because we all went in hard for the ball we became tagged with that "Dirty Leeds" label' would be adequate. In fact, the truth was more complicated. When faced by teams willing to stand toe-to-toe with them, Leeds always tended to incite the wrath of opposition supporters because to them the game would appear one long succession of Leeds' fouls. In fact, the foul tally in the Everton match shows Leeds committing twelve to Everton's nineteen – but it was the manner in which Leeds *carried* themselves. United never seemed to care about their reputation, they never retreated when the opposition attempted to turn the tables and they knew just how far to wind up the opposition without winding up the referee. It didn't matter if the match statistics exonerated them; they were such perfect villains. From this point on, the team the Sheffield United programme called a 'travesty of soccer' was pilloried on a truly national scale.

How far ahead of its time this team was – the modernism of their methods and the crowd reactions they provoked – is highlighted by Leeds' visit to Old Trafford in early December 1964. Like the Everton game a month earlier, this, too, was halted by the referee for ten minutes with Leeds 1–0 ahead, but on this occasion because a malfunctioning steam engine passing the ground had disgorged a huge cloud of smoke over the stadium. Leeds United were the future of football, the trailblazers of the now ubiquitous 'professionalism'. No wonder they perturbed so many people.

Other teams had been just as unpopular with opposition supporters, but what made this Leeds side so uniquely loathed was how much they managed to rile opposition players. In one of the autobiographies George Best gives a good example from that Old Trafford encounter of their adventurous aggression: 'As the two teams walked down the tunnel,' he wrote in *The Best of Times*, 'I felt a terrific pain in my right calf as someone kicked me with brute force. I turned. It was Bobby Collins. "And that's just for starters Bestie," he said.' Reprehensible, obviously, and entirely contrary to the spirit of the game, but one can't help being amused by the sheer audacity of the man – and the naked malevolence of the act.

Collins knew that fear worked. If a player is intimidated, the likelihood is that he will give his opponent more time – a footballer's most precious commodity. Collins took it further than most would dare, far too far for some tastes, but it was highly effective. Over the next five years, as Manchester United conquered Europe and George Best was at his peak, he tore countless teams to shreds, but for all his sublime ability he never once dominated a game against Leeds United. It wasn't because Best was physically frightened by Leeds, simply that Leeds were prepared to use every weapon at their disposal to stop him playing, whether physical, psychological, tactical or, like the tunnel assault, borderline criminal.

But it wasn't a cowardly approach. Nobby Stiles, Best's protectorin-chief, took his team-mate's revenge. 'Every time you come down our right-hand side and kick George, you filthy bastard,' he shouted at Collins, slamming him into the perimeter wall in a forceful tackle, 'I'm going to friggin' well hit you like that, only harder.' Collins got up to score the only goal of the game. He had started it, taken the retribution as fair punishment, continued to hound Best despite Stiles' injunctions and still led his team to maximum points. That was the hyperactive impudence that came to characterize Revie's Leeds.

From December the Championship race was distilled down to three teams. In the absence of Liverpool, who were preoccupied with Europe, Manchester United, Chelsea and Leeds uncoupled themselves from the pack and careered away. The psychological implications of breaking away so early are interesting. Often it is not the 'Cup Final' encounters with one's rivals that cause a team to crack, but the pressure to keep on accumulating points against the makeweights. Every Saturday at 4.45 p.m., win, draw or lose, the players come into the dressing room to be told how the other two have got on. If your result is better than the other teams – elation. If worse – depression. And if the results are similar, the status quo prevails for another week and the stress levels build. Normally, this scenario does not occur until Easter, by which time there are only a handful of games left to play. Knowing that one slip-up could cost you the title even as early as December is a more demanding situation altogether. But perhaps Leeds' success the previous year, when they had led the charge for promotion, lessened the attritional desperation of constantly attempting to keep pace with Manchester United and Chelsea. Their victory at Old Trafford put them in second place behind Chelsea; then, with amazing aplomb, they embarked on a sixteen-game unbeaten run which took them into late spring as leaders and short-priced favourites for an improbable title.

The boldness of Revie's perseverance for so long without a recognizable centre-forward deserves scrutiny. To camouflage the attacking weakness of his team, he demanded a greater fluidity than had hitherto been the norm in English football. This innovation had been the making of him as a player, but here he adapted the 'Revie Plan' for most players in his team, so that when Leeds' attacking thrust was coming from the full backs or centre-half, as it so often did, then Collins, Giles and Johanneson, nominally attackers, would drop back to cover. Revie encouraged his players to do things that had never previously been part of their job descriptions, and although he was lucky in their readiness to follow him, his own daredevilry should never be underestimated. It wasn't quite free-flowing 'total football' on the

Dutch model, because it was based far more on defensive discipline, but it did share an awareness of the individual's responsibility to think on the hoof, to plug the gaps left by a less rigid positional function. If this meant Collins retreating to take Charlton's place in defence and the dangers of Charlton getting caught upfield, Revie was prepared to accept this. Manchester United and Chelsea were formidable challengers, both capable of more classically coherent attacking football than Leeds, but neither had, as Richard Ulyatt argued, 'a greater driving force than Leeds have in Don Revie, none of them possesses team spirit in a greater degree. Team spirit and ambition mean as much as skill and experience in football of every class.' Heart, balls and brain; Revie was mixing a pretty potent cocktail.

For a novice team to sustain its title challenge for so long was remarkable enough. Complicating matters further was the club's first notable run for fifteen years in the FA Cup, a competition in which United's dismal lack of achievement had become a running joke in the city. After efficiently dispatching Southport in the third round, Leeds were drawn to face Everton in the fourth, a tie which, given the bad blood between the two teams, chilled the hearts of most aesthetes. Predictably, the mutual animosity was still rife and the 1-1 draw was marred by countless fouls. For once, Leeds came off the worse, being reduced to ten men after Bremner was stretchered off with a gashed leg. Fortunately, he recovered to take part in the replay at Goodison Park three days later, a far less fractious affair even though the crowd, at over 65,000, was comfortably the biggest the team had ever seen. Charlton and Weston scored the goals in the 2-1 victory, but the match's most decisive feature was the defensive cover provided by Leeds' terrier-like midfield. Easy wins over Shrewsbury and Crystal Palace put them in the semi-finals for the first time in the club's history, and then sod's law saw them drawn against Manchester United, the very team that had spent the last five months doggedly shadowing them.

All winter Revie had remained steadfast in his decision to wait for Peacock's return before admitting that Leeds could win anything; in truth, he was right to err on the side of caution. Throughout January and February, Leeds' form had been scratchy, grinding out five draws in six games, with the partnership of Storrie and Weston only contributing two goals. However, in those days draws were not the devalued currency that they have become since the winning imperative was enshrined in the three-points-for-a-win formula. Back then they still retained respectability, indeed honour. Fortuitously, after several frustrating delays, Peacock finally re-emerged in late February to score four times in a run of five victories that consolidated Leeds' position at the top of the table. His presence revitalized Revie's team as an attacking force, knitting the whole side together with his precise and intelligent play. Significantly, in the ten league games he managed to play in all season, the team scored 27 goals compared to the 56 they scored in the thirty-two games he missed. Put another way, he was worth a goal a game more to the team when he played. Leeds had stayed in the race through their energy, organization, will and impudence. Now, belatedly, Revie could unleash them in the way he had so painstakingly and expensively plotted.

It was Revie's misfortune that in both competitions Manchester United stood between his team and success. At Hillsborough his semifinal virgins belied their inexperience by embroiling themselves in a ragged, violent 0–0 draw. This was another game held up as an example of Leeds' wickedness, usually by Manchester United propagandists who conveniently forget their own cadre of cloggers. On this occasion, however, Leeds were more sinned against than sinning. Nobby Stiles' early dreadful tackle on Albert Johanneson set the tone for the game, which quickly degenerated into a series of skirmishes, on and off the ball, between Jack Charlton and Denis Law, and Billy Bremner and Pat Crerand. The *Yorkshire Post*, never as fanatically pro their local club as most other provincial newspapers, soundly castigated Busby's team for the calculated ferocity of their approach. 'For a side so packed with talent, their behaviour was shabby in the extreme... Saints would have been hard pushed not to retaliate. Leeds are no saints.' If this uncharacteristic rough-house treatment was meant to distract Leeds, it didn't work, but with Johanneson limping for the majority of the game and Best absent through injury, both sides lacked real penetrative pace.

The replay, too, four days later at Nottingham Forest's City Ground, was deadlocked at 0–0 as the two sides punched and counter-punched to little effect. In the 89th minute, however, Johnny Giles floated a free-kick from inside the centre-circle into the penalty area, where Bremner, with his back to the keeper, somehow contorted his neck to glance the ball, at point-blank range, past a flummoxed Pat Dunne in the Manchester United goal. On the sidelines Kenneth Wolstenholme observed that 'Don Revie's gone mad', knowing that leaving it so late to score was the best way of guaranteeing victory. It was an impressive piece of skill from Bremner but no mystery that the chance fell to him to deliver the sucker punch, so regular was his uncanny habit of contributing at critical moments. Not for him the meaningless fourth or fifth in a comprehensive drubbing. His goals always seemed to matter. With the final against Liverpool four weeks away, Revie let the city go wild at the thought of Wembley, but he withdrew his players to a quiet Dales hotel to focus on the first part of a highly improbable 'double'.

Wins against West Ham, Stoke and West Bromwich Albion in eight days took Leeds into their decisive home game against Manchester United in buoyant mood, having beaten them twice already that season. Their confidence of sealing the title was not misplaced, since a win would have put Leeds five points clear with four games to play. Bremner, however, was suspended, and though Jimmy Greenhoff manfully endeavoured to fill the gap in midfield, Leeds succumbed to a 1–0 defeat. It put them squarely on the back foot in the race, since Manchester United emerged from Elland Road only a point behind Leeds with a game in hand.

The only consolation that weekend was the announcement that Bobby Collins had been elected Footballer of the Year, a controversial choice, but as the *Observer*'s Hugh McIlvanney saw it, entirely merited: 'Even those who feel that his conduct is often less than exemplary admit that he is a footballer of great skill and dedication and that his accomplishments in the last two or three years were so remarkable as to make him an obvious candidate for this award.' If this was not to be the only piece of silverware to grace Elland Road that season, Collins would have to inspire his flagging team-mates one last time to win all their remaining fixtures and exert maximum pressure on Matt Busby's team. Since the Football League, in their wisdom, refused to alter the schedule for the last four games – Monday, Tuesday, Saturday and Monday – four games in eight days, it proved a punishing and impractical assignment.

By virtue of Manchester United's game in hand, Leeds stayed in first place until their final game kicked off, away to bottom-placed Birmingham City. In the preceding week they had faced three quasi-derby games, a double-header with Sheffield Wednesday and an away fixture at Sheffield United. They had lost at Hillsborough while still without Bremner, but bounced back to win at Elland Road and Bramall Lane. Going into the Monday night fixture at St Andrews, Leeds still held a one-point lead but had a marginally inferior goal average to Manchester United, who still had two games to play. Within an hour, Leeds' whole season had completely disintegrated. Birmingham scored three times. Revie, Bremner remembered later, instructed them to 'take it steady' and conserve their energy for Wembley. Well aware that Manchester United were beating Arsenal at Old Trafford, he knew the game was up.

In the 65th minute a penalty award changed the course of the game. Giles scored, Revie became re-energized, Reaney made it 3–2 and, with four minutes to go, Charlton equalized. If they could score again, Manchester United would at least have to get a point at Villa Park two days later. But even with eight white shirts in the Birmingham penalty box and two sweepers to keep smashing the ball back, Leeds were unable to clinch the goal that would have kept the race alive. Not for the last time, they would not settle for the classical anti-climax, the disastrous and embarrassing cock-up. Their refusal to accept defeat led them to tantalize their fans further, revitalizing hope when there should have been none, not capitulating despite the odds stacked against them. Manchester United duly took the title on goal average. Both sides had identical records, except for the six extra goals Manchester United had scored. Ultimately, Peacock's long spell on the sidelines had been critical all along. Revie hid his disappointment well, magnanimously telephoned Busby to congratulate him and, in an unpopular move, ordered the team straight onto the bus to head south, five days early, to prepare for Wembley.

This was Revie's special time, the time he loved most. Secluded with his players in the Selsdon Park Hotel near Croydon (later the birthplace of Ted Heath's strange 'Selsdon Man' project), he could escape the distractions of running the whole club and indulge himself in organizing his famously innocent diversions of indoor bowls and dominoes. But on this occasion it was counter-productive. The consensus among his squad was that they should have been allowed to go home instead of being holed up in a Surrey hotel for days on end with nothing to do. Bored and out of sorts, they became over-focused on the technicalities of their game plan and overwhelmed by the magnitude of the task ahead.

Cup Final day came, and even before Revie had led his players out at Wembley to greet the Duke of Edinburgh, the tension they felt was palpable. In the tunnel Bill Shankly, at the head of his Liverpool team, turned to Bobby Collins, an old adversary from Merseyside derbies, and asked 'How are you, Bobby?' 'I feel awful,' Collins replied. Billy Bremner vividly remembered the game being like a nightmare where he was running away from someone but could never find the speed to elude them. Too many Leeds players had off-days, notably Johanneson and Peacock, and with Jim Storrie hobbling injured on the peripheries and Gerry Byrne, the Liverpool full-back, playing for all but the first five minutes with a shattered collar-bone, the match was a woeful spectacle.

So preoccupied with containment did Leeds seem to be that, for the whole of normal time, they barely created a single worthwhile chance. Without Gary Sprake's goalkeeping they would have lost easily. Danny Blanchflower, writing in the *Sunday Express* afterwards, went as far as to accuse Leeds of not fully entering into the spirit of a Cup Final game but this is a harsh judgement. If anything, Leeds were stage-struck. Nevertheless, Hugh McIlvanney put his finger on it when he observed that 'a welter of self-conscious method did not conceal the shameful poverty of imaginative football'. The 30,000 fans who had travelled to London tried to keep the players going by their incessant chanting of 'Leeds, Leeds, Leeds', but it was only in extra time that the game stuttered into life. Leeds would have settled for a 0–0 draw, but Roger Hunt's goal for the Reds meant that caution, at last, had to be dumped. Revie ordered Bremner upfield to replace Storrie and encouraged Charlton to try for better fortune against Ron Yeats than Peacock had enjoyed. Eight minutes later Charlton, in the centre-forward position, headed down Norman Hunter's clipped cross-field pass to Bremner, who hit a heavy half-volleyed shot with the outside of his right foot. It sped, unstoppably, into the top right-hand corner of the Liverpool goal. United's first ever goal at Wembley was a memorable example of Bremner's artistry and his unyielding drive. One of the few players to have performed on the day, it was typical of him to come up with something when all seemed lost.

The goal thrust Revie into something of a quandary. If he could keep both Charlton and Bremner in attacking positions, then maybe Leeds could snatch an undeserved winner. Alternatively, he could bring them both back and play for a draw. But the team had played so poorly that his first instinct was to split the difference: recall Charlton into his conventional role while Bremner stayed up-front. It left Leeds tactically compromised, allowing too much space for Liverpool to exploit without the compensation of any additional attacking threat to keep their midfield and defence occupied. Six minutes into the second period, Ian St John headed the decisive goal past Sprake and, for all their efforts in the last nine minutes, United were unable to get off the canvas a second time.

In defeat, Revie was sanguine. As Ron Yeats marshalled his line of players up the steps to receive the Cup, the Leeds United manager strode onto the pitch to console his depressed players. Despite two tro-phies having been snatched from them in less than a week, Revie exuded defiant pride. Bremner, the goalscorer, was in tears. 'Don't let it worry you, Billy,' Revie told him, 'We will be back and next time you'll be skipper and we'll win.' Jack Charlton also remembers Revie telling him, 'We'll win it next year.' As a player, Revie had watched Manchester City lose at Wembley in 1955, only to lead them to victory himself in 1956.

Back in Leeds the following day they were feted at a huge civic reception. There, Revie rejected the slur that his team had over-achieved for most of the season but lacked the class to win any-thing. This had not been a once in a lifetime opportunity, a romantic swan song for a team past its peak. Leeds United were a work in progress and, as Jack Charlton put it with amazing *sang-froid*, 'there would be plenty of chances in the years to come'. Runners-up medals in both senior competitions and a place in Europe were hardly trifling spoils from a first season back in the First Division. With a strong foothold secured and base camp estab-lished, the assault on the summit could begin.

SEVEN

RUNNING ON THE SPOT

I f the Champions League, that fool's paradise which lends relative failure the trappings of success, had existed in the mid-1960s, the next three seasons would have seen Leeds United rewarded with the reputation of an elite club. Back then, second best meant second best. Unable to translate potential and progress into silverware, they were branded perennial 'chokers' and, to use a cricketing analogy, 'flat track bullies'. What would now be hyped as a considerable achievement was then brutally dismissed as inadequate.

Such a verdict presupposes that Leeds began the 1965/66 season as a mature team, yet how often have we seen a club play beyond its potential for a season in the top division before struggling? In recent years both Bradford and Ipswich have been examples of football's equivalent of the 'difficult second album' syndrome. Revie's aim was to win something and win it quickly; instead, he had to settle for the steady development of his team as a force in European football. Almost forty years on it can look like three seasons of worthy but essentially fruitless endeavour. Nonetheless, it was a period that provided his players with the education which equipped them to establish Leeds United as consistently the best team in England. While over the next ten years all their main challengers peaked and troughed, some reaching heights that Leeds could not achieve, one must remember that on the very day Leeds won the First Division title for the last time under Revie's leadership, Manchester United were relegated. While Revie was in place, Leeds bucked the cyclical trend of decline and renewal that afflicted not only Manchester United but also Manchester City, Liverpool, Arsenal, Chelsea and Everton. That his precocious charges had three years of disappointment to make up for undoubtedly helped him to do it.

The desperation to net that first trophy, any trophy, contributed to their ultimate frustration. A scatter-gun approach left them giving equal priority to every fixture in every competition, often thrusting them into the latter stages of tournaments just when fatigue began to take its toll. Norman Hunter has argued that when they accepted that they were unlikely to win every competition in a season, they invariably had more success; but when the honours' board of a club was as barren as United's, it is understandable that Revie did not want to limit ambitions.

From 1965/66 to 1967/68 Leeds were runners-up in the league once and fourth twice, FA Cup semi-finalists on two occasions, semi-finalists and losing finalists in the Fairs Cup, before finally winning the Fairs and League Cups in 1968. It was a formidably harrowing apprenticeship for them to serve, particularly coming on top of their twin setbacks in 1965. It was made all the more difficult to bear once the sympathy of the media had evaporated, leaving them open to ridicule as 'chokers'. Those who favoured the psychological explanation for their fate as eternal bridesmaids were wide of the mark. It was much more mundane than that. In the three seasons they played 186 matches, with Revie picking his strongest XI on all but four occasions. At the crucial times the players were totally knackered. Bremner has dismissed the import of such end of season congestion when they often had to face three or four games in a week; all that mattered to him was that they were young and fit. It's the sort of thing footballers tend to say, but it failed to take account of mental exhaustion. Winning a trophy in 1968 meant Revie at last had the courage to compromise. They were later attacked for the bunker mentality they adopted in relations with the outside world, but one has to say that it was pretty obvious why they did it, considering all the barbed jibes of opposition supporters and press alike.

In the summer of 1965 Revie chose once again not to get involved in the transfer market. His one longstanding target, Alan Ball, had a prohibitive value placed upon him by the Blackpool Board and, though he was eventually allowed to leave the following year, Revie was unable to persuade the Leeds Board to sanction a fee of over £100,000 for his services. It was the only really serious disagreement Revie ever had with Harry Reynolds, but maybe, in hindsight, it was for the best. While Ball was an outstanding player, he was extremely unpopular with opposition crowds. Leeds had enough trouble on that score. Imagine the stick had the vociferous ginger World Cup winner slotted in alongside Bremner, Collins and Giles in the Leeds midfield black hat brigade! Furthermore, it is doubtful that he could have had more impact than Peter Lorimer, who, after three years' careful grounding in the reserves following his premature debut, was now considered ready for a starting place.

With Storrie still nursing the injury sustained in the Cup Final, Lorimer took over alongside Peacock, Revie having finally lost patience with Don Weston. United got off to a roaring start in the league, top of the table after five games, with Peacock in such excellent form that after a three-year hiatus he earned an England recall. An ecstatic Revie claimed, 'I couldn't have been more pleased if I'd been selected myself.' 'People were saying we had bought a "boner"', he went on, but Peacock's form had proved them all wrong. Given Peacock's frailty, this boast was somewhat ill advised, as his knees were clearly not strong enough to withstand the torture of two games per week. By the end of January 1966 no amount of courage, Revie's patented soapy massages or injections could get Peacock ready to play. From then until March 1968, when he finally accepted the doctors' admonishments and retired, he only managed to play a further nine times. Without him, Leeds were never as potently fluid. Leeds' excellence in defence often allowed them to smother games once they had taken the lead but, valiantly though Belfitt, Greenhoff and Madeley tried to give the attack some teeth, United could never reach the dynamic attacking heights without a sophisticated, conventional centre-forward to act as a spearhead. Revie's long prevarication over his replacement significantly undermined his team's chances until he finally settled on Mick Jones of Sheffield United in September 1967.

One doesn't have to be much of a code-breaker to identify who Hugh McIlvanney was referring to in his wish list for 1967, published in the *Observer* on New Year's Eve 1966. 'The losers in football in 1967,' he wrote, 'should be and probably will be those teams who have tried to devalue skill and flair and to make physical endeavour and functional efficiency the supreme virtues. Sooner or later, they will be made to realize that the First Division is not an athletics meeting.' He singled out Best, Law, Charlton and Liverpool's Gordon Milne as the players who fought successfully against this tendency, but no specific mention was made of any of Revie's charges.

Leeds' reputation in Britain was still poor. At best, still in thrall to the gung-ho spirit of the domestic game, the big hitters of Fleet Street conceded that they were a very difficult team to beat. Abroad, however, was a different story. Their first forays into European competition were received with plaudits from coaches and journalists more au fait with the defensive arts.

October 1965 saw United's debut in the InterCity Fairs Cup, the precursor to the UEFA Cup. Facing the top Italian side Torino at Elland Road was as difficult a baptism as they could have faced. Nereo Rocco, Torino's manager, so stocky he was almost cuboid, remarked that 'Leeds were a fine team' with 'a simply magnificent crowd'. Neither verdicts would have occurred to English commentators. Revie pulled the oldest trick in the book by sending out his players in unfamiliar shirt numbers in the hope of disrupting Torino's rigid man-to-man marking system. It didn't take the Italians long to work that out. Revie's little ruse gave Leeds the initial attacking impetus but Torino rallied to make the score 2–1 as United, naively, continued to press for a third goal.

La Gazzetta dello Sport called them 'steam-roller Leeds': Revie, it went on to say, 'showed he has learned about the continental kind of play'. For the away leg Harry Reynolds had to charter two planes from Yeadon to take supporters to Turin, a sharp turnaround from the indifference of recent years. To the incongruous strains of 'Ilkla Moor' from their fans, Leeds held out for a 0–0 draw in a frenzied game that revealed a new maturity to their counter-attacking style. It was all the more impressive since Collins was appallingly injured when Poletti jumped on him while he was lying on the floor, 10 yards from the ball. As Collins lay screaming in pain, his femur shattered by the assault, the Italians attempted to bundle him off the pitch in order to restart the game – at which point a free-for-all broke out. It says a lot for the mental toughness of the other Leeds players that they steeled themselves throughout the remaining 40 minutes. *La Stampa*'s correspondent was enormously impressed with the way Leeds held out. 'This was the fastest game in Italy for a long time,' he wrote. 'Leeds are a robust, determined team, full of willpower and exceptional ability. This team has told us something about British soccer that we've not heard for years... all the team seemed to be spurred by fire.'

Here we have the crux of Leeds' domestic difficulties. They were a team that appealed to Italian tastes but not to British ones. They didn't adhere to the strict disciplines of *catenaccio* but they put into practice much else they had learned from their earlier encounters with Serie A teams. They gave their defensive focus a British twist: a hard-running, seemingly helter-skelter ability to hit teams on the break. It made them a highly effective European outfit. Such a technical approach with its occasional exuberant, emotional edge was neither fully appreciated nor even understood at home. The British palate would eventually catch up.

Leeds' victory had come at a very high price. The foul that broke Collins' thighbone was so vile that the two players' wives up in the stand, Vicky Bremner and May Bell, burst into tears at the sight. Collins, as one would expect, took his injury stoically, but the long months of recuperation loomed ominously for Revie and his team. While Beryl Collins flew out to Italy to retrieve her husband, Revie was left with the problem of replacing his inspirational skipper. His decision to switch Giles inside rather earlier than he had hoped (Giles was in fact to keep this position for the next ten years) left him with the recurring problem Revie had thought he'd solved with his purchase: what to do with the right-wing berth?

For the first time in nearly two years the manager had to resort to the chequebook, signing Mike O'Grady, a player now largely forgotten but one whose versatility on either flank proved extremely useful over the next four years. With Johanneson's continual injury problems largely consigning him to a bit-part role from then on, the £30,000 paid out to Huddersfield Town for the England international proved an astute move. Giles, meanwhile, took to the centre with relish. 'Only then,' he told Leeds, Leeds, Leeds, 'did I feel I was playing in my best position.' The traumatic transition from Collins to Giles was seamless in football terms but it left a huge hole at the heart of the team. This talented but raw and callow side had been driven on by the martinet in the size two boots. Now they were on their own.

Bobby Collins returned from his fractured femur for one game at the end of the 1965/66 season and started the following season back in his old place in the heart of midfield. However, the injury had essentially been so severe that it would have ended a normal player's career. Even at thirty-six, Collins did not allow a little thing like chronic pain to get in the way of him and his addiction to football, but with his mobility severely hampered, he only made a handful of further appearances that season before being granted a free transfer at the season's end. He moved on to Bury and continued to turn out regularly until the age of forty-one during spells in England, Scotland and Australia before three short appointments managing Huddersfield Town, Hull City and Barnsley in the early 1970s and 80s.

The willingness of more than 200 supporters to pay in excess of £50 for what amounted to little more than a day trip to Italy seemed to suggest that Leeds' long tribulations with their capricious public were coming to an end. Ten days later a large crowd assembled at the airport to welcome Collins and his wife home, similarly revealing a real affection for the club. Yet nothing was ever quite straightforward for Leeds and their fans. Although the average attendance had reached a healthy plateau of around 36,000, enough to give Reynolds and his Board great comfort, from match to match it still had an alarming propensity to oscillate wildly, reaching the heights of 50,000 when a real challenger was in town but dropping as low as 25,000 when the division's duffers turned up.

This kind of fluctuation bred an air of uncertainty in the club, leaving directors, staff and players more than a little perplexed. Torino's Rocco had commended the club for its wonderful, scrupulously fair crowd, but it didn't always seem that way to Revie and his team. Against Blackburn Rovers in 1965, Leeds sauntered to a 3–0 lead after only 25 minutes. They were rewarded by their own supporters with a slow hand-clap for failing to extend that margin in the second half. Revie was enraged: 'They were three goals up after going headlong on a most tiring afternoon for football,' he complained. 'They came off lathered in sweat and had the match well in hand. I was appalled!'

A furious debate broke out among the fans as to the main cause of this lack of respect. Some regulars from the paddock stands accused the 'Johnny Come Latelys' of the Scratching Shed. Others bizarrely blamed the poor tannoy system that drowned out the half-time entertainment from 'The Minstrels', a deeply non-PC act that belted out honky-tonk tunes for no apparent reason. If the crowd could have heard their popular standards, it was said, they would have joined in, but the lack of amplification scuppered the crowd's momentum. One letter-writer in the *Yorkshire Evening Post*, 'Scotia', went so far as to claim that it was a response to Leeds' rough tackling – 'Staying away altogether if this sort of thing goes unchecked is the next logical step. We had been assured that United would play like gentlemen.' (It begs the question, 'By whom?') This plaintive appeal for sportsmanship was not representative of the majority of the crowd. They had come to expect conspicuous effort and were simply bored as United cruised easily to victory. It does reveal, however, the difficulties faced by 'new' or emerging clubs. The only way of hooking a large and appreciative audience is by winning. This always eases the identity transference from a fickle public to its football team. It wasn't until the season of their first title win that Leeds United could be said to have truly established itself in its own city.

Now led by Jack Charlton, who had reluctantly resumed the captaincy, United's first European campaign went from strength to strength. In the second round SC Leipzig were beaten 2–1 away on a pitch covered in six inches of snow rolled flat enough to make play of a sort possible. Their bold performance in the heartland of Honecker's republic was enough to secure the tie before a pallid 0–0 draw back at Elland Road. During the next home tie against Valencia, a dozen policemen had to restore order as a fourteen-man brawl erupted. Leeds' stand-in captain was well to the fore as he sought retribution after a sly off-the-ball kick from Vidagany. Both players were eventually sent off after a ten-minute break had allowed the teams to cool down, but Leeds still managed to equalize Valencia's early goal through the type of long, rasping shot that became Peter Lorimer's party piece.

The Football Association's rather predictable response was to convene a special inquiry into Charlton's conduct, but, much to their chagrin, the Dutch referee appeared as the defence's key witness, exonerating Charlton of any culpability for starting the altercation, if not for marauding after the defender like a dyspeptic giraffe to gain his revenge. This charitable intervention did not save Charlton from a £20 fine, which did nothing to improve the FA's dysfunctional relationship with the club. Revie was even more aggrieved to learn that the Spanish FA took no action regarding the two Valencia players sent off. Those members of the press who travelled to Spain for the second leg sanctimoniously hoping to condemn further carnage were to be disappointed. O'Grady's fine goal put Revie's European initiates into the quarter-finals.

Sandor Balogh, the manager of Hungarian side Ujpest Dozsa, whose team Leeds annihilated 4–1 in the home leg of their quarter-final, was quick to endorse United's favourable continental impression: 'I thought the way, right to the end, that the whole team was running about both in attack and defence was simply fantastic.' By the time the away leg came around, Revie's men were so knackered that he had to cancel training. A brisk morning walk along the banks of the Danube was deemed sufficient and this welcome relaxed approach left them limber enough to secure the tie with an undemanding 1–1 draw.

For the semi-final Leeds were back on the Peninsula, drawn against Real Zaragoza. Leeds stuck to an overly cautious gameplan: Lorimer and Terry Cooper were dropped even though both had scored in the previous round, and this most awkward of matches was chosen for Greenhoff and Eddie Gray to make their European debuts. Conscious that Leeds had made all their running in the competition to date at Elland Road, Revie concocted a 4-5-1 system designed to allow only the two wingers to get forward in support of the isolated Jim Storrie. Most reporters thought these tactics a bit of a dog's dinner. The idea was to stifle the opposition's five-strong forward line, and it nearly worked, but after Leeds had lost a goal and seen Giles sent off, it needed Johanneson to score in a one-on-one with the keeper to save Revie's face. He missed.

Always one to dig his feet in if criticized by those he considered football ignoramuses, Revie picked the same team for the home leg but gave them a more adventurous shape. Johanneson and Charlton scored in a 2–1 victory, and with the away goal rule still a pipe dream, Charlton was summoned to the centre-circle by the referee to toss a red and white disc to decide the venue for the play-off. In front of a jubilant home crowd of over 45,000, Charlton called correctly.

Perversely, the third game, with a place in the Final at stake, drew a smaller crowd to Elland Road than the previous fixture. Revie's confidence was high but a spot of off-field gamesmanship beforehand spectacularly rebounded on him. According to Eddie Gray, who was now dropped to make room for Lorimer's return, the manager had become convinced that Zaragoza would struggle in heavy conditions, so a few hours before kick-off he arranged for the local fire brigade to saturate the pitch. After only fifteen minutes United had conceded three goals. It was a classic case of the biter being bitten. There was no way back from such a defeat, and Leeds' first European Cup campaign was over. Revie refused to moan, however, and accepted that a superior team had outclassed his inexperienced lads. 'We gave all we had but it was nowhere near good enough,' he admitted sadly. It was far better than anyone had predicted. He had learned a lot, his players adored the whole European experience and he vowed that next year they would go further.

To his intense disappointment the next season's European jaunt turned out to be another staging post in a convoluted learning process rather than the culmination of his strenuous efforts to transform his contenders into winners. Over the course of three seasons, Leeds would laboriously drag themselves from Fairs Cup semi-finalists to finalists to winners – first bronze, then silver, finally gold. Imagine the fortitude this feat took, the sheer resilience of Revie and his team, cursing their luck but never each other, overcoming the desolation with a freakishly detached appreciation of the progress they had made and their faith in the principles and methods that had carried them thus far. It was a lot to endure without the abuse on top. It was one thing to fall short after an arduous campaign: that was something he could correct. It was quite another to be called muffers, bunglers, lemons and Jonahs for doing so, with that hint of a psychological frailty impossible to rectify. Revie, revealing his superstitious side, maintained that the club was cursed with bad luck. It made him all the more adamant that he would not change, and if a 'fuck the world' attitude was occasionally discernible in his team's play, it was entirely understandable.

The route to the final in 1967 would be remarkably similar to the season before, encompassing another trip to Valencia, a much heralded return to Italy, the fortuitous spin of a disc and complete mental and physical exhaustion. The team hadn't changed much either. After Collins had failed to make an effective comeback, Charlton, wearing lightly the celebrity England's World Cup win that summer had bestowed upon him, assumed the mantle of senior professional. His colleagues respected him and probably had more genuine affection for him than they had for Collins, but they didn't defer to him and definitely weren't frightened of him. Indeed, the practical jokes at his expense continued apace. Leeds were very much a team of equals now, and it took a while for them to assimilate the responsibility that this demanded.

Much of the speculation around the city at this time centred on Revie's strange reluctance to give his team one last shove towards success by signing someone of Collins' calibre to replace the erstwhile captain. He believed his players already had everything it would take to win trophies and, with Matt Busby's advice as his touchstone, had based his team on a strong core of homegrown players. His view of teamwork was that it only thrived in the absence of ego. The fear that this could be diluted by the injudicious purchase of an outsider, someone not schooled in the Leeds way, made him hesitant. He recognized that he was in a dangerous position. Just one bad signing at this point could upset everything if the bad habits the player brought with him proved to be infectious among Revie's still impressionable squad. For now, he preferred to keep Reynolds' money in the bank.

Every season for the past four years one or more of the young professionals in the reserves had been promoted to the first-team group, most of them achieving 'regular' status within a few months of their debuts. In 1966 it was the turn of Eddie Gray and Paul Madeley to graduate from cameo or understudy appearances to holding down their places. Madeley, Revie's model pupil, was an immaculate presence in the dressing-room and arguably the most important player in United's squad. His elegant athleticism, unhurried and apparently effortless, earned him Revie's nickname of 'The Rolls-Royce'. In four years Revie had reaped seven first-team regulars – Sprake, Reaney, Madeley, Hunter, Lorimer, Gray and Cooper – from Cocker and Owen's prodigious nursery. As if to emphasize how much the situation had evolved at Elland Road, Leeds' inactivity in the transfer market demonstrated the move away from the short-termism that had dominated the early part of Revie's tenure, to the placid, patient confidence of the middle part. It was only later, when he had grasped that the 1966 vintage was the last great year before the blight set in, that he decided to solve the problems in Leeds' attack by more conventional means.

Revie's perfect centre-forward would have to meet some pretty exacting criteria. Perversely, the manager wasn't looking for a predatory goalscorer, someone from the Jimmy Greaves mould. He wanted someone who was prepared to sweat, to keep running, with the physique to shield the ball; someone who was dominant in the air, courageous, unselfish and, above all, persistent. He knew that the others in his team, mainly the midfielders but also Charlton, would continue to score, so he needed someone as much to help them score more as much as to grab 20 goals a season himself. In Greenhoff and Belfitt he had two players who together combined all the attributes but individually fell short of Revie's ideal.

Belfitt was the workhorse personified: a strong runner with a neat first touch but who lacked pace, power and consistency. Greenhoff was a languid, graceful striker who seemed to glide through games. The fans loved him, as they always love those whose skills are unattainable. Some looked at Belfitt and thought, 'I could do that.' Everyone knew that what Greenhoff had was out of their reach. Nonetheless, their records were similar and though, of course, Greenhoff went on to have a good if not great career, it was Belfitt who came closest to fitting Revie's requirements. He was the prototype Mick Jones.

Their limitations notwithstanding, both men featured strongly in Leeds' second Fairs Cup ordeal. A bye in the first round meant that it was a more compressed event for the team that year, and by walloping DWS Amsterdam 8–2 in the second round, United had the luxury of concentrating on domestic affairs until mid-January. A makeshift Leeds team sealed the return tie with Valencia in Spain, with Terry Hibbitt, deputizing for the injured O'Grady and Johanneson, giving an impressive performance on the left wing in a 2–0 victory. Having only played four games, two of them walkovers, Leeds strolled into their quarter-final tie with Bologna in irrepressible form.

After an FA Cup replay on the Monday night, Leeds took the 5.30 a.m. Tuesday flight to Italy. Revie had argued that the Fairs Cup should take precedence and the Cup game be postponed, but much to his exasperation the FA's view that forty-eight hours was ample preparation time prevailed. To say that the team were jaded would be an understatement, but they rallied well, with Bremner and Giles toiling splendidly to provide defensive cover and Cooper, on the wing, providing an effective outlet to give the midfield and defence an occasional breather.

In a pulsating home leg Giles' eighth-minute penalty levelled the aggregate score. Both sides, uncharacteristically, went all out for the winner, but even in extra time the decisive goal never came. Although penalty shoot-outs to decide deadlocked games have lost all their lustre since England's travails in the 1990s, at least they have an element of skill attached to them. Leeds v Bologna came down to the toss of a disc, not this year to decide the venue for the replay, but actually to settle the match! Bulgarelli, the Bologna captain, after three and a half hours of exertion, made his first mistake. He called 'red'; the disc landed white side up and for the second year in succession Leeds' progression was down to good fortune – not a bad record for a supposedly jinxed club!

The Fairs Cup semi-final against Kilmarnock took place on the Friday night before the FA Cup Final. In the space of 30 minutes Rod Belfitt produced the finest performance of his spasmodic Leeds career by scoring a hat-trick. The Scots managed to scramble two goals back, but when Giles scored Leeds' fourth, the tie was essentially over. With such a commanding lead, United casually strangled the away leg, blockading their own goal with ease to ensure their place in the Final. The old football mantra 'if you can't win, make sure you don't lose' was not welcomed by observers who preferred teams to entertain – the journalist John Rafferty dismissed them as 'a team which plays sternly but unattractively, who hope to win but above all do not want to lose'.

Were Leeds stifled by their manager's wariness? As the great Sir Humphrey Appleby put it to Jim Hacker in *Yes, Minister*, 'A cynic is what an idealist terms a realist.' A fixture backlog throughout Europe had resulted in the Final being postponed until the beginning of the next season. Unlike some of his sanctified contemporaries, Revie felt no obligation to the game in its wider context. He couldn't afford such affectation. All that mattered to him was that his players embarked on their holidays with a Cup Final to look forward to. He wasn't frightened of losing, as so many of his detractors maintained: he hated it.

The Final was against the powerful Yugoslavian side Dinamo Zagreb, the pride of Croatian nationalism. No team likes playing such important games at the beginning of the football season, but even Revie had to admit that by August, Leeds were in far better shape than they were in May. After seven weeks' holiday and five weeks' training, tiredness was no longer a plausible excuse. The problem this time was momentum. UEFA weren't quite as unsympathetic as the FA would probably have been, and scheduled the final ties for the last week in August, allowing Leeds three league games to find some form. Having been such good starters in the past, however, United chose this moment to stutter. They could manage only one goal in a wretched run of a draw and two defeats that preceded the away leg of the Fairs Cup Final.

Stuck in this rut, Revie had instructed them to keep it tight for the Final and play on the break, but two Dinamo goals, more than Leeds had ever conceded away in Europe, rendered his strategy useless. The omens for the home tie a week later were also inauspicious. Though Leeds had managed the first victory of the season in their home game with Fulham on the intervening Saturday, Bremner had been sent off and sections of the crowd, renowned more for its tetchiness than for its savagery, erupted in a full-scale fight with opposition fans and the police. There had been a few isolated incidents before: one arrest for a serious offence – throwing a beer bottle at a Sheffield United player the previous season; several more for trivial stuff like swearing and throwing toilet rolls; and one for a fan who pelted the Sunderland bus with biscuits. The Fulham game marked a significant escalation in violence. After United's capitulation in Yugoslavia, the home leg of the Fairs Cup Final hardly helped matters. Dinamo Zagreb cannily held out for a 0–0 draw, with the same tactics Leeds had flirted with in the first game, and United were consigned to their fourth runners' up spot in three seasons. It was becoming difficult to tell who was getting more frustrated, the team or its supporters.

There can be no doubt that the crowd's behaviour had deteriorated over the past five seasons. On the back of their strong showing, Leeds had begun to attract a sizeable teenage crowd keen to associate itself with success. When this did not materialize as quickly as anticipated, the hostility shown to opposition players and referees increased, in place of the sportsmanship that had so charmed Torino. This intensified the atmosphere at Elland Road, a trend not helped, arguably, by the conduct of some of the players.

Revie had always intended that Bremner would eventually be captain of Leeds United, but Collins' injury and Charlton's reluctance to give up his superstitious ritual of always being last man on the pitch – an example of how Revie's bizarre notions were spreading through his squad – thrust the arm-band on Bremner prematurely. He had everything a good skipper should have – 'for the sake of Leeds United' as the song 'Glory, Glory Leeds United' put it, 'he would break himself in two' – but he was also easy to provoke, quick to argue and could rarely resist retaliation when kicked. Watching the home tie against Zagreb, Arthur Hopcraft identified a correlation between Bremner's performance and the new viciousness abroad at Elland Road. 'The affection for Bremner among the Leeds crowd,' he wrote, 'is the most vivid current illustration of one of the most constant aspects of football addiction: the fans' appointment of villains to be cherished for their personality. Bremner is a highly gifted player but he draws most approval from the crowd when his temper breaks into, and overtakes, the game.'

It is easy to see why Bremner remains the supporters' favourite ever player. This tendency to lose control when riled was always indulged by the fans – because most of them liked to imagine themselves reacting in the same way. He was the supporter on the pitch. Crowds always respond to players who wear their emotions so openly, but he can't be blamed for their lack of control. The exasperation at Leeds' predicament ate away at them both. He had given everything for the cause for eight long years and was always involved in everything that went on. Failing again aggravated the tense and volatile sense of perpetual anti-climax that the club just could not shake off. The incitement was mutual.

So much work, so much improvement, yet the breakthrough looked as remote as ever. The catalogue of misfortune in Europe was mirrored at home: runners-up in the league in 1965/66, followed by two fourth-placed finishes and, more heartbreaking still, back to back FA Cup semi-final defeats in 1966/67 and 1967/68. The loss to Chelsea in 1967 was the most galling. Although Revie was sporting his lucky blue suit, a garment as fabled in Leeds as the golden fleece is among Antiquarians, United still lost 1–0 after a pernickety decision by referee Ken Burns. The dapper Don's favourite outfit was a plain serge, single-breasted suit usually complemented in the midst of winter by the ubiquitous sheepskin jacket. It seemed to comfort him to wear it but the luck didn't always rub off on his team. Lorimer had 'scored' from a free-kick in the dying moments, but since Chelsea's wall had not retreated the full 10 yards, a rule more honoured in the breach than the observance, the 'equalizer' was expunged. Even Kenneth Wolstenholme, a man not noted for his scorn for referees, was moved to remark in his televized commentary, 'You'll have to look in the rules book backwards to find a reason.' Leeds surrounded the referee but the prolonged protestations proved fruitless. The free-kick was retaken, easily cleared, the game lost and another entry found its way onto Revie's long ledger of grievances with the FA and its officials.

So often when it came down to the referee's discretion at crucial junctures, Burns here, Tinkler in 1971, Michas in 1973, not to mention Kitabdjian in 1975, Leeds lost out. Like the old joke, some maintain that Don Revie wouldn't have been so paranoid if those buggers hadn't been out to get him! But the referee's decision was not the main reason why Leeds lost to Chelsea. They were outplayed on the day, with Tony Hateley having a field day in the absence of Jack Charlton. Banging on about bad luck avoided the issues – Leeds hadn't had a centre-forward to speak of for nearly two years and their centre-half was injured. United's continued inability to cash in when things were going well was making the club and its supporters neurotic.

As the 1967/68 season progressed, the urge to silence the critics, to ram their doubts back down their throats, became Leeds' over-riding motivation. To do it, Revie had to sacrifice his sentimental dream of a team made up from homegrown stock and finally acknowledged the gaping hole in his side. In late September, on the back of profits approaching £150,000 in the previous two seasons, he broke the club's transfer record and signed Sheffield United's Mick Jones. Jones would become the unsung hero of Leeds' golden period: his tirelessness and extraordinary, some would argue foolhardy, courage gave a fluency to the team that had been absent since Peacock's demise.

At first, the centre-forward's ungainliness seemed to suggest that Revie had made a spectacular misjudgement, but the one-on-one sessions he put Jones through and the extra classes run by Owen and Cocker quickly brought results. By the middle of the season, after such a dour, defensive dormancy, the team sprang into life, wreaking an awesome 7–0 revenge on Chelsea, a team in farcical disarray after Tommy Docherty's resignation.

It was, perhaps, fitting for such a 'new' club to mark its coming of age in the newest competition. The League Cup, that bastard child of Alan Hardaker, could never match the kudos of the FA's showpiece, but Leeds, ravenous for success, could not afford to be choosy. In 1966 the club had succumbed to the greatest humiliation of Revie's tenure, drubbed 7–0 by West Ham, yet bounced back the following season to record easy wins over Luton, Bury, Sunderland, Stoke and Derby en route to the Final. The Football League has exhibited a genius for bad marketing throughout this tournament's troubled existence but in

1968 its profile was even lower than it is today. Although the previous year was the first time it was awarded a Wembley Final, it was still played on a Saturday afternoon, marooned in the middle of a full domestic programme and, of course, thanks to Hardaker's suspicion of television, without coverage.

Just as well that it was so neglected, for Leeds' victory over Arsenal was undoubtedly one of the worst games ever played at Wembley: tedious, scrappy and entirely devoid of subtle or imaginative play. Overly cautious, the two teams simply tried to batter each other into submission. Terry Cooper's goal after seventeen minutes was the only highlight on the newsreel footage, a goal he claims to have dreamt of scoring on each of the three nights preceding the match, a tale which gained great currency at Elland Road in the prevailing climate of portentous obsession.

The goal itself was hardly supernatural. It came as a result of Jack Charlton's recently devised tactic of standing on the goal-line in front of the goalkeeper for in-swinging corners, a controversial ploy that was thought to contravene the 'spirit' of the game. In his autobiography Charlton explains how he stumbled across the idea while trying to wind up his brother, who was playing in goal in a knockabout session with the England squad. It so enraged the saintly Bobby that Jack persuaded Revie to try it out. Once the Leeds defence had found it impossible to cope with during training, Revie sanctioned its use in matches, causing mayhem in the opposition's six-yard box for years to come. It was a brilliant plan, because even the very best goalkeepers – Gordon Banks and Pat Jennings – hated it, and as often as they punched Charlton in the head while the ball was being delivered, he was still able to flick the ball on or lay it off, leaving the keeper embarrassed and exposed. The victims of this mugging complained continuously of obstruction, but the truly clever thing was that Charlton's size was the real impediment and not how he put it about. It was a ruthless exploitation of the physical advantage he enjoyed. On that March afternoon in 1968 Charlton knocked down Eddie Gray's corner from his patented position for Cooper to volley in. For the remainder of the game, Leeds defended staunchly, not risking anything but not needing to.

At the final whistle, Bremner, foregoing the triple somersault so de rigeur today, performed a modest forward-roll in the centre-circle before the whole team converged on him. Revie, racing to join them, was captured by photographers in a rare expression of unalloyed delight; but the strongest emotion the players recall from that day was an overwhelming sense of relief that they had finally prevailed. At the rousing civic reception in Leeds' city centre, Revie, with something to offer the crowd at last, spoke like a man freed from an onerous burden. It was an infectious feeling. Indeed, United's record immediately afterwards suggested that this was the watershed moment in the club's fortunes. Sadly, the earlier disappointments were only preludes to more trauma ahead.

EIGHT

WHITE RIOT

f the League Cup, that peculiarly ugly, squat trophy, acted as a kind of confidence transfusion for United, it also marked their transformation from the biggest also-rans in British football to an elite club. In the seven years it had taken Revie to net Leeds' first prize, much had changed, but in a city still more enthralled by Harry Ramsden than Hare Krishna, the club was some way off the flamboyant spirit of the decade. Although the Wembley win did not convert Leeds United to the path of righteousness, it did change the media's perception of the team and its transgressions – from brute force to gamesmanship, white-collar sharp practice instead of blue-collar barbarity.

Revie's cautious inclinations were not dispelled by the victory over Arsenal. Control freaks find it difficult to discard rigid plans, since it makes a football match an unpleasantly nerve-wracking experience, one they feel unable to influence from the dugout. Only George Graham, the closest in spirit to Revie of all his successors, had the nerve to use a similarly ruggedly defensive system policy for such a prolonged period when managing Arsenal in the late 1980s. It takes a suspicious nature, courage, imperviousness to criticism and an unassailable stature within a football club to pull it off; Revie had all in abundance.

United's Board, meanwhile, had been steadily developing the club's infrastructure with a succession of ground improvements and wage rises, all funded by the higher attendances Leeds' progress was attracting. Sadly, the forgotten co-architect of Leeds United's rise,

Harry Reynolds, was no longer around to see his scheme blossom. Crippled by arthritis, he had reluctantly resigned from the chairmanship at the beginning of the 1967/68 season, and though he had insisted on making the painful journey to Wembley for the League Cup Final, he was ultimately too ill to take his seat. Reynolds was succeeded by Albert Morris, the wallpaper magnate who had worked so tirelessly to tighten the club's finances, but he died only three weeks after presiding over Leeds' first ever Cup victory from the royal box at Wembley. Percy Woodward, vice-chairman for more than twenty years, was left as the principal benefactor of Reynolds' and Morris' five-year hard slog.

Alderman Woodward, more Old School than his predecessor, never seemed to enjoy the same affinity with Revie and the players as Reynolds had. Arguably, this was because Reynolds had bestowed too much power on Revie who, now the finances had been straightened and the club established, did not really need the Board any more. There was still respect, but much of the warmth disappeared with Reynolds. Woodward didn't learn from the former chairman's mistaken attempt to take on the Leeds fans, and his only significant contribution during his first year in the Chair was a Canute-like effort to arrest the tide of increasingly poor behaviour on match days. 'I would not take my grandchildren to Elland Road,' he proclaimed, 'and wouldn't recommend anyone else to do so. The abusive language which one always expects to hear a little of has developed into sheer filth and must be stopped.' Fat chance! The new breed of football fan was unwilling to accept an outdated concept of appropriate etiquette; and in any case, no measures were imposed to stamp it out. The only voice anyone listened to at Elland Road these days was Don Revie's.

The manager's stated ambition at the beginning of the 1967/68 season had been to win 'any two' of the four available trophies, an uncharacteristically optimistic assertion from one usually so keen to dampen down expectation. With the League Cup safely in the cabinet by the beginning of March, the 'Quadruple' was still on. However, the FA Cup ended those hopes when a blunder by Gary Sprake gifted

Five-year-old Jacqueline Cocks shows the Leeds United players just how to do it. Left to right: Alan Peacock, Bobby Collins (captain), Norman Hunter, Billy Bremner and Jim Storrie. Empics/Topham Picturepoint

Above: A rare photograph of John Charles in the new all-white strip. His return in the summer of 1962 quickly descended into farce. Allsport

Left: Albert Johanneson in happier days before the 1965 Cup Final. Yorkshire Post

When undersoil heating was still an Elland Road pipe dream... This shot from February 1963 shows the ground staff using straw and fire in a futile attempt to thaw the frozen pitch.

Below: Singularly unlikely revolutionaries, the Leeds United board celebrate United's return to the First Division in 1964. Left to right: Robert Roberts, Percy Woodward, Sydney Simon, Harry Reynolds, Sam Bolton, Albert Morris and Manny Cussins.

Left: Les Cocker attends linesman Bill Troupe as referee Ray Tinkler looks on. The linesman had been hit by a missile in the aftermath of the 'riot' during the fractious game against West Bromwich Albion in April 1971.

'It's up to you, West Yorks, West *Yorks*!' Billy Bremner takes the microphone at the banquet following United's draw with Chelsea in the 1970 Cup Final.

Right: The much-mocked indoor bowls sessions became famous when England players used them to ridicule Revie's squareness. Here Allan Clarke takes on Les Cocker as the obviously enthralled Giles, Hunter, Charlton and Cooper await their turns.

Yorkshire Post

Come in, number 15. Yorkshire's Republican Army, in Patrick McGoohan mode, welcome Duncan McKenzie into the fold, summer 1974.
Andrew Varley

Left: Smoking in bed: Jack and Billy in a Wolverhampton hotel on the Sunday morning after the 1972 Cup Final.
Andrew Varley

Norman Hunter, Allan Clarke and Eddie Gray in the Cracked Egg Café on Elland Road, listening to the radio for the FA Cup Fifth Round Draw in 1972.
Andrew Varley

Below: Les Cocker and Arsenal goalkeeper Geoff Barnett tend to a stricken Mick Jones, Wembley 1972.
Andrew Varley

Above: Don Revie, in his lucky blue suit, and his nemesis Bob Stokoe, in even luckier tracksuit, lead their teams out at Wembley for the 1973 Cup Final between Leeds and Sunderland.
Empics

'Sports casual', early-1970s-style, as United set off for their ill-fated trip to Salonika for the 1973 Cupwinners' Cup Final.

Below: Another Paul Trevillion-designed pre-match gimmick.

Below: The last reunion. Don Revie takes his leave of Elland Road in the company of his 'sons' in Spring 1988. The last gathering of the clan drew (left to right): Norman Hunter, David Harvey, Joe Jordan, Mick Bates, Paul Madeley, Terry Cooper, Bob English, Jack Charlton, Johnny Giles and Bobby Collins. Revie is flanked by his two favourites, Allan Clarke and Billy Bremner.

Yorkshire Post

1974 League Champions – Don Revie and Billy Bremner mark the end of their relationship in style.

Yorkshire Post

Everton a late winner in the semi-final and United's form in the league tailed off dramatically. After dragging themselves from twenty-second in September to first by mid-April, four consecutive defeats handed the title to Manchester City. Much as the year before, the Fairs Cup offered their best chance of success.

It was a strange year for Leeds in Europe; the players hardly required their passports at all. Encompassing ties against Hibernian, Rangers and Dundee, the draw was more like the Texaco Cup than a bona fide continental jaunt. United's 2–1 victory over Dundee in the semi-final left them on course for Revie's target but, like the previous year, the Final was postponed until the beginning of the following season, affording Leeds the opportunity for a sort of meaningful Charity Shield to kick-start a campaign by winning something.

One would have thought that the home leg of a European Final, even if it was televised live, would draw in more than half of Elland Road's capacity. Despite scheduling the fixture for the first week in August, the locally traditional annual holiday, it didn't help the shameful attendance of 25,268, illustrating the city's curious ambivalence towards its team. Even more exasperating was that their opponents, Hungary's Ferencvaros, were among the top three sides in Europe and boasted a clutch of world-class players, including the peerless Florian Albert who had torn Brazil apart in the World Cup Finals just two years earlier.

One of the most notable features of the Leeds players' conduct was that instances of showboating were rare. The public's unreliability had polarized the team and its crowd. Players did not dally after scoring to milk the crowd's applause because they were primarily playing for each other, not for the capricious spectator. Accusations of insularity were essentially accurate, but this came from their insecurity and anger at the lack of faith shown in them.

The meagre crowd witnessed a typical Leeds 1–0 display, with Paul Madeley, United's key player in this, their introverted period, operating as an auxiliary midfielder to repel the attacking talents of Albert and the sublime Varga. Jones had been Cup-tied for Wembley but compensated now in his first Final appearance by scoring the decisive goal after another Charlton goal-line flick-on from Lorimer's in-swinging corner. Ferencvaros persisted with their muted counter-attacking game for far too long but came close to equalizing on several occasions. It was a tactic Leeds were comfortably familiar with. A more expansive, attacking style could well have opened up their defence, but by deciding to battle it out, Ferencvaros chose United's strongest suit.

In spite of this, most experts confidently predicted that the one-goal advantage would not be enough for Leeds to survive the second leg. Originally, this was supposed to be played the following week, but the Warsaw Pact's invasion of Czechoslovakia earlier that year now led to a lengthy delay and even the prospect of the tie being declared void. Many clubs can claim all manner of bizarre reasons for post-ponements. Indeed, the subject has become the staple of radio phone-in shows over the last few years – but few could boast that the intervention of General Secretary Brezhnev and Cold War tensions almost handed them a European trophy on a plate. Revie and the Hungarians were adamant that the game should go ahead, and once UEFA, or EUFA as it was still known in the UK, had withdrawn their provocative proposal to segregate Eastern and Western European teams in future, the match was officially sanctioned for the second week in September. It turned out to be the most valiant performance in the club's history.

The common view beforehand was that Ferencvaros, probably the best team in Europe according to Bill Shankly and Sir Matt Busby, would humble United in Budapest's NEP Stadium. Leeds, however, put on a resolutely defensive display, which saw all ten out-field players entrenched between the penalty area and the half-way line for prolonged periods of the game. Jones, at the apex of this system, gave the lead by harrying all four Ferencvaros defenders, with the two wingers Hibbitt and O'Grady tucking in to pack the mid-field. Attacking play was restricted to set-pieces and the occasional unsupported foray from Jones or Lorimer. Leeds were too preoccupied with fortifying Sprake's goal to hazard even two players up front to try to extend their lead. Initially, the Hungarians played smoothly, passing the ball around, creating space, trying shots, but once Cooper had acrobatically cleared off the line and Sprake, enjoying the finest game of his perversely variable career, had thwarted fine attempts from Albert, Szoke and Novak, they abandoned their natural game.

For much of the second half Ferencvaros continued to carve out chances. Yet United kept their nerve, with Sprake, briefly hereafter known as 'the Hero of Budapest', showing why Revie kept faith with him in spite of his famous blunders. Thus, already eight games into the following season, the team finally put the previous one to bed by becoming the first British club to win the Inter-City Fairs Cup, an achievement that had the *Sketch*'s correspondent, a certain Mr J. Bean, extolling them as 'the most professional side ever to cross the channel'. After collecting the trophy from Sir Stanley Rous, President of the Fairs Cup Committee, the United party, led by the Earl of Harewood, celebrated back at their hotel with the press corps and the solitary fan who had hitch-hiked his way to the game. It was the customary Leeds knees-up, a few drinks and everyone doing their party piece, all 'Cushy Butterfield' and 'Ilkla Moor'. By the time they got home the following day there had been a sea-change in the way they were perceived. Having done to foreigners what they had done to domestic opposition for years, they had finally become accepted by the English press, as much for their spirit as for their prowess. Desmond Hackett of the *Daily Express*, usually a critic, wrote: 'When tired limbs screamed rebellion over extra exertion, there was not one Leeds player who failed to drive himself in that further yard of effort.' This sort of acclamation had been long overdue.

Ten thousand fans turned up on the Headrow to welcome Leeds home. At the reception the Mayor, partaking in the party atmosphere, made light of his disability by conducting the communal singing with his crutches. Once the players had gone into the Town Hall for the banquet, however, 300 supporters embarked on a mini-riot, trampling flowerbeds, stopping traffic and chanting obscene songs before being dispersed by the police. The club professed its habitual profound sense of shame and disgust at some of their fans' antics, but if their continuing immaturity would be a cause for concern for years to come, the new maturity of the players promised an exuberant future.

The key to learning how to win was that those players who were mature in age and temperament – Charlton, Giles and Bremner – were now joined by those mature in experience – the likes of Madeley, Cooper and Gray. At the beginning of the 1968/69 season the whole first-team squad, with the twin exceptions of Charlton at thirty-three and Giles at twenty-eight, were twenty-five or under. In the past this naivety had hindered them, but winning two trophies made up in know-how and assurance what they had previously lacked in worldliness. Revie had fulfilled the target set down in the summer of 1967: they had won two competitions, albeit the junior ones. In 1968 he narrowed his ambition to just one, the title he knew Leeds needed in order to fight their way into English football's pantheon. It was time, he calculated, for the League Championship.

Bremner recalled the thinking behind it with remarkable nonchalance: 'When you haven't won anything, you're delighted to win *something*; but as soon as a new challenge is offered, you have to climb higher. And so we climbed that little bit higher, in going for the League.' They would do so with the best domestic record of the century to date, with just two defeats, a twenty-eight match unbeaten run and an unprecedented number of points. All sports psychologists tell their clients that 'peaking when it counts' is all that matters, and after five years of close calls, or, more charitably, preparation, United incontrovertibly peaked when the situation was at its most advantageous. Manchester United and Liverpool were on the wane with their current personnel, Manchester City hadn't the resilience to establish a dynasty, Arsenal and Everton were fine-tuning their rebuilding programmes, and Chelsea and Tottenham were locked in the inconsistency that still confounds them today.

In previous seasons Revie had utilized his squad in full; for 1968/69 tinkering was out. He used only twelve players with any regularity: Sprake, Reaney, Cooper, Bremner, Charlton, Hunter, O'Grady, Madeley, Jones, Giles, Gray and Lorimer. Of all of them, Madeley was the anomaly. So self-effacing was he that in 1975 he turned down the England captaincy. In the Leeds side his versatility overshadowed his contribution. Most people assume that he slotted into the team whenever a first-choice player was injured or suspended. In fact, he rarely missed a game for ten years, frequently substituting in a position that wasn't his own. Nevertheless, Revie would always find a place for him even if everyone else was available. That he did not settle into a specific role barely mattered. His modesty has hidden his surplus of ability – composure, intelligence, fierce in the tackle, strong in the air, neat passing and box-to-box stamina. For half the season he deputized in defence, but for the rest he played in preference to Lorimer, patrolling the centre of midfield, unselfishly giving Giles and Bremner more leeway to attack. Ostensibly then, for half the title-winning season Leeds played with only Jones up front; but though the team was far more potent when Lorimer was selected, the defensive superiority that Madeley helped establish was a critical component in their triumph. United would not win many honours for entertainment, but the deployment of Madeley's calm industry gave them the decisive tactical edge in many crucial games.

United's pattern of play developed from Collins' idea of communal responsibility into the effective use of small communities of players on either side of the pitch. Hunter, Cooper, Giles and Gray formed the left-side society, working the ball in triangles and quadrilaterals between them before seizing on the space created to unleash an attacking move. Charlton, Reaney, Bremner and O'Grady replicated this on the right side, only less predictably. If Jack saw an opportunity to take the ball 70 yards, he could not resist trying to do so. Generally, the system was marked by the uncanny ability of Bremner and Giles to play the killer ball once the opposition had been beguiled into committing too many midfielders to win the ball back. If they found themselves in trouble, Jones was the outlet, with the on-rushing midfielders giving the centre-forward a multiplicity of options. All season long, Leeds tormented opposing teams, making them expend their energy in pursuit of the ball. It was a demoralizing experience, cruelly inflicted, but it provided for a captivating spectacle once a fortnight at Elland Road. The technique of creating and exploiting space, coupled with the unstinting support of colleagues for the man in possession, had long been the hallmark of Cocker and Owen's training ground sessions; it was soon proliferating throughout the First Division.

United hit the top of the table after nine games, in a fine run of seven wins and two draws. Although a blip came in the autumn, with two defeats and three successive draws, over the long winter months they gradually clawed their way back. Liverpool, not quite at their best, was still a formidable competitor, hanging on to first place until late February. That month, temperatures fell to arctic levels, causing many postponements. Fortunately, Leeds had a special, if primitive, approach to ground maintenance. The playing surface was covered with tons of straw; flaming braziers thawed out a frozen surface, allowing them to play while other teams were left idling. Seven wins on the trot enabled United to pull ahead as Liverpool foundered against Nottingham Forest, Arsenal and Stoke City, all teams that Leeds did the 'double' over that year. Acknowledging the stress that had undermined them before, Revie was moved to pay tribute to his boys' 'skill and courage to play fine football despite the tensions at the top'.

Norman Giller of the *Daily Express* agreed: 'Knowing that the South has yet to accept them as worthy of wearing the English crown... Leeds, this season, have clothed their game with clean tactics as well as a high degree of skill.' Given the abysmal record of southern clubs in the post-war era it was a little presumptuous of the south to try to impose standards on the north, but London still liked to delude itself that it was at the heart of the game. Getting knocked out of all three cup competitions early also suited Leeds' ultimate purpose: by the time it came to the run-in they had played far fewer games than in any of the three previous seasons and were far fresher. They had eight games to survive in April.

Victory over defending champions Manchester City and hard-fought draws at Hillsborough and the Hawthorns took them to Highbury to face the scrutiny of the sceptical London media. Arsenal, looking for vengeance for 1968's League Cup defeat and reeling from the humiliation of their catastrophic loss to Swindon Town in the 1969 Final were anxious to dent United's championship aspirations. The match eventually turned on referee Ken Burns' decision not to send off Gary Sprake for thumping Bobby Gould in the face after the burly centre-forward had clattered into the goalkeeper. The players felt that Burns owed them one after the 1967 FA Cup semi-final and, amazingly, he obliged. Just as Leeds had been stupefied by that earlier decision, so here most spectators thought his discretion beggared belief. Goals from Jones and Giles, the latter rounding the Arsenal goalkeeper Bob Wilson and walking the ball into an empty net, secured the win. It put them in an almost unassailable position at the top of the League with just four matches to go.

Sprake may have avoided being brought to book for his disreputable behaviour, but the whole team was nevertheless roundly condemned for spending so much of the game wasting time. With the title deemed a foregone conclusion, compliments were of the backhanded variety. 'Leeds would be deserving rather than popular champions,' wrote Brian Glanville. 'One has to admire them but it's still hard to like them. If they're not as ruthless as they were, they make up for that in cynical histrionics.' Desmond Hackett also disapproved of the lengths they would go to ensure success: 'Some of their dying swan acts were so obvious, even the referee ignored them. Leeds certainly merit the Championship awards but they do not rate any Oscars!'

The allegation that Leeds deliberately attempted to manipulate and pressurize referees is impossible to refute but has to be understood. In Europe, United had been on the receiving end of 'gamesmanship', or 'cheating', time and again. Indeed, earlier that season Mike O'Grady had been booked for being head-butted in the face by Napoli's Omar Sivori, who had then cleverly dived to the floor more quickly than his victim. They had learned that it was up to the referee to make the decision, and if occasionally he made mistakes that harmed you, then evening it up by trying to influence the mistakes he made in your favour was entirely logical. It was all part of the 'new' game, amoral not immoral. Yet Leeds did not pioneer its introduction to British football. It had seeped in with every European campaign undertaken by British teams as they were shown what was required to compete successfully. Leeds could not see the sense in being hypocritical, kicking their way on the continent and adopting angelic postures at home. They rigidly applied the same methods at home as abroad. Whether people liked it or not was never the issue. If Leeds could get away with it, it was in.

A win at home to Leicester City, followed by a draw at Goodison Park on a night when Liverpool were held at Coventry, left Leeds five points clear with two games to play. Technically, only Shankly's team, with three games left, could catch them. Fate (or the fixture compilers) decreed that United's penultimate match, on the Monday night after the FA Cup Final, took them to Anfield. A point, and the title would be theirs. The legend of that night in Liverpool has grown to apocryphal proportions, but witnesses insist it actually happened: the Anfield crowd displayed incredible sportsmanship towards Bremner and his team.

The match was played in a furious atmosphere. In front of the inevitable Liverpool onslaught, Leeds did not quaver. Madeley dropped deep to help out his beleaguered colleagues at every opportunity, frustrating Liverpool's forwards with a grim display of organized obduracy. Reaney and Cooper had been detailed to sit tight on Callaghan and Thompson, Liverpool's two wingers, forcing the main thrusts to go through the middle where there were massed ranks of white shirts. Clear chances were missed, but in the end Leeds hung on to win the point that guaranteed them the championship. It was fitting that their defensive ability, the basis of all they had achieved, clinched the title for Revie.

What happened next has become part of Leeds United folklore.

Beforehand, Revie had instructed Bremner, if they should get that decisive point, to lead the players after the game towards the Kop. Bremner took some persuading, but after they had celebrated before their own travelling support, Bremner duly marched his men forward. The ground fell silent, but instead of being lynched, the Leeds team were surprised to find themselves being loudly hailed as 'champions' by the 27,000 Koppites massed in front of them. The players stayed put for 20 minutes, soaking it all in, larking around, jumping on one another and paying their tributes to both sets of fans. They had been derided and despised for such a long time that one could not blame them for basking in the adulation. 'Being cheered by a rival crowd – any rival crowd – was a new experience for us,' Eddie Gray recalls. 'This in itself was as much of a turning point for Leeds as the Championship achievement.' Back in the dressing-room, where Shankly had provided a crate of champagne, Revie clearly felt flattered by the two extraordinary events of the evening: 'The reception given us by the sporting Liverpool crowd was truly magnificent,' he said, 'and so, for that matter, was our defence tonight. It was superb in everything.'

Eight years after he had been appointed, almost as an afterthought, at a woefully undistinguished club heading for insolvency, Revie had taken Leeds to the top of the domestic game. All the brickbats he had had to endure, all the strain, were made worthwhile by the hospitality of the Kop. Shankly, an incurable romantic where football was concerned and not one to bandy around accolades where they were not deserved, gave Leeds his stamp of approval. 'Leeds United are worthy champions,' he proclaimed. 'They are a great side.' That was good enough for Revie and his team. The respect of their fellow professionals was all they craved and now they revelled in the novel experience of popularity. They were underdogs no more. A psychological weight had been lifted. 'That wonderful night at Anfield saw our burning faith in ourselves justified,' Billy Bremner reflected. 'At last we were well and truly vindicated.' The irksome oiks, Revie's 'Little West Riding Hoods', had joined football's aristocracy.

NINE

HIGH AND DRY

evie, an exultant Manager of the Year, had every right to celebrate that summer of 1969. His team had dumb-founded the critics, rewriting the record books for number of points accumulated and fewest defeats in a season. 'All these successes,' he wrote, 'made the past failures more easy to bear, and to look back upon without anger or anguish.' It was like the end of a terrible journey, all the rancour obliterated by the pleasure of finally arriving. Never one to allow himself an easy ride, however, he limited his enjoyment of the moment to a few short weeks before announcing to his players that his ambition for the 1969/70 season was 'the miracle'.

Only a few days after they'd returned from their holidays, Revie set them the target of the League Championship, the FA Cup and the European Cup. It's a reflection of the esteem in which they held him and their own self-belief that no one summoned a Corporation van to come and take him to the nearest asylum. A 'double' was dif-ficult enough; only one team had managed it all century. But the 'treble'? That, surely, was ridiculous. It is clear that even he did not think it was a realistic ambition; indeed, he conceded subsequently, 'the deliberate aim of a treble was nothing short of fantastic'. By constantly upping the ante at the start of each season, though, he was trying to insure against stagnation. 'It was said that our man-ager could rest easy now, because the footballing world had acknowledged us as true Champions,' reflected Billy Bremner. 'Rest easy? Don't you believe it!' Satisfaction was a dangerous emotion in management, and Don Revie refused to permit his players that luxury. The League Championship was no pinnacle. In their minds they had only just begun.

To emphasize his intent to lead an unprecedented charge at all three major trophies, Revie bought himself a present. The one weakness his team had persistently displayed was their lack of an out and out goalscorer, a genuine 20-goals-a-season star. In their title-winning season only Mick Jones had reached double figures. If Leeds were to prosper in the European Cup, Revie urgently needed someone to capitalize more heavily on the chances created by his illustrious midfield. To this end he shamelessly badgered relegated Leicester City to release Allan Clarke, a dead-eyed finisher with just the requisite hint of cruelty about him. Like all his major deals, it was meticulously researched, with the player's temperamental suitability to join the Leeds fellowship always being the clinching factor.

Clarke was a magnificent footballer – quick, assured, intelligent, opportunistic and so conspicuously secure in his own ability that it was commonly assumed that he was in love with himself. His unruffled, straight-backed running style betrayed the natural arrogance of the thoroughbred centre-forward, and if his single-mindedness would later lead him off at odd tangents (during his unhappy stint as Leeds manager once advocating the birching of unruly Leeds fans and volunteering to administer the thrashings personally), it added a withering dimension to United's play. It was the first time since Collins that Revie had invested in something approaching the finished article; he had to demolish the domestic transfer record to do it, but the days when the Board would quibble at such an outrageous outlay had long since passed. For £165,000, or the price of thirty new Barratt homes in those days, Leeds United had finally purchased their own bespoke Jimmy Greaves.

Goals from Charlton and Gray in the Charity Shield against Manchester City got Leeds away for the second successive season with a trophy to brandish at yet another civic reception. Their early form in the league, however, was a little rickety. Clarke's brio undoubtedly added punch to United's attack, but playing with two out and out forwards on a regular basis for the first time in years took some time to get accustomed to. Clarke's introduction also coincided with Lorimer's permanent inclusion in the team on the right side in preference to O'Grady – to give Leeds more attacking options than ever before – but it curtailed the freedom of Bremner and Giles to advance as much as they had in previous seasons.

Lorimer was not an orthodox midfield player or winger. Although he possessed enough defensive nous to stay in position when necessary, his inclination to attack distorted the rigid tactical template that had been the basis of United's defensive dominance. From now on it was neither 4–4–2 nor strictly 4–3–3, but more like 4–3½–2½ as Lorimer ploughed forward to support Clarke and Jones at every opportunity. This is what Revie meant when he said he'd let the team 'off the leash' after the first title. Lorimer's role was the embodiment of the concept and he, more than anyone, was responsible for injecting the dynamism into Leeds' play that characterized the last five years of Revie's tenure.

It was a long haul through autumn and winter in the league. Not until the middle of January, when they put together seven victories in eight games, did they finally get back to the top of the table. With Clarke in the team, they were scoring more goals per game than ever before, but with Madeley often playing at full-back in the absence of the injured Cooper, they were also shipping more goals than usual. Madeley was a competent full-back – indeed, most of his twenty-four England caps came in this position – but without him as a shield in front of Hunter and Charlton, the whole defence was far more vulnerable than the year before.

With only eight clean sheets all season in comparison to the twenty-four in 1968/69, it is pretty obvious that allowing the players their heads to play in a more open fashion significantly weakened the foundations of the Championship winning team's success. Revie grasped the nettle because he was confident that a greater attacking verve would compensate for the extra licence in defence, a psychological switch from never wanting to lose to always wanting to win. In a poor First Division with Liverpool and Manchester United in decline, this strategy should have brought back-to-back titles. That it didn't was due more to Leed's elongated runs in the FA Cup and Europe than the dogged Everton team who ended up as eventual Champions. By early March, Leeds' programme was so congested that six of the team, the club physician warned Revie, were on the verge of nervous and physical collapse. Revie's appetite for the 'treble' was in danger of running his shattered team into the ground.

An atypically dull, scoreless draw with Liverpool on 7 March left Leeds still in top spot, having only lost two games all season, a 3–2 reverse at Goodison Park back in August and a wretched Boxing Day defeat at Newcastle. Everything seemed to be on course for a spectacular finish. The partnership between Jones and Clarke was flourishing, with the former scoring more goals in fewer games than in previous seasons when he'd been forced to toil alone. Clarke and Lorimer also thrived, contributing 31 goals between them as United's reliance on the 1–0 victory was thrillingly abandoned. Underlining their dominance with a glut of three, four, five and six goals per game performances, Leeds were playing a style of football at this high-water mark of their season that looked unstoppable. In January they had humiliated third-placed Chelsea at Stamford Bridge in a 5–2 rout, following this up with another five-goal performance to blow West Bromwich Albion away.

The transformation in Leeds' style was a natural corollary of their new maturity – the movement off the ball had become increasingly subtle and the options available to the man in possession were manifold. Gone were the days when the best route to goal was behind the full-backs and a cross into the penalty area. Now United were shooting from distance, feeding the rapacious Clarke in the inside-right or inside-left channels, hitting the ball over the top for Jones and giving Lorimer the opportunity to blast the ball from anywhere in the opposition's half. It was all based on Bremner and Giles' ability to control the pace of the game, and this they achieved with apparent ease on the hard pitches of autumn and winter. Once the spring thaw had set in, however, the mud bath surfaces cancelled out the advantages possessed by teams with superior techniques. With the levelling effect of those awful pitches plus the fixture pile-up, the twin toll they exacted on the Leeds players' legs blew Revie's dream apart.

United's debut games in the European Cup had been a less than taxing experience. With only four rounds in total before the Final, it was by far the least gruelling of all the major tournaments. In the four games scheduled before Christmas, Leeds cruised past the Norwegian Champions SK Lyn Oslo 16–0 on aggregate and twice thumped their old Hungarian adversaries Ferencvaros 3–0 to book their place in the quarter-finals. On the competition's resumption in early March, Leeds were drawn against Standard Liège, coming through as 1–0 winners in both difficult legs. This victory set up a semi-final tie with Celtic, then on course for their fifth successive Scottish title and recognized by the less parochial English journalists as the best team in Britain by a comfortable margin. United's run in the FA Cup followed a similar pattern. Leeds kicked off their campaign at Elland Road on 3 January 1970, celebrating the announcement of Revie's OBE in the New Years Honours List two days earlier by beating Swansea Town 2–1. Victories over non-league Sutton United, Mansfield Town and Swindon Town eased their passage into the semi-final before they faced their real significant test – Manchester United.

It was at this point, in mid-March, that a choice clearly had to be made. Despite some players' subsequent assertions that Revie had never prioritized the League that year, knowing it to be a test too far on top of his other aspirations, this is just retrospective justification. After all, they were top with just seven games to go. Leeds weren't in an impregnable position, but had the League been all they had had to go for, they would have made a better fist of it than they actually managed. Revie, as he points out time and again in his 'Green Post' columns and in the *Leeds United Book of Football*, published in the summer of 1970, definitely wanted all three trophies. It was only at this point in the season, with a World Cup looming, allowing no prospect of extending the season beyond April and Norman Hunter's injury in the second leg against Standard Liège uppermost in his mind, that pragmatism dictated he should concentrate on the two cups.

In an ideal world, two wins would get them the FA Cup, and two wins and a draw the European Cup. The League would require far more effort, and, since they'd already won it once, the other two competitions had greater novelty value. So it was that Leeds came to give Everton a helping hand towards the title by running up the white flag. Cramming the team with reserves Yorath, Hibbitt, Belfitt, Lumsden, Galvin and even the long-marginalized Johanneson for the last six League games reveals just how much United had switched their focus. United's second-string team picked up only 3 points from a possible 12, earning the club a £5,000 fine for fielding an uncompetitive team from the Football League, who refused to believe Revie's claims of an injury epidemic. Interestingly, the 9 points lost in this spell were the precise difference between themselves in second place and Everton in first at the end of the season. This sacrifice at such a late stage was completely understandable given what was at stake in the other two competitions. However, it now required the winning of at least one of them to justify such a cynically cold-blooded compromise.

As ever, nothing ran smoothly for Leeds United. Instead of the usual one FA Cup semi-final, the famous '90 minutes to Wembley', it took Leeds three games and five hours to get past Manchester United. As in the 1965 epic, Bremner finally conjured up the only goal deep into the second replay to guarantee Leeds' progress to Wembley. In between the instalments of this saga, United were fitting as many as three other games a week into their crowded schedule. Fortunately, once the tie was resolved, with the League now surrendered, United's first-choice team were given a break of six days before their home tie with Celtic. This, predictably enough, provoked the wrath and sanction of Alan Hardaker, and Leeds were duly censured for sending out the reserves in the league match on the Monday that preceded their Wednesday semi-final and for the two league games they were ordered to play on the Thursday and Saturday of that very same week.

The first 'Battle of Britain' between Leeds and Celtic did not go according to plan. All managers prefer to have the away leg first, giving their team the cushion of a home leg to right any wrongs in front of their own partisan crowd. Leeds, though, were drawn at home first and turned in a lacklustre display in front of a crowd, again puzzlingly below capacity. Leeds went behind within 90 seconds and never really got back into the match, prompting Phil Brown to write in the *Yorkshire Evening Post* that 'the elastic had gone'. Jimmy Johnstone gave Cooper a roasting at left-back, and with no Norman Hunter to support him, 'the world's best full-back' seemed to droop under the pressure. Things grew worse after 70 minutes when Bremner headed the ground and had to be stretchered off with concussion. Like the rest of his team-mates, he just wasn't himself. Left in the dressing-room completely disorientated, he spent the remaining 20 minutes of the match wandering in and out of the club offices.

They were lucky to get away with only a 1–0 defeat after such a thorough trouncing, but Revie, at least, refused to be downbeat about his team's prospects in the second leg despite all the praise of Celtic's mastery. The *Glasgow Evening Times*' verdict that Celtic 'whipped this most "professional" of teams in every phase of the game' was not for Caledonian audiences only – every national newspaper concurred. On the same night Everton secured the First Division title, and there was some gloating from the *Daily Mail* that Leeds had abandoned this prize for Europe and got stuffed twice in the process. Leeds, however, knew that their revised destiny was still in their own hands. With first class seats booked aboard the 7.25 a.m. Yorkshire Pullman to London, where he would sort out United's hotel arrangements for the forthcoming FA Cup Final prior to the evening league game at Upton Park, Revie trudged off into the night with a defiant air. 'We never give up hope,' he said, challenging United's detractors to bet against them. It was do or die at Hampden Park.

Before revenge could be plotted, the small matter of the FA Cup Final had to be surmounted. Bridling at the Football League fine, Revie picked a handful of first teamers to start against West Ham in the week before Wembley and was rewarded by Paul Reaney fracturing his leg in a trademark crunching tackle. It was not a good omen but at least Norman Hunter was pronounced fit enough to start at Wembley, allowing Madeley to move over from centre-back to right-back. United's record at Wembley, especially for entertainment, had been dreadful. The 1965 Final found them sleepwalking, unable to get their normal rhythm going, while the 1968 League Cup Final had seen them outbore Arsenal in a bleak battle. Most pundits expected Leeds in the 1970 Final to pick up where they'd left off and try to smother Chelsea. This was certainly what Chelsea would have you believe, keen to play up the contrasts between their image as Emperors of urbane Kings Road cool and Revie's humourless, cloth-capped whippet-fanciers. In fact, the match turned out to be a classic.

For much of the game, Leeds, wearing red socks for the benefit of black and white television viewers to distinguish them from Chelsea's affectation of wearing white ones, took the game to the West Londoners on a gloopy porridge of a pitch. In all the match reports much was made of the fact that the Horse of the Year Show had been held there recently; but all that mud and sand did not spoil the game. Leeds had hardly put it together in weeks, but they seized this occasion to return to the top of their game, with Giles orchestrating attack after attack, Lorimer keen to try his luck from anywhere within 40 yards of goal and Eddie Gray giving David Webb the sort of treatment Johnstone had inflicted on Cooper the previous week. Many felt that it was Gray's Cup Final: certainly the torment he inflicted on the Chelsea full-back must rank as one of the finest examples of wing-play at the Wembley showpiece. For all that, it wasn't enough for United to win an incredibly open game.

Having scored a soft goal midway through the first half when Charlton's tame header somehow trickled past two Chelsea defenders, United were caught just before half-time by an equally daft goal when Sprake dived over a frail shot from Houseman. The Leeds keeper was left sheepishly looking at his feet while Charlton screamed at him in despair. In the second half Leeds took control, keeping Chelsea's midfield at arm's length while constantly probing their defence. Seven minutes from time, Jones thumped the rebound from Clarke's diving header into the bottom right hand corner of Peter Bonetti's goal, prompting Kenneth Wolstenholme to pronounce that the Cup was finally bound for Leeds. Mystifyingly, however, Leeds comprehensively failed to fall back and defend their lead for the last few minutes, and some slack marking allowed Ian Hutchison to equalize with just three minutes left. Revie later claimed that he had been trying to get a message to Bremner to tell him to 'shut up shop' but had been prevented from doing so by 'seven London policemen' who had blocked his way. Whatever the reason, it was an extraordinary lapse at a crucial moment.

Extra time was duly survived by both sides as caution took hold for the first time in the match, making it the first ever Wembley Cup Final not to produce a winner on the day. And so the purgatory continued, though the players were at last permitted some leeway and allowed to break curfew and attend the Café Royal banquet that night – a strange event seeing they had nothing to celebrate. Revie must have felt punch drunk but still found the spirit to give a speech thanking the FA Chairman, Andrew Stephen, for his praise of United's 'epic World Cup class' display. Turning to more pressing matters, he reminded his team that, after their night in the hotel, it was straight back to Leeds in the morning and off to Glasgow on the Monday where 'I'd give a year's wages to beat Celtic.' The players waggishly challenged him to put the said sum in the players' pool in the event of their success, a wager he cheerfully accepted. Amid much merriment and no little booze, United let off steam after another disappointment. Forty-eight hours later they were bound for a Glasgow hotel with the bingo coupons at the ready again.

Predictably, Revie's pre-match briefing was preoccupied with how to stop Jimmy Johnstone inflicting the same sort of damage for a second time. With the left-footed Hunter now back to support Cooper on the vulnerable side of United's defence, Revie's plan revolved around the two players dropping off to cover the winger, constantly 'double-teaming' him in the wide areas so that he would lay the ball off rather than take two men on. Initially, the plan worked, with Johnstone far less influential than he had been at Elland Road, and when Bremner whacked in a 30-yard shot after 15 minutes to level the tie and silence the 136,000 crowd, Elsie Revie's housekeeping for the year was seriously endangered.

Not for long, however, as Celtic went berserk, peppering the Leeds' goal with relentless frequency. Sprake, keen to atone for his Wembley horror show, was in fine form, but even he couldn't stop the tide forever, and Celtic sneaked back in front with a John Hughes goal just after half-time. Shortly afterwards, the Leeds' goalkeeper was stretchered off after a collision with Celtic's goalscorer. 'There seems to be no end to the misfortunes of Leeds United,' lamented Kenneth Wolstenholme. David Harvey, Sprake's replacement, had little chance with Celtic's second – the only time Johnstone was left one-on-one at the back, crossing for Murdoch to slot home from close range. Now Leeds required two goals in less than half an hour; utterly exhausted, and prostrate in the face of Celtic's onslaught, they could only let the match peter out in a comfortable victory for the Scots. Essentially, the tie had been lost in Leeds, but that didn't stop the disappointment on the night, a disappointment subsequently exacerbated when in the Final, Celtic succumbed to the rank outsiders Feyernoord, not even giving United the consolation of being knocked out by the eventual victors. After sixty-one intense games and with a team on the verge of collapse, Leeds had come up with precisely nothing. Their whole season and, some speculated, their sanity, hinged on the sixty-second game, the FA Cup Final Replay.

Two weeks after their setback in Glasgow, United regrouped at Old Trafford for the rematch with Chelsea. The game's 'highlights' have been replayed so often, usually as a staple of those 'I Loved it When Dirty Bastard Footballers Ruled the World' shows so beloved by Channel 4, that it's widely thought to have been a bloodbath. In fact, for most of the first half nothing untoward actually happened apart from Ron Harris's deliberate scything assault on Eddie Gray just after

Mick Jones had opened the scoring for United. Leeds simply out-classed Chelsea for much of the game, but halfway through the second half, as Leeds tried to protect their lead in the face of some ferocious pressure from Chelsea, the game degenerated into a kicking match. It was then that referee Eric Jennings should have stepped in, as Hutchinson, McCreadie, Houseman and Cooke seemed intent on sending Bremner to hospital, committing thirty-five fouls in total to Leeds' eleven. Typically, the Leeds skipper was not averse to a spot of retaliation, which only served to raise the temperature as battles raged between Giles, Hunter, Clarke and Charlton and their opponents.

Perhaps Jennings was too mindful of the occasion and didn't want to sully his big day out by sending players off, but his tolerance of a staggering number of filthy tackles, players squaring up to each other and sly cracks around the head was beyond comprehension. In the end Leeds were caught out with 12 minutes to go, in a finely worked move that left Osgood free to head the ball home for the equalizing goal. Extra time saw Chelsea starting to take charge for the first time in 210 minutes of football, and after 14 minutes of the first period, David Webb, the victim of the Wembley torture, headed in the winning goal from Charlton's miscued header. With 16 minutes to save their season, United threw everyone forward but couldn't break Chelsea down. Clutching their losers' medals, the disconsolate players trooped back to the sanctuary of their dressing-room, heads bowed as if grieving.

Nine months on from Revie's original target, they had fallen tantalizingly short of every goal. 'Leeds, like Sysiphus, have pushed three boulders almost to the top of three mountains,' wrote Geoffrey Green most poetically in *The Times*, 'and are now left to see them all back in the dark of the valley.' It had been their greatest ever season, but Leeds had won nothing. Consolation was impossible. Ultimately, it had proved far too tough an ordeal. Learning his lesson, Revie vowed never again to be so unrealistic. Patience, he now understood, was a virtue in football, too.

TEN

NO LOVE LOST

ootball should have been the last thing on the Leeds players' agenda that summer. The club doctor diagnosed that they all needed a complete break from the game. Characteristically, his advice, after the mental and physical torture of that harrowing season, was only heeded by a few members of the team. Paul Madeley, offered a late berth in Sir Alf Ramsey's World Cup squad bound for Mexico, turned down the opportunity, sensing he would only feature in the rarest of circumstances, but Allan Clarke, Terry Cooper, Norman Hunter, Jack Charlton and Les Cocker all made the trip. Typical of the year they had just endured, it proved to be another heartbreaking experience.

Ramsey's selections weren't the only representatives of Leeds United along for the World Cup ride. The BBC had engaged Don Revie as a 'colour man', appearing alongside David Coleman throughout the tournament. Billy Bremner and Johnny Giles also went to Mexico, just for the fun of it. For these football 'junkies' some dazzling football and the free-flowing Cuba Libres were as restorative as any conventional rest. What better way to get last season out of their systems than by watching Pelé, Gerson and Tostao, and arguing and debating long into the night with journalists about the game they loved?

England reached the quarter-finals of the tournament and went two goals up against West Germany; but then Ramsey's dream of retaining the World Cup turned sour. For the first time he experimented with tactical substitutions, with Norman Hunter one of those foolishly introduced in midfield in a premature attempt to close out the game. As Don Revie could have told Sir Alf, a defensive mindset is not something a team could easily adopt in the middle of a game. It had to be part of the original battle plan. Never one to use substitutes when all the outfield players were fit – except as a late time-wasting exercise – Revie believed that the best eleven players to finish a game were invariably the ones who started it. It would certainly have been a better strategy for Ramsey, no matter how exhausted Martin Peters and Bobby Charlton appeared. As it was, West Germany clawed their way back into the game and mugged England in extra time with a Gerd Muller winner. From his position high in the BBC commentary box, Revie refrained from criticizing Ramsey, but his natural caution would never have allowed him to chance such a half-baked gamble so early in the match. Terry Cooper was the only member of the Leeds contingent with a regular starting place: the defeat ruined his hopes of becoming the second Leeds player to win a World Cup winners medal.

In spite of the disappointment at England's exit, those hazy colour television broadcasts from Guadalajara and Mexico City changed English football. The inspirational attacking style of the exuberant Brazilians demonstrated exactly how the game was supposed to be played. The fear of losing, which had shackled so many teams, was shown for the cowardice it was. Even Revie was heavily influenced by it and recognized the implications for his own team. It would take some time to implement a new fearless philosophy, so strongly ingrained had their defensive habits become, but in 1970 a new Leeds United began to emerge. The conservatism he had clung to like a comfort blanket during the club's rise was about to be cast aside once and for all.

Remarkably refreshed from his working holiday in Central America, Don Revie was not to be sidetracked by the offer of a £100,000 contract to manage Birmingham City in the summer of 1970. His side was fast approaching the peak of its powers and fate could never again be so malignant. Or so it seemed at the time. Yet the agonies of the previous season would see his limited squad reveal its remarkable powers of recovery once more.

Meanwhile, the manager's vain attempts to buff up his team's public image continued. On being voted Manager of the Year for the second year running, Revie was typically self-effacing: 'If this award had been open to Britain, and the Scottish FA had the good sense to let their own managers be nominated,' he declared, '...the Manager of the Year would certainly have been Jock Stein of Celtic.' He wasn't saying anything new. By Revie's criteria Jock Stein would probably have been Manager of the Year every year from 1965 to 1974!

Then Revie turned to his own club, penning an article in which he defended his team against accusations of gamesmanship. Its style, like his BBC punditry – awkward, earnest, plaintive even – is characteristic of his mindset: 'Some time before Leeds United won even the first of the several honours that have come our way,' he wrote, 'I told a gathering of our players that it was not sufficient merely to become champions. Of equal importance in my book was to behave like champions, off as well as on the field.' After his paean to Stein, Revie now cleverly revealed his ecumenical streak, crossing the sectarian divide by citing Willie Struth, a former manager of Rangers, as his role model. The appeal of Struth to a father figure like Revie is obvious: 'There is the story about how he [Struth] used to order any player with hair nearing his collar to attend upon the hairdresser; how he roared out two players found in the cheaper seats in a Glasgow cinema with the blast "As Rangers players, you will occupy seats befitting your position."' The use of 'attend upon', an archaism even in 1970, is telling. It speaks of a man trying too hard to convince his detractors. Furthermore, it's difficult to see how a certain player's preference for the stalls at the Leeds Odeon would make him a less worthy recipient of a championship winners' medal. It's true that Revie shuddered at tabloid reports of Chelsea players lording it in the Kings Road, but playing the 'standards and values' card shows him endearingly out of touch.

As for the accusation that Leeds were more physical than skilful: 'totally unfair', said Revie. Bizarrely, he even called George Best in Leeds' defence: 'I recall George Best being asked how he rated Leeds. He replied: "Their strength is that they have no weaknesses: they also possess a tremendous team spirit and players of great individual skills." I like to think that George was echoing the thoughts of most of the people in football, but for a long time we had to suffer other things being said about us, and bear it with dignity.' At the very least Revie is quoting Best out of context. In later years the player's biannual roughhousing by Revie's defenders – and particularly Paul Reaney, the player Best least liked to play against – left him far more equivocal about the Elland Road club. In his latest autobiography, *Blessed*, Best concedes that Leeds turned into a decent team, but he remains most preoccupied by their antics as 'masters of the black arts': his former team-mate Johnny Giles, 'Once went over the top and caught me so fiercely that the impact tore open the tie-up holding the pad at the top of my sock and his boot went through everything into the bone.' ('None of the bad things I did,' Giles has since admitted, 'of which I am now thoroughly ashamed, helped my club win a single title. Indeed, quite the opposite.' The enmity between the two Uniteds did not stop Revie being mentioned in the Old Trafford boardroom as a possible successor to Matt Busby, when attempts to lure Jock Stein from Celtic came to nothing.)

For Revie, who so wanted to be liked as well as respected, being champions was about 'wearing a crown with dignity'. He would never wholly convince the press or win their respect. Like many other managers, he vehemently asserted that he didn't care what 'non-football' people wrote but he was nakedly hypersensitive to anything less than gushing praise. Even the most successful managers protested that they wouldn't have particular newspapers in the house. Yet long before the advent of PR departments at football clubs, all mysteriously had a photographic recall of every word of even the mildest criticism. Alex Ferguson didn't invent blacklisting and feuding with certain journalists! Refusing to acknowledge that he'd never win his critics over, Revie wasted an awful lot of time trying to argue his case.

The first five league games were all won, with Manchester United, Everton and Spurs among the beaten sides, but a goal-less draw at Highbury on 1 September would prove to be more significant than it then appeared. Leeds would eventually lose the title to Arsenal by a single point. Worse, they would do so while accruing more points – 64 – than any other club finishing second in a championship race. Even so, deprived of Bremner, Reaney and Gray for large chunks of the season through injury, Leeds did well to keep their title challenge alive for so long. With only two points for a win, Leeds were at one stage 7 points clear at the top. Once again, however, the wheels would come off. Whether through arrogance, complacency brought on by over-preparation, or just plain bad luck, Leeds would again come up short – at least on the domestic front.

The season turned on two infamous matches, which still cause the more seasoned Leeds supporter to shudder. The first remains one of the biggest FA Cup upsets of all time. The second witnessed one of the most notorious refereeing decisions the domestic game has seen.

On 13 February, Leeds travelled to Layer Road, Colchester, for the FA Cup fifth round, convinced that they only had to turn up to win. They led the First Division by three points; their opponents, Colchester United, were half way down the Fourth. 'So one-sided did the contest appear,' said one report, 'that even the ritual pre-match tub-thumping about Davids overcoming Goliaths appeared more spurious than usual.' Revie, meticulous as always, had his opponents watched but, blessed with the courage of true no-hopers, Colchester were surprisingly disrespectful towards their lofty visitors. Before the tie, their thirty-four-year-old centre-forward, Ray Crawford, had remarked: 'I always score against Jack Charlton.' It was no idle boast. Pushed and prompted by their captain Brian Lewis, Colchester harried Leeds from the off. On the cramped Layer Road pitch, the arch-intimidators were thoroughly intimidated. Crawford, who had won a championship medal with Alf Ramsey's Ipswich nearly a decade earlier, scored twice in the first 28 minutes. One goal was hooked in while Crawford was lying on his back, adding to the first half's general air of farce.

After the interval, Lewis delivered a high and hopeful cross, and, with Sprake and Reaney dithering, Simmons managed to scramble a third. At last Leeds came to life. Hunter and then Giles pulled goals back, but it was too little too late. In the 17 minutes that remained they could not contrive an equalizer. For Gary Sprake the game was but one of many televised nightmares. He was at fault on all three goals, coming to claim the ball when he should have stayed on his line. 'We always felt we could trouble them,' Crawford later explained. 'Dick Graham, our manager, reckoned Sprake was vulnerable coming to crosses and basically that's what we tried to exploit.'

Notwithstanding Revie's best efforts, Leeds' downfall prompted an outburst of national rejoicing. His critics leapt at the chance to savour the club's embarrassment. 'The rest of English soccer could join Colchester in celebrating the new-found truth that the last dregs of romance have not been drained from this competition,' opined a breathless *Daily Telegraph*. 'Leeds had used familiar tactics: tackles had been ruthless, fouls stealthy and sophisticated. In these drab days when a footballer's action seems always to be prompted by cold, commercial instinct, it was the first breath of spring to watch the Colchester players galloping over to their manager and lift him high at the final whistle.' For the Leeds supporter it was a game to be spoken of only in whispers.

Even before their historic FA Cup reverse, home defeats against Tottenham and Liverpool in the early weeks of 1971 had piled the pressure on Leeds. Once again, Revie had to pull his team off the floor, and once again, he did so with aplomb. Five of the next six league matches were won, before defeat at Stamford Bridge at the end of March. Yet Leeds had never managed to pull clear of the grindingly consistent Arsenal, who were developing the habit of grabbing late winners to sustain their challenge.

On 17 April, Leeds hosted West Bromwich Albion in one of the best-remembered matches ever screened by *Match of the Day*. A home win was critical to Leeds' title hopes, but Ray Tinkler's freakish refereeing performance thwarted the club's ambitions once again, when he waved play on, even though Albion's Colin Suggett was sauntering back to the halfway line at least 10 yards offside. Tony Brown, almost embarrassed, squared to a clearly incredulous Astle, and for Leeds the match was lost. 'Tinkler,' said Don Revie afterwards, 'ruined nine months of work.'

It's a measure of just how much Revie's team were loathed that their setbacks remained so long in the memory of their detractors. Fully fifteen years on, with the club once again struggling in the Second Division, one excitable journalist even went so far as to blame Leeds' behaviour that day for 'setting the tone of national moral decline'. The reaction of the Leeds players and fans to Tinkler's decision was, fumed David Miller of *The Times*, 'the definitive moment of moral corruption in English soccer, from which point the domestic game moved steadily downwards. Leeds United under Don Revie stood for everything that was reprehensible in sport,' he fulminated, 'from gamesmanship to physical intimidation and were blatantly beyond the effective control of either the Football League or Football Association. Revie and his chairman, Percy Woodward, disgracefully suggested that Tinkler's performance – which I have to say was lamentably inadequate – had justified the crowd's reaction.' For Miller suspension was an insufficient penalty for the Leeds players who remonstrated with Tinkler. 'They should have been prosecuted by the police for provoking public disorder.'

Forfeiting a title that had seemed for the taking all season was surely punishment enough. Three league games were left and Leeds won them all. A late and controversial Jack Charlton goal was enough to beat Arsenal at Elland Road and keep the championship race alive. This time a debatable offside decision had worked in Leeds' favour, but it would not be enough. Nearly 52,000 crammed into White Hart Lane for the decider, a Spurs–Arsenal North London derby. Fifty thousand more were locked out. Arsenal needed at least a goal-less draw for the title, while a defeat or a scoring draw would hand the title to Leeds on goal average. A goal from Ray Kennedy at the death sealed a ninth straight win and an eighth championship for the Gunners. The game finished 1–0 to the Arsenal, as it had done so often that season. Rather bathetically, Leeds received the news in Hull where they were playing a testimonial match for striker Chris Chilton.

Football people are fond of repeating the cliché that championships are always deserved. Back in 1971 clubs had smaller squads and had to play more games, which makes it doubly difficult to argue. It is also true, however, that Arsenal were nothing more than middling title winners. Though he was gracious in his tribute to Bertie Mee, this must have compounded Revie's disappointment.

Superbly organized and ultra-functional, Arsenal would win more matches that season than any title winners before or since. They would end it with not only the title, but also the FA Cup, becoming only the second team since the previous century, after North London rivals Tottenham in 1961, to win the 'double'. Their glory was fleeting. Arsenal had finished tenth the previous year and been knocked out of the FA Cup in the third round by Blackpool. A year later they would finish fifth and in 1974 they were tenth again. Even in 1971, when it all came together under the captaincy of Frank McLintock, Arsenal still managed to lose 5–0 in the league at Stoke.

Even as United's domestic aspirations unravelled in sharp contrast to 1970, there was some recompense for Leeds in Europe. In the Inter-City Fairs Cup, Sarpsborg of Norway and the Czechs of Sparta Prague were swept aside comfortably. Leeds had to rely on the away goals rule to ease past Dynamo Dresden after losing the second leg 2–1, a bruising encounter which saw red cards for the normally placid Mick Jones as well as the East Germans' Geyer. There was more controversy in the quarter-final against Vitoria Setubal of Portugal. A dubious late penalty gave Leeds a last-gasp 2–1 win at Elland Road, and a 1–1 draw in Portugal – Lorimer the scorer – saw Leeds through.

The win secured a high-octane semi-final battle with Liverpool. Revie gambled, returning Bremner to the fray after three months out with injury. Once again the Scotsman proved himself the little man for the big occasion, scoring with a diving header to give Leeds a 1–0 home win. At Anfield Revie rolled back the years, instructing his team to put up the shutters, and a goal-less draw was enough to put his team through to their third European Final.

The Fairs Cup, then only sixteen years old, had conspicuously failed to inspire the Leeds public: for the rounds Elland Road had been less than half full. Leeds' ground was still a long way from being one of football's great theatres, especially on European nights. Even in the early 1970s the ground was still partly uncovered at one end, the so-called 'scratching shed' not being demolished until 1975. Despite these unglamorous surroundings, however, the indifference of Leeds supporters to the greatness in their midst exasperated Revie. He wanted his team to be a 'magnetic drawing card' wherever they went. Maddeningly, though, Elland Road was crammed only for the biggest names. As few as 31,000 turned up for a league game against Crystal Palace during the championship run in. Some 17,000 more came when Leeds beat Arsenal in the penultimate match. Twenty years later Colin Welland could still write that Leeds was an oval-ball town without appearing absurd. Indeed, it was only during David O'Leary's ill-fated four-year reign that football came to dominate in the same way that it did in Liverpool and Manchester. Leeds under O'Leary won nothing, yet they were a far more popular draw than Revie's side, one of the finest post-war club teams, ever were. For all O'Leary's detractors, in his last three seasons the ground was almost full for every league game for the only time in Leeds United's ninety-year history.

Beating Juventus to win a European trophy is the stuff of which football managers' dreams are made, but for Revie achieving this feat would be a rather anti-climactic experience. Like United's previous two Finals, the 1971 showpiece was delayed, this time until June, detaching the event from the ebb and flow of the season. In Turin for the away leg of the Fair's Cup Final the teams had endured a frustrating interlude when the first leg was abandoned after 51 minutes owing to a waterlogged pitch. The game was replayed three days later and Leeds earned a creditable 2–2 draw. The scorers were Paul Madeley, with an uncharacteristically flashy 35-yard drive, and substitute Mick Bates, thrown into the fray after an injury to Mick Jones.

The Italian side did manage to pull in 42,000 to Elland Road for the home leg, a tight affair where the outcome was always in doubt. This time, though, Leeds finally enjoyed the run of the ball. Allan

Clarke rifled in a low shot on the turn to give Leeds the lead, but Juventus were quickly level, Pietro Anastasi sliding in the equalizer past an advancing Sprake. The nip and tuck continued, with Giles and Cooper impressing for Leeds. As Juve's attacking threat gradually abated, Leeds settled into the familiar – and dangerous – habit of playing out time. But there were to be no last-gasp shocks this time. Leeds hung on to win on away goals. The result was hard on Juventus, who had gone through the entire competition without losing a match. 'After all the knocks and setbacks the boys have suffered,' commented a relieved Revie, 'it is time they had a few breaks. Juventus are a world-class side, and we could never relax.'

This second Fairs Cup was Leeds' fourth trophy in four seasons. They became the first and only British team to win the trophy twice. It was a commendable record, but still the air of disappointment lingered. While the victory was celebrated, expectations had grown considerably and it seemed scant reward for everyone's efforts over the last two seasons. Now almost all the players agree that they should have won more. They always worked diligently to ensure that the club was unfailingly in pole position each spring, but more often than not they fell short of the target Revie set them at the start of each campaign. The European Cup was Revie's ultimate goal, and to win it they had first to qualify, which meant securing a second league title. Anything else would be gratefully received but it would still be second best. Of course, after two unsuccessful Final appearances, the FA Cup still tantalized the whole club, but coming second again in the Championship race remained the bigger blow to Revie's ambitions. He knew his team's appetite had not diminished and was convinced that their dreadful luck with Tinkler's perverse performance was the main reason why his dream had imploded. Next season, he resolved, would be different. Next season they would not allow themselves to become hostages to the arbitrary rulings of a wilful referee. If Arsenal could win the 'double', he calculated, then so could Leeds.

ELEVEN

CATCHING THE BUTTERFLY

common criticism of Revie, not least among Leeds supporters who remember the wilderness years of the 1980s, is
that his team grew old together because the manager paid
insufficient attention to maintaining the pedigree of his
stock. Too constricted by years of over-indulgence of his
players, it is alleged, he was never going to be comfortable wielding
the axe. Therefore, we are told, he dodged the issue and decamped to
England. If we are to believe this, then Revie's personality fits his
'Godfather' caricature perfectly, a sick-making combination of ruthlessness and gross sentimentality. It's a case that fails to stand up.

No doubt, Revie would not have enjoyed telling Billy Bremner, in
particular, that he was no longer an integral part of his team. But he
had done it to countless of his protégés before – Greenhoff, Collins
and O'Grady for example. He was on the brink of finally 'shafting'
Sprake. All the evidence suggests that it is something he would have
been able to cope with. In 1971, in any case, the average age of his
squad was still well under thirty: that his players were not yet suffering from burnout was a perfectly rational assessment. Moreover, he
gradually introduced two Scots who would become the backbone of
the side. He was not unaware of the need to spice up the team with
youth before he left.

In 1970, on the recommendation of his fellow Scot Bobby Collins,
Leeds signed the eighteen-year-old Joe Jordan from Morton. The gap-
toothed Jordan did not make his debut for another year but was
quickly being groomed as the natural successor to Mick Jones. He

displayed the same muscular, hard-running technique and was equally strong in the air, and he was not to play a supporting role for long. After Revie's departure, he became a permanent fixture in the side, following the knee injury that ended Jones' career before his thirty-first birthday. Another recruit from north of the border was the 6ft 4in Gordon McQueen, a former goalkeeper pencilled in to replace Jack Charlton, who turned thirty-seven in May 1972. McQueen recalled Revie's fondness for his countrymen: 'At one stage there were no fewer than seventeen Scots in the first team pool. I joined at round about the same time as Joe Jordan and we were in the reserves together.' Revie's concern for his brood had not diminished after a decade in charge. 'His man management was wonderful,' said McQueen. 'He made sure our families were well looked after when they visited. He would invite our parents down to watch us play and put them up in nice hotels without telling us. He had so many lovely touches. As far as football was concerned he was a strict disciplinarian. But the players loved him and, as the saying goes, would run through a brick wall for him.'

Another Celt breaking through into the first team was Terry Yorath, a converted rugby union scrum half from South Wales. Yorath, a prosaic midfielder, never enjoyed much of a rapport with a Leeds support by now used to the filet mignon of Giles and Bremner. His lack of pace also drew disdain from some quarters. Nevertheless, the former apprentice was to make himself a regular in the later stages of 1973/74, filling five positions. Unkindly, some supporters pointed out that Leeds didn't start losing until he became a fixture. Yorath was unfortunate, perhaps, that his ascent coincided with the turbulence of the immediate post-Revie era.

Despite a sprinkling of new blood, however, it is still remarkable to note how thin Revie's squad remained, despite so many years at football's top table. Leeds played fifty-five competitive matches that season with only twenty outfield players, several of whom were very much on the fringes. One was John Faulkner, possibly Revie's most quixotic acquisition. The Orpington-born centre half had impressed the opposing manager while playing for Sutton United in the 1970 FA Cup, despite a 6–0 mauling for the non-leaguers. Both his league appearances were undistinguished, one marked by an own-goal and the second, against Manchester City a fortnight later, by a fractured kneecap. Faulkner's only other appearances for Leeds were against Belgian side Lierse in the club's European campaign in late 1971. Acutely conscious of his limited resources, Revie had opted to field a weakened side at Elland Road after Leeds won the away leg 2–0. The tactic backfired spectacularly, Leeds losing 4–0 on home turf. Faulkner may have appeared totally out of place alongside Norman Hunter and Paul Madeley, yet Revie's judgement was not totally awry. The player's unhappy spell at Elland Road came to an end when he joined Luton Town, helping the Hatters win promotion to Division One in 1974. Other bit-part players were Jimmy Mann, Keith Edwards, Chris Galvin and Nigel Davey. Astonishingly, Leeds' playing reserves would actually be depleted further in the course of the season, Revie opting to raise some cash by selling Terry Hibbitt to Newcastle for £30,000 and perennial substitute Rod Belfitt to Ipswich for £40,000.

In late 1971 Revie did make one abortive bid to strengthen the squad, and it was to prove a boon for headline writers. Asa Hartford, an attacking midfielder then playing for West Bromwich Albion, was lined up as cover for Giles and Bremner and actually trained with the Leeds squad. But the £177,000 deal was scuppered when Hartford failed his medical due to a heart defect. The club's caution was misplaced. Hartford's career continued unhindered at Manchester City and Everton, and he also won fifty caps for Scotland. Forever after, though, the player was doomed to carry the unwanted tag 'hole in the Hartford'.

Revie may have had little quality to spare, but this did not prevent 1971/72 becoming ranked by most aficionados as Leeds' finest. 'By then we were the best team in Britain by a long way,' said John Giles. 'There was a beauty about that team. By 1972 there was no team in the world that we feared.'

The repercussions of the West Bromwich Albion debacle the

previous season were to prove costly, however. The FA Disciplinary Commission investigating the pitch invasion that followed Astle's 'goal' took a dim view of post-match comments by Revie and chairman Percy Woodward inferring that referee Tinkler's woeful performance had partly justified the crowd's reaction. It fined Leeds £500 and forced them to play the first four home matches of the following season at neutral grounds. Revie and Woodward were also censured, though both apologized to the commission.

Leeds were unbeaten in exile, taking six out of eight points on their travels. At Leeds Road, Huddersfield, United drew 0–0 with Wolves and beat Crystal Palace. Newcastle were thrashed 5–1 at Hillsborough, while the first ever First Division game played at Boothferry Park, Hull, saw Leeds draw 1–1 with Spurs. Leeds returned to Elland Road in style on 18 September, a Peter Lorimer goal enough to see off title challengers Liverpool. Unfortunately, away from home Leeds had been unable to recapture the consistency of the previous season. Five league games were lost before Christmas, including the visits to Sheffield United, Huddersfield Town and Southampton. At the turn of the year Leeds would hit a path of imperious form, which turned the public perception of the club on its head. Pragmatism gave way to poetry as Manchester United, Southampton and Nottingham Forest were demolished by displays of huge swagger and panache.

After seven years in the First Division, the team knew their regular opponents inside out and believed in their own innate ability to triumph over them. It was time to throw away their inhibitions. The first casualty, as Norman Hunter recalled, were Revie's beloved 'dossiers'. No one dared tell him to his face that they'd stopped listening, but the players were of one mind: all this irrelevant homework on the opposition was now a weekly chore to be endured.

The felicitous presence of television cameras at the home games against Manchester United and Southampton left the viewing public in no doubt about the cultural revolution that had taken place at Elland Road. The former were dispatched 5–1 on 19 February, the game notable for a Mick Jones hat-trick and Eddie Gray nutmegging George Best in front of the dugouts. 'George nutmegged lots of people in his time,' said the self-deprecating Gray. 'I don't think he worried about that.'

The humbling of Charlton and Best should, perhaps, be put into context. Manchester United, by then enduring the unhappy reign of Frank O'Farrell, had come into the match on the back of five successive defeats, but still the triumph was no fluke. A fortnight later came the performance Revie rated as the finest of his reign – the 7–0 demolition of Southampton. This produced one of *Match of the Day*'s most repeated passages of play, when Leeds played keep-ball with their humiliated opponents. Allan Clarke began the torment, playing a self-consciously lazy pass to Bremner, who picked up the hint. Leeds then strung together thirty passes without interruption, the whole movement interspersed with a string of outrageous flicks and feints by Giles and Bremner.

Barry Davies' spellbound commentary gives a flavour of the moment: 'To say that Leeds are playing with Southampton is the understatement of the season,' he intones. 'Poor old Southampton just don't know what day it is. Every man jack of this Leeds side is now turning it on – oh, look at that! [as Giles flicks the ball onto Clarke's chest, his left foot arced behind his right ankle]. It's almost cruel. The Elland Road crowd are lapping this up. For the second home match running Leeds United are turning on a brilliant show and the other team are just not on the park. [Revie, chewing fiercely throughout, is impassive alongside Mick Bates in the dugout.] One has to feel some sympathy for Southampton, but the gap between their position and Leeds is an almighty chasm.' Even the *Daily Telegraph* would join in the plaudits: 'Leeds, with their breathtaking efficiency, left no doubt about the sheer quality of their football. With John Giles and Billy Bremner juggling in midfield, Leeds, as manager Don Revie has claimed, had more than a passing resemblance to Real Madrid in their prime.' It was a supreme moment. Eleven years after he'd made the decision to switch the club strip to all-white in homage to Real

Madrid, Revie had finally received the one compliment he always hoped for.

In early 1972 Revie had become commercially involved with Paul Trevillion, a football illustrator and budding inventor. Persuaded that the best team in the country were not getting the plaudits they deserved, he accepted Trevillion's suggestion that, by adopting a few gimmicks to bypass the press and whip up the hysteria of the public, United could quickly reverse the years of negative publicity.

In short, the project was the full-scale marketing of the team – not to sell replica shirts (the souvenir shop was still full of programmes, badges and the odd woolly hat), but to manipulate its image. It involved madcap but funny schemes like the pre-match salute, the sock-tags, group warm-up callisthenics, culminating in the choreographed kicking of plastic footballs into the crowd. Strangely, it worked. The most memorable part was the salute. The team would run out of the tunnel two minutes before their opponents, giving the crowd ample opportunity to barrack the visitors when they appeared shortly afterwards. The players would then form a line either side of the centre spot and salute each part of the ground in turn, milking the applause. And all before they had kicked a ball.

Trevillion's rituals merit a mention in *My Super Football Book 1973*, which quite absurdly gives Revie sole credit for them. 'The idea of the "Leeds Wave",' it notes, 'was the idea of manager Don Revie in 1972. Arguably the greatest club side in Europe, they also bring some showmanship to the occasion. The manager also decided they should perform warm-up exercises before the match to entertain their supporters. Other teams derided the idea, but the Leeds players entered into the spirit, cavorting around the ground displaying their names to the fans.' Thirty years ago football shirts were adorned with a number, the club crest and nothing else, but Trevillion had special tracksuits made, with each player's surname embroidered on the back. After the match the players would throw their number-bearing, autographed sock-tags – another stylistic affectation – into the crowd, 'to be snapped up by souvenir hunters'. Years later, when the club had sunk into mid-table and crowds had dwindled, all this performance would come to seem faintly embarrassing. Few mourned when the whole routine was quietly dropped.

Leeds' detractors were not about to disappear, of course. Witness this passage from the *Scotsman*, from an article entitled 'The Bad Guys Are in White', published as late as 1996:

> It was no coincidence that the first person to be given the tag of 'utility player' was a Leeds man [an allusion, presumably, to Paul Madeley]. The truth is the entire team were utility men. There were frills around the fringes, supplied by Terry Cooper and Eddie Gray, but the outfit as a whole was sterile and surgical. When each cog played its part, as happened in the 7–0 demolition of Southampton, the Leeds machine was the most productive in British industry. But it happened all too rarely, and the latter years of Revie's reign saw the emphasis on power at the expense of finesse. The bludgeon, as represented by Joe Jordan, replaced the scalpel.

In fact, the reverse was true. Leeds had by this time come to rely on their talent to carry them past opponents who were almost always their technical inferiors. How could Giles and Bremner, players of complementary brilliance at the heart of the midfield, ever be dismissed as 'utility players'?

At home that 1971 season Leeds were all but impregnable. Just two points were dropped in the seventeen games actually played at Elland Road, but a record of just one win in three away ensured that Revie's team would be one of a gaggle of clubs vying for the title. Among them was Derby County, managed by his future nemesis Brian Clough. Ironically, and contrary to the *Scotsman*'s theory, it was United's fresh willingness to attack away from home that was cited as the cause of their undoing, by leaving them exposed at the back.

In the FA Cup, meanwhile, Leeds were making steady progress towards their second Final in three years. Liverpool were shut out at Anfield in the fourth round and conquered in the return at Elland Road, Allan Clarke scoring both goals in a 2–0 win. But it was the sixth-round tussle with Spurs which is best remembered, though the margin of victory was modest. Only an outstanding performance by Pat Jennings saved the North Londoners from a drubbing. Reporting in the *Observer*, Hugh McIlvanney enthused that Leeds' football was 'breathtaking in its scope and fluency, alive with dazzling improvisations... There was scarcely a weakness to be seen and excellence was everywhere.'

By the end of March, Leeds were, as so often in the past, still on course for the 'double', as the season once again hinged on half-a-dozen critical games. Yet again, however, the team were hamstrung by their perennial twin bugbears – too many games and too many injuries. The former certainly contributed to an ultimately decisive setback on All Fool's Day. Leeds were forced to play fellow title contenders Derby just twenty-four hours after taking on West Ham at Upton Park, where two goals from Eddie Gray had salvaged a point. Add in that the Baseball Ground more resembled a ploughed field than a football pitch, as it usually did in those days, it came as no great surprise that Leeds succumbed. Revie's tired troops were helped by the return of Giles after a groin strain, but the fast and tense match was no place for the flowing football which had so distinguished Leeds in the preceding weeks. Conscious that their energy would sap later on, United began at a frantic pace. Giles had a goal disallowed after nine minutes, but that was as close as Leeds came to going in front. Six minutes later a cross from Alan Durban was met by the head of striker John O'Hare and Derby were in front. The goal triggered an onslaught on the Leeds goal, earning a string of corners, and only two trademark goal-line clearances kept Leeds in contention. Derby got the clincher they had long threatened in the 69th minute when Kevin Hector released John O'Hare for a clear run at Gary Sprake. O'Hare's shot was blocked but the ball rebounded from Sprake's body, cannoned off a retreating Norman Hunter and trickled into the net.

Refusing to capitulate, United kept their titles hopes alive with a comfortable home win against Huddersfield Town and a rare away triumph against their bogey team Stoke City. Leeds were almost at full strength, but there was one hugely significant absentee: David Harvey replaced the injured Gary Sprake. After nearly 380 appearances, Sprake's Leeds career was almost at an end, although this was not evident at the time. He would make just three more appearances before being sold to Birmingham City in October 1973. The fee was £100,000, then a record for a British goalkeeper.

Sprake is very much the prodigal son of the Revie family. Rather ungraciously, Revie himself admitted that Leeds might have won more had he replaced his goalkeeper earlier. Despite a decade of shared hotel rooms and shared ambitions, the Welshman is the one member of 'the family' who has no interest in reliving past glories. Perhaps this is partly because he continues to be remembered more for his occasional failures than his considerable achievements.

A rare interview with the reclusive Welshman in 2001 carries an unexpected note of pathos. Since he was forced out of football with a back injury in 1976, the intervening years have not been kind to Sprake. Now fifty-six and living in Solihull, he has had two heart attacks, a triple by-pass and a blood clot on the lung, which saw him 'die on the operating table'. He has also been through a divorce and spent ten months on the dole. He has not been back to Elland Road since 1977. 'I've had invites,' Sprake was quoted as saying, 'but I was never much for watching from the stand even when I was a player. And I haven't seen much of the lads I used to play with. I suppose you drift apart.' Sprake is being disingenuous here. Being persuaded to 'corroborate' allegations against Revie in support of those long-standing match-fixing rumours, which earned him £15,000 from the *Daily Mirror* and the cold-shoulder from all his former team-mates, is the real reason for his self-inflicted exile.

For Terry Cooper, like Sprake, that particular Saturday at Stoke marked the beginning of the end of a lengthy and distinguished Leeds career. In Cooper's case there was to be a brief post-script. He reappeared in 1974, winning an England recall from Revie, but injury struck once more and he never returned to being a Leeds regular. Revie, who rated Cooper 'as the world's number one left back', tried hard to remain positive as his season began to unravel once again.

Dropping three points out of four at West Ham and Derby could have been fatal to Leeds' title hopes, but results elsewhere kept them in title contention ahead of the looming FA Cup semi-final against Birmingham. 'Somebody up there likes us after all!' said Billy Bremner. 'Such a nail-biting finish is good for the game and whoever wins the title will be worthy champions.' Bremner's upbeat message is undermined by the facts. Winning at Stoke did not advance Leeds' cause one bit. Derby remained top by a point, while Liverpool and Manchester City stayed in touch just a point behind Leeds.

If Leeds were going to miss out on the Championship, there was little doubt that Revie favoured Liverpool over both Derby County and Manchester City. His admiration for Shankly knew no bounds and in this relationship, at least, the warmth was mutual. 'The Liverpool players are totally loyal to Bill Shankly because he is totally loyal to them,' Revie said. 'That situation does not exist in as many clubs as you might think. One of the reasons I admire Shankly is that he never criticises his players publicly, even when things are going badly. Some managers tend to be difficult to please... in fact they give the impression they are never satisfied with their players. I know how disheartening this can be to a team.' This is a veiled dig at Brian Clough and Malcolm Allison, the antitheses of Revie's 'ideal' manager. In fact, he detested the pair of them – hated their brashness, the way they turned into braggarts as soon as a camera came anywhere near them, their 'holier than thou' sermons on how the game should be played, and the implied criticisms aimed at his team. Unfortunately for Revie, in 1972 the Derby manager was to have the pleasure of delivering the perfect rebuttal.

For the moment, however, the Leeds manager was more concerned with overcoming Second Division Birmingham to reach his third FA Cup Final in eight years. With the previous season's humiliating Cup exit still fresh in his mind, Revie was taking no chances against a team he knew Leeds ought to beat comfortably. 'Without wishing to appear pompous, it is asking a lot of any side to match Leeds for skill.

That's why nearly all our Cup opponents from lower divisions have attempted to nullify our flair at the expense of our own creative ability.' Refusing to risk anything, however, he ordered Maurice Lindley and Syd Owen to prepare the usual 'dossier' on Birmingham. Billy Bremner's verdict was forthright. 'If we don't go through, it will be our own fault, not that of our "spies". If we can't beat Birmingham, we don't deserve to win.'

His insouciance turned out to be justified. Leeds won 3–0 at Hillsborough in a match dubbed a 'Saturday afternoon saunter' by the *Yorkshire Evening Post*. Birmingham had made a rather desperate bid to psyche out Leeds by emulating their trademark warm-up, but their cheek was about the only thing they got right all afternoon. It was over as soon as Mick Jones opened the scoring after 18 minutes. Six minutes later Birmingham were caught square at the back as Eddie Gray fed a through ball to Peter Lorimer, who put Leeds further ahead with a low shot into the corner. Jones' second, on 64 minutes, rounded off a comfortable passage to Wembley.

By Monday the ever-cautious Revie was encouraging his team to forget about Wembley and concentrate on the League. While his men were on duty at Hillsborough, Derby and Liverpool had cruised passed Huddersfield and West Ham respectively. Leeds were now fourth, three points behind Derby but with two games in hand. 'This week is one of the most important of the season,' said Revie. 'It brings two away games and if we can collect points from these games we shall be well on the way to the title.' Losing away to Newcastle wasn't as calamitous as it first appeared, as Derby were beaten by Manchester City, and in United's next game the imperious Giles kept Leeds in the frame by converting a penalty at West Bromwich Albion for a 1–0 win. With two league games left, Leeds were still fourth, two points behind Manchester City, who had completed their league programme. Derby and Liverpool were a point ahead of Leeds, with one and two games outstanding respectively.

With the FA Cup Final looming, Leeds once again approached League secretary Alan Hardaker to have the club's outstanding fixtures rescheduled. Once again Revie was rebuffed, apparently because the move would have compromised England's commitments in the European Nations Cup and Wolves' clash with Spurs in the UEFA Cup. To Leeds' supporters it seemed as if the League's principal remit was to stop the club winning trophies. Those with long-enough memories place Hardaker alongside Ray Tinkler and assorted other officials among the gallery of rogues whose actions are felt to have prevented Revie's team from fulfilling its potential.

Hardaker, Football League Secretary from 1957 to 1979, has been dead for over twenty years, but retrospective accounts of his reign suggest Leeds' infuriated followers may have had a point. A blunt and autocratic man, he began his autobiography, *Hardaker of the Leagues*, thus: 'One of the few things I have come to be certain about in football is the impossibility of attempting to be a just and forward-looking administrator as well as generally popular. For every person who thinks a decision is right, there is another who will condemn it as a sin against the game in general and himself in particular.' He made a virtue out of seeking to prove his own dictum. The late Bryon Butler recalled some of the various titles by which he was variously described: '"the great dictator", "football's godfather", "a cross between Cagney and Caligula", "the League's answer to Idi Amin" and, most fancifully, "St Alan of St Annes". Hardaker always referred to himself as "only a paid servant whose job is to implement decisions and rules",' Butler himself observed, 'but it's fair to say that, as an enforcer, he didn't believe in tip-toeing through life simply to avoid treading on a few feet.' Whatever Hardaker's merits, his personal enmity toward Revie ensured that the club would receive no favours while he was in charge. His successor, the lugubrious Graham Kelly, is frank about the two men's estrangement, pointing out that 'Hardaker loathed Revie with a vengeance that can only have been reserved for a fellow Yorkshireman who he felt had twisted his way to the top.'

So it transpired that Leeds had to win three critical games out of eight if they were to capture the 'double' – with Hardaker doubtless praying that they would slip up. The first game in the sequence saw

46,565 fans pack Elland Road for the home game against Chelsea, Leeds' biggest gate of the season. A 2–0 victory left United needing only to beat Wolves a week later to capture the title. Ironically, Brian Clough's Derby had done Revie a huge favour by beating Liverpool with a single goal at Anfield. Clough, showing his usual chutzpah, had played Steve Powell at right-back at the age of sixteen. 'How many managers, how many clubs would have been prepared to do that?' he crowed later. The Rams were now top but had completed their forty-two-match programme. With one game to go, only Leeds, one point behind, and Liverpool, two adrift, could topple them. At last Revie was moved to admit: 'I think we have a chance now of the double.' The bookies agreed. Leeds were 5–2 on to win the league, with Derby available at 7–2 and Liverpool 6–1. Revie's team were even money to lift both trophies, with Ladbrokes ruefully admitting it stood to lose 'a lot of money' if Leeds won either.

With the Centenary FA Cup Final to be played on 6 May, another queue was forming at Les Cocker's treatment table. Giles, Clarke and both full-backs, Madeley and Reaney, had picked up knocks in the Chelsea game. Eddie Gray, who had missed the match with a thigh strain, was also struggling to get fit. Giles' groin injury was the biggest worry. In the event, however, Revie was able to field a full-strength team, with the exception of long-term casualty Terry Cooper. But he was taking no chances. His players were ordered to rest; even golf was ruled out of bounds.

No one was expecting a pretty game. Even Revie admitted that the 1968 League Cup Final clash had been 'an often bitter, niggling affair, which must rank as one of the worst games seen at Wembley'. This time he expected better, but it was hardly going to be a beautiful marriage of contrasts. 'It is never easy to get the better of Arsenal because they are extremely well-organised,' he said. 'Arsenal are never more dangerous than when they are pinned deep in their own half. They have the ability to take opponents by surprise with quick, incisive counter-attacks.'

Despite Revie's characteristic habit of heaping praise on the opposition, there was a steely determination in the Leeds camp not to let a third FA Cup Final slip away. 'I dread the thought we could go another season without winning something,' Revie commented in the run up to the game. In those days the match was the only domestic fixture to be screened live on television, and the competition was at or near the high-water mark of its prestige. Losing the 1970 Final against Chelsea, Revie now admitted, had been 'the biggest disappointment of my life'. Losing a European Cup semi-final was, apparently, less of a blow.

As if to remind Leeds of what was at stake, the Football Association had arranged for all the past-winners of the Cup, including Arsenal, to parade their colours around the stadium. The Queen and Duke of Edinburgh were also in attendance, paying one of their relatively infrequent visits to a football match. Captain Bremner, nevertheless, had little time for such pre-match fripperies. 'I believe it was all a bit of a shambles,' he recalled, 'which did not surprise me. The only professional point was when Tommy Steele led some singing.' Predictably enough, the match would not mirror the grandeur of the occasion.

In the first half the Gunners' counter-attacking strategy very nearly paid dividends. Harvey, the only player in the Leeds team not to have played at Wembley before, brilliantly saved a 30-yard deflected drive from Frank McLintock. Then, on the half-hour, a lunging Paul Reaney cleared a shot from Alan Ball off the line. Jack Charlton, who would be thirty-seven the following Monday, was having one of his finest games in twenty years as a Leeds player. At the other end Leeds were endeavouring to follow Revie's instruction to attack, and were to make twenty-one scoring attempts to Arsenal's twelve, but with Peter Storey keeping a tight rein on John Giles, and Frank McLintock resolute at the back alongside Peter Simpson and Pat Rice, they were finding the going tough in the early stages. It was not until the final minutes of the first period that Leeds contrived any clear-cut openings. The first saw a clever ball from Bremner beat three Arsenal defenders before landing at the feet of Allan Clarke, who found Jones near the edge of the area. His low shot beat Arsenal's stand-in keeper Geoff Barnett, but passed just wide of the post. Just before the interval, Leeds came even closer to scoring. A Lorimer cross from the right was met by a header from Clarke, which beat Barnett but hit the cross-bar.

Arsenal had the first real opportunity of the second half, when McNab headed into the side netting from an Armstrong cross. But with Giles and Bremner gradually gaining the ascendancy, the match was approaching its defining moment. On 53 minutes Mick Jones ran on to a pass from Peter Lorimer down the right. After gliding past McNab to the by-line, Jones supplied a measured cross to Allan Clarke, who was running in towards the penalty spot. Clarke's diving header beat Barnett down at his left-hand post. The strike prompted a wild exhibition of delight and relief among players and supporters. 'I knew as soon as I connected it was a goal,' said Clarke. 'I had time to see the goalkeeper first and pick my spot and I followed it all the way in.'

For Revie the memory of so many near-misses extinguished any spontaneous display of satisfaction. He merely rose from the bench and gestured as if to say, 'Keep it calm, keep your discipline.' There were still 37 minutes to go. He needn't have worried. Leeds played with more confidence after the goal and had numerous chances to add to their lead. Most of Arsenal's increasingly desperate attacks petered out on the edge of the Leeds area. There was to be just one final scare. On 70 minutes Charlie George sent a stinging shot past Harvey, which cannoned against the bar. Simpson, racing in, stabbed the rebound wide. After the disappointments of 1965 and 1970, victory brought Revie joy unconfined. 'I have waited and sweated a lot of years for today but it has all been worth it,' he said. 'This is the second happiest day of my life: the first was when we beat Liverpool to win the Championship.' The hardest part, he said, had been to tell Gary Sprake he wasn't playing: 'Gary accepted it. It is all part of the family spirit at this club.'

There was to be a pause before his players could at last lay their hands on the FA Cup. In the 88th minute of the game Mick Jones had collided with Barnett, dislocating an elbow. Bremner delayed climb-ing the steps to collect the trophy while Jones was receiving treatment on the pitch. Eventually, however, he could wait no longer. 'I wiped my hands on my shirt and [the Queen] gave me a lovely smile,' said Bremner. 'I think she said, "Very well done, you have earned it", but you don't really take it all in when you've got thousands of people just waiting for you to lift the trophy in the air.' Jones did make it up the steps, his heavily-strapped figure one of the game's most enduring memories. Aided by Norman Hunter and clearly in agony, he collected his medal while his team-mates postponed their lap of honour.

For forty-eight hours at least, this particular Leeds triumph would not bringing a swinging hangover in its wake. The traditional post-match parade was postponed until the following Thursday and the players were absent from the celebration banquet in London. That event was hosted by FA chairman Dr Andrew Stephen. He was also chairman of Sheffield Wednesday, the last Yorkshire side to win the FA Cup, in 1935. 'We are all delighted with this young man's [Jones] determination to be presented to the Queen,' Dr Stephen commented rather pompously. 'It was very much appreciated in the Royal Box.'

For once even the London papers were generous in their praise. 'Leeds, the most consistent team in European soccer for the last eight years, carried off [the Cup] in a final which eventually was one-sided,' conceded our old friend David Miller, then of the *Sunday Telegraph*. The doyen of sports writers, the *Observer*'s Hugh McIlvanney, wrote that 'Leeds... outplayed Arsenal to an extent that was inadequately reflected in the scoreline. It was Leeds whose football was the more controlled, whose ideas were more inventive. Once Leeds had settled, and especially after their goal, they dominated Arsenal completely.'

It was then the consensus in footballing circles that no side which had not won the FA Cup could lay claim to true greatness. Now this victory confirmed Leeds' status as one of the great post-war sides. Revie's comparison with 'Real Madrid in their pomp', alluded to in the match programme, no longer seemed quite so vainglorious. 'They were held in awe by a generation of schoolboys,' recalled the

Independent's Jonathan Rendall in a retrospective on the Revie years, following Leeds' promotion back to the First Division in 1990. 'In 1972, Esso Petrol Stations ran a promotion in advance of the Cup Final. Thousands of silver alloy coins, each containing the name of previous winner, were given away to be mounted in a plastic collectors' album. There was one coin – that for the Centenary Cup winners – that was bigger than all the others. For weeks before the match, the allotted spaced for it yawned at the head of the album. Inevitably Leeds filled it. They even had their own currency, and devalued your own [team's].'

Leaving their wives – and the Cup – behind, Revie's players were back on the road within an hour of the final whistle. Their destination was the Mount Hotel near Wolverhampton, where they were to prepare for Monday's 'double' decider. At dinner that night Wolves legend Derek Dougan, ironically as it turned out, presented Allan Clarke with the Golden Boot for scoring the winning goal.

Leeds limped into Molineux two days later, visibly wilting after eight highly charged matches in a month. Jones was already missing and three other members of Revie's meagre squad would not have played had the match not been so momentous. Eddie Gray took to the field with one of his thighs bound in tape from knee to groin, while Clarke and Giles both had painkilling injections. Clarke, limping throughout, would eventually make way for Terry Yorath, leaving Leeds without either member of their first-choice attack. Bremner started the match at centre-forward, with Mick Bates taking his place in midfield.

Revie's men should have been too much for Wolves, even though their opponents played with the type of passion (in what was for them, after all, a 'dead' game) that Sir Alex Ferguson would later amusingly term 'perverse'. Leeds were expected to play a containing game to get the point that would have won them the Championship. Wolves were in the middle of a two-leg UEFA Cup Final against Spurs and would surely be happy to play for a draw. For once Revie was to cast caution aside. In his newspaper column, he declared that Leeds would go all out for victory, notwithstanding his player's tired limbs. 'I reckon it would be soccer suicide to adopt a negative style of play,' he said with unconscious irony. 'Teams can always be relied on to raise their game when they play against us. Wolves prefer opponents to play defensively because it means their own flaws at the back are not exposed.'

This was the year, however, that Revie was to suffer a double-whammy at the hands of officialdom. Hardaker's intransigence had already placed a formidable obstacle in his path, and now appalling refereeing would yet again thwart his ambitions. That evening at Molineux, Bill Gow of Swansea earned his own entry in the Elland Road book of infamy by denying Leeds three penalties. The most blatant offence came on 23 minutes when Bernard Shaw got both hands to the ball to stop Allan Clarke from shooting. Gow was unsighted but the linesman, J.C. Collins, was having none of it. 'It was one of his first games and he froze,' said Norman Hunter. But Leeds should already have been in front. Gow had waved play on after goalkeeper Phil Parkes brought down Allan Clarke early on. In the second half Shaw was the guilty man again, handling a Lorimer shot, but once more Gow ignored Leeds' pleas. By that time Leeds were a goal down, even though they had dominated the match. From Wolves' second corner – Leeds had already had seven – Francis Munro shot through a crowd of players into the net. Dougan returned to haunt Clarke and Leeds on 65 minutes, putting Wolves 2–0 up against the run of play. Bremner renewed Leeds' hopes a few minutes later, scoring from a Paul Madeley pass, but with Jack Charlton up alongside his captain in attack, their frantic final efforts were unavailing. Wolves full-back Gerry Taylor decided the championship in the dying moments, clearing off the line after Yorath had lobbed the ball over the head of goalkeeper Parkes. Once again, when it had seemed far easier to prevail than fail, Leeds were left cursing their luck. It was over.

They were not the only footballers feeling bitter that night. At Highbury, Leeds' FA Cup Final opponents had denied Liverpool the win that would have taken the title to Anfield. In the 88th minute, with the Liverpool supporters chanting that Leeds were losing at Wolves, John Toshack fired home – only to be ruled offside. Bill Shankly slammed referee Roger Kirkpatrick for a 'diabolical decision' that 'cost us the championship'.

Derby's players received the news of their unexpected triumph on the beach in Majorca, where they had repaired for a close season break with assistant manager Peter Taylor. Brian Clough had taken his family to the Scilly Isles. Taylor, wrote Clough, 'convinced them the title was ours, but I can't honestly say I shared his confidence. I expected Leeds to get the result because Revie was the most thorough of men who, wherever possible, left nothing to chance.' With Leeds and Liverpool faltering at the last, some tagged Derby unworthy champions. Clough, unsurprisingly, disagreed. It must have been doubly galling for Revie that Clough and not his old friend Shankly was the beneficiary of Leeds' misfortune. The Derby manager had already carved out an alternative career as an eccentric and outspoken TV pundit, and United's 'cynicism' was the frequent subject of his barbs. On one occasion he had even called for Revie to be fined and Leeds kicked out of the First Division, an appeal that was to guarantee him a frosty reception at Elland Road just two years later. 'Leeds in those days cheated,' says Clough, 'and I was more than happy to draw people's attention to the fact.'

Alan Hardaker was evidently of the same mind, and it is hard for many to look beyond him as the real architect of Leeds' demise on that May evening. The Leeds players certainly think so, though Revie's penchant for making influential enemies hardly helped their cause. 'He [Revie] didn't want to make friends,' Peter Lorimer told Bryn Law of BBC Radio Leeds, a revealing comment about someone who so painfully wanted to be liked. 'One of the biggest things he did wrong for himself as a manager was to become a great enemy of Hardaker, who made things tremendously difficult for us. Alan Hardaker had a personal thing about Don Revie, but Don was that kind of man. He could make enemies. He was such a professional and if there was any rule he could use, and he was entitled to use it, he would go for it.'

Norman Hunter believes this very professionalism backfired on the fateful May weekend, when Revie's players were prevented from celebrating their Cup win. 'What the gaffer should have done is let us go out and get absolutely smashed,' he told the same interviewer. 'We'd have gone in the steam room on Sunday and been fine by Monday.'

Alcohol and professional football were more comfortable bedfellows then, players getting 'stoned', as Jack Charlton misleadingly puts it, to relieve the tension towards the end of the season, but there had never been any chance of Hunter getting his wish. The most the players could look forward to was a meal in a motorway service station on the way up the M1. The manager had also decreed that the players would be allowed a morning in bed on the Sunday, followed by hot baths and massages. The evenings would be spent playing bingo and carpet bowls. Monday morning would see some light training, with the players then going back to bed for a light tea.

As if the loss of the double that night at Molineux wasn't enough to leave a sour taste in every Leeds fan's mouth, the whole sorry episode was exhumed five years later by the *Daily Mirror* as the third plank of evidence in their attempt to prove that Don Revie was corrupt. Adding to the claims of Stokoe and those conveniently anonymous Newcastle players about the two games at the end of the 1961/62 season, *Mirror* reporters Richard Stott and Frank Palmer alleged that Revie had enlisted Mike O'Grady, by now himself a Wolves player, as a 'fixer', paid to offer his new colleagues £1000 per man to gift the title-decider to United. The article was based on interviews undertaken with O'Grady and Gary Sprake (the recipient of £15,000 from the *Mirror*), which appeared to corroborate the allegations. However, when the case was investigated by the police and the FA, both parties found that Revie had no case to answer. When the *People*, the *Mirror*'s sister paper, repeated the claims, egging the pudding by alleging that Bremner kept trying to find takers for the 'bribe' in the course of the game, Bremner sued for libel. At the trial Sprake was forced to retract his version and Bremner was duly awarded £100,000 damages by the court. As for O'Grady, in 1990 he told Revie's biographer, Andrew Mourant, that he felt pressurized by the journalists into talking to the *Mirror* but now refused to substantiate the paper's story. It's a strange tale, full of claims and counter-claims, but given the court's verdict and the findings of the police and the FA, it's difficult to see how we're supposed to believe in Revie's guilt. It just doesn't add up.

While Bremner emerged as the victor from this tawdry saga, Revie is still the loser. Mud has continued to stick to him, allowing those who feuded with him in the 1960s and 70s to exploit the immunity provided by his death to trot out all manner of wild accusations without needing a scrap of proof to back them up. Malcolm Allison, for example, interviewed by Rob Steen in *The Mavericks*, is allowed to say that Revie 'used to leave £300 or £400 in an envelope in the referee's room and they could take it or leave it. I'm just talking about a little thing called bribery.'

Over the thirteen years Revie was manager of Leeds and nearly 500 games in all competitions, wouldn't at least one referee, one might think, have corroborated Allison's claim? Yet the allegation is left unchallenged. Revie's death has meant his reputation is fair game for anyone. The lessons to be learned from all this are simple. Don't walk out on the England job and sell exclusive rights to your story like Revie did, thereby making enemies of all the other newspapers, and, above all, don't die early.

After their shattering reverse at Wolves, Revie's men returned to Leeds for what threatened to rank as one of the most anti-climactic trophy celebrations ever. The event only made an inside page of the *Yorkshire Evening Post*, though the local paper did its level best to place an upbeat gloss on proceedings. 'The team might have been forgiven for viewing the prospect of a "triumphant" return to Elland Road with some cynicism,' it reported. 'They need not have worried. As they emerged from the Queen's Hotel, the roar of the 1,500 people in City Square must nearly have dislodged the Black Prince from his horse.' To their credit the Leeds supporters, who had shed copious tears for their team just two days previously, turned out en masse to salute the team's Wembley achievement. And it's just as well they did; the FA Cup had never been to Leeds and it hasn't been back since. The fans lined the route of the traditional open-topped coach as it wound its way down Wellington Street, Gelderd Road and Lowfields Lane to Elland Road, where 35,000 'raised a cheer worthy of a Wembley crowd'.

Revie's battle-weary platoon made a strange tableau for the photographers, with Terry Cooper grinning from his wheelchair and Mick Jones with his arm in a sling, but they were genuinely touched by their reception, which momentarily threatened to get out of hand. About 1000 fans invaded the pitch as the procession made its way towards the Kop, and Revie threatened to take the team off the field unless they withdrew. Mystifyingly, some fans also 'celebrated' with a demonstration of unilateral hooliganism, smashing windows in shops and offices around the ground.

The manager, so often maddened by the citizenry's blasé attitude towards their football club, shared his players' gratitude towards those well-wishers who had behaved themselves. 'I just didn't believe it would be like this,' he said. 'These supporters make me feel very proud to belong to Leeds United.' For the acquisitive Revie, however, that pride was clearly contingent. Within a year he would be breaking bread with the chairman of Everton to discuss a possible move to Merseyside.

TWELVE

YESTERDAY'S MEN?

leven years into his regime, Revie's team had now won five major trophies, but if they were to achieve the immortality he felt was their due, the manager knew time was running out. In 1971 Revie had expressed the hope that Leeds could remain one of the top clubs 'for perhaps the next two or three years'. It sounded a conservative assessment at the time, but it proved to be spot on, since there was no conveyor belt of stars to replace those that left or retired. By mid-1970, when the team he built was complete, Revie had spent £500,000 on players such as Allan Clarke, Mick Jones and John Giles. He had also sold shrewdly, recouping close to £300,000. Even at their peak in the 1971/72 season Leeds United did not have the financial clout of Everton or Spurs, never mind Manchester United. It was the old problem of the city's divided loyalties: quite simply, not enough people came to watch Leeds to provide the revenue for a huge transfer kitty with which Revie could make a successful team into a successful club. He dreamt of a dynasty but was well aware that permanently securing Leeds' place at the top table was a forlorn hope, given the fluctuating crowds and the strange ambivalence of most new supporters.

'Leeds have spent the best part of a million pounds on ground improvements and expect to spend more,' wrote Peter Morris in *The Team-makers: a Gallery of the Great Soccer Managers*, published in 1971. 'But they must keep a successful team to justify it. Always, you have the uneasy feeling that if Revie were to leave Leeds and the club began a slide down, there would be a startling reversion to the days when the club nearly dropped into the Third Division.' Morris's prescient work was spot on. Leeds narrowly avoided just such a fate in the late 1980s before the club's renaissance under Howard Wilkinson. In 1972 Don Revie realized he had at best a couple of years to cash in with his present team before some difficult choices had to be faced. Then, either he would have to go or he'd have to ditch the majority of his team.

Perhaps it was inevitable that Revie would eventually leave. By 1972 Revie's talent for finding raw talent through the club's widely envied scouting system, especially in Scotland and the north-east, and then inculcating it with his peculiarly puritan work ethic, seemed to have exhausted itself. The clock was ticking, and the players knew it, too. 'I think when we've all finished, Leeds might have a good team,' reflected Allan Clarke, 'but they'll not have a great team.' (The job of Revie's eleven successors has been to prove Clarke wrong, and none has yet managed it, though Brian Clough's record suggests that he might have, had he approached the task with Peter Taylor at his side and a little more sensitivity.)

Leeds, with their fickle fans and provincial directors, were always struggling to keep pace with the scale of Revie's ambitions. 'If you think small then you stay small,' he had reasoned after taking the job. Whether haggling over his salary or trying to sell his best players, the Board thought small too often. 'What you put into the game you take out, otherwise there'll be no returns,' Revie used to tell young players coming into the club. 'You can earn a lot of money in ten or fifteen years and at the end be financially secure for life if you are prepared to work hard. This is common sense.' Even in 1971 Revie was explaining to one writer how he was going to build a football academy at Leeds – a hostel 'where youth players would learn the game and at the same time prepare themselves under qualified teachers for a life outside it when their playing days were over'. The Leeds manager would eventually get his academy, but Revie did not live to see it. It would be another twenty years before Howard Wilkinson masterminded the facility at Boston Spa, near Wetherby, which has produced – among others – Harry Kewell, Jonathan Woodgate and Alan Smith. Revie, 'the Don' in more than name, would have been the ideal figurehead for such an institution. More attuned to the training ground than the boardroom, his influence was all pervading. 'Revie is the epitome of industry,' said an impressed Peter Morris. 'Visit Elland Road any day of the week and you'll meet him as like as not in heavy sweater and tracksuit trousers, his face bathed in honest sweat, perhaps blowing just a little. He will subside into his office chair to talk to you, but all the time you can see the man is positively itching to get on with it and he looks curiously out of place behind his desk – a grizzly bear perched on a cocktail bar stool.'

In August 1972 as he embarked on another campaign, Revie had the team he wanted. What he needed was the run of the ball, an even break from officials and a season relatively free of injuries and suspensions. Even if that was likely to be a forlorn hope, he can't have expected it all to come crashing round his ears within the year. By the end of the most curious season in Leeds' history, however, it seemed that the 'glory years' were behind them.

There was just one major addition to the squad, though this was the season that would see Joe Jordan and Gordon McQueen emerge as first-team regulars. Signed as a central defender, the versatile Trevor Cherry became the only non-international in Leeds' first-team squad when he moved to Leeds from Huddersfield Town for £100,000. Cherry had captained Huddersfield to the Second Division title in 1970 and would eventually replace Terry Cooper as Leeds' left-back for Revie's last two seasons.

The season opened in depressing fashion, Leeds losing 4–0 at Chelsea to record their worst opening day performance for twenty-four years, although there were some mitigating circumstances. Jack Charlton was injured and Norman Hunter and Allan Clarke both missed the game through suspension. Roy Ellam, another new signing from Huddersfield, partnered Paul Madeley in central defence. With Cherry in for Cooper, Leeds' makeshift backline was dealt a further blow when Harvey left the field with concussion. Mick Jones was carried off with a twisted ankle and Peter Lorimer took over in goal. Damage limitation was the most Revie could hope for.

Normal service was resumed at Sheffield United the following Tuesday. With thirty-seven-year-old Charlton back at the heart of the defence and Harvey back in goal, Leeds won 2–0. Another victory followed, at home to West Bromwich Albion, but Leeds' stuttering start would eventually prove fatal to their championship aspirations. Just five of the first eleven games were won, already prompting murmurings in the press that Revie's ageing team was over the hill. 'I think they must accept that Giles and Charlton are past their peak, and that Bremner's overworked batteries are running low,' wrote the *Guardian*'s Eric Todd. 'Leeds have achieved many things but now... the writing is on the wall.'

The obituaries were premature, but two defeats by Liverpool before Christmas were portentous. The Anfield club was soon to assume the mantle of England's premier club, a title they would not relinquish for the best part of two decades. One of those defeats came in a hotly contested League Cup replay in extra time at Elland Road on 22 November, but Shankly proclaimed the result a mixed blessing, with fixture congestion threatening to get in the way of his own title ambitions. 'The losers of this match may well be the winners in the end,' he remarked. He was wrong.

In the league Leeds had bounced back from another home defeat by Liverpool in September by thrashing champions Derby 5–0, but there was a *fin de siècle* air about the club after two successive defeats. Ten thousand fewer fans turned up to watch the Derby game, and worse was to follow on 16 December when only 25,000 showed up for the home game against Birmingham City, though Leeds' form by that time had begun to recover. Revie was entitled to wonder whether the Leeds public deserved him.

The team's indifferent form did not help, but events surrounding the clash with Manchester United on 18 April provided abundant evidence of another potent incentive for some fans to stay away. 'Soccer Fans Blaze Terror Trail in Leeds' was the splash headline of the local paper the day after the match. Crowd trouble was the now the rule rather than the exception in games involving Leeds, and never more so than when their hated trans-Pennine rivals came to town. For the less belligerent supporters the simple task of getting to and from the ground had become a hazardous obstacle course. Even taking care to remain in the thick of one's own fans was no guarantee of safety. On that particular Wednesday evening one Leeds man was kicked unconscious on Boar Lane, in the heart of the city, by eight youths wearing the colours of his hometown team. He had been reckless enough to protest that they had been jostling his pregnant wife.

On the field the ordeal of chasing honours on several fronts was yet again proving Leeds' undoing. Revie's men turned in a listless display and Manchester United, fleetingly rejuvenated under Tommy Docherty and unbeaten for six matches, won 1–0. It was a devastating blow to Leeds' championship hopes. Bremner summed up the mood in the dressing room: 'We felt pretty sick. Our dressing room was like a morgue. Nobody spoke. We genuinely felt we had a good chance of catching Liverpool and winning the title. I felt more disappointed for the gaffer than anyone else. He had set his heart on having another crack at the European Cup.'

Injuries and suspensions had again taken a heavy toll on Revie's squad in early 1973, but although Trevor Cherry had filled the gap vacated by Terry Cooper, even as the fixtures piled up the manager was not to be tempted back into the transfer market. His rivals were less reluctant, another ominous sign. Defeat by Manchester United left Leeds eight points adrift of leaders Liverpool with five matches to go but two games in hand. Crystal Palace were dispatched 4–0 at a barely half-full Elland Road a few days later, a result which merely delayed the inevitable. Fittingly, it would be Liverpool who would finally put an end to Leeds' title hopes two days later. A crowd of 56,000 packed Anfield to salute Liverpool's first trophy in seven years. Goals from Kevin Keegan and Peter Cormack duly delivered it against a Leeds team deprived of several first-team regulars.

Losing out to his old pal Shankly was a sight more palatable to

Revie than their fate the previous year when they had surrendered the Championship to the odious Clough, and Revie had no hesitation in adopting magnanimity in defeat. The United team formed a 'guard of honour' as the victors left the field, in conscious imitation of the long ovation they had received from the Kop in 1969. 'I am far from broken-hearted,' said an unusually stoical Revie. 'Deep down I didn't really expect Leeds to finish top. Naturally we would have liked to win the championship but, next to ourselves, I think Liverpool are the side we would most like to see achieve it.' The Liverpool manager, shrewd as ever, was not slow to acknowledge the significance of his encounters with Revie's team. 'We have now beaten Leeds three times this season, and some teams haven't managed that in eight years,' he quipped.

Leeds had been playing catch-up all season, but Revie had other reasons to be sanguine about losing the league. By that stage his team were progressing toward two Cup Finals, and he had good reason to be confident of winning them both.

The European Cup Winners' Cup was a competition Leeds had never previously entered. Their early passage was relatively comfortable, despite a lacklustre performance against the Turkish side Ankaragucu in the first round, where they had to rely on a Mick Jones goal to earn a 2–1 aggregate win in front of a paltry 22,000 crowd at Elland Road. More comfortable aggregate victories followed against Carl Zeiss Jena (2–0) and Rapid Bucharest (8–1). In the semi-final Leeds were paired against the Yugoslavs Hajduk Split, a far tougher proposition. The attendance for the home leg, played first, was a dispiritingly low 32,000. Leeds' poor crowds had become something of an embarrassment even to their own supporters.

They sparked an anguished debate on local television. On *Look North*, the local BBC TV news magazine, one fan came up with the novel theory that Leeds' gates were lower than their rivals' because Yorkshire folk demanded value for money. In the *Yorkshire Evening Post* another penny-pincher concurred: 'After seeing United shut up shop when one or two goals up, I have often wondered if we should all go home at half-time.' Perhaps the most bizarre explanation for the sparsely populated terraces came from the fan who questioned the siting of United's ground. 'I am convinced it's at the wrong side of the city,' he speculated. 'The soccer centre of Leeds is north of the river [Aire], and certainly the amateur and schoolboy game is much stronger there.'

Those who did manage to struggle across town witnessed a disciplined performance from Leeds in the home leg of the semi-final. A supremely fit Hajduk had played with swagger and confidence, but an Allan Clarke goal gave United a narrow advantage to take to Yugoslavia. Unfortunately for Leeds, the man now hailed as the best close-range finisher since Jimmy Greaves would miss both that game and the final – should Leeds qualify. The England striker was sent off at Elland Road for retaliation after being tackled from behind by the defender Boljat. The Hajduk player escaped without a caution. Revie was 'surprised' UEFA handed Clarke a two-match ban instead of the customary one-game suspension, but there was no right of appeal.

Revie came to consider United's performance in Yugoslavia the equal of his team's finest in Europe, the 1968 Fair's Cup Final triumph against Ferencvaros. The game was played just two days after the Anfield defeat, which finally put an end to Leeds' championship hopes. Eddie Gray was also absent, along with Clarke. As a tired Leeds side arrived at the ground, they were taunted by the notoriously volatile Hajduk fans, with the prediction of a 5–0 hammering. Captain Bremner smiled and shrugged his shoulders. His highly experienced team were not to be ruffled. Leeds played a controlled, defensive game, restricting their opponents to just one clear chance. In fact, it was Leeds who contrived the better openings. On 20 minutes Peter Lorimer crashed a drive against the foot of a post, and in the second half a Mick Jones effort was clawed round the post by the Split goalkeeper. In the final act of the game Giles drilled a shot into the net, only to see the goal disallowed because the referee had blown the final whistle as the ball went in. Revie hailed his team's feat as 'fantastic... at a time when many people are once again trying to write us off'. Again, however, victory came with a sting in the tail.

Bremner had picked up a caution and would also miss the Final. Now it was on to Salonika – and their ninth Cup Final in nine years. A scratch Leeds side would, for once, be the underdogs against AC Milan, the only club to have won both the European Cup and Cup Winners' Cup.

In the FA Cup it had taken a second replay at neutral Villa Park for Leeds to beat Norwich City. Allan Clarke scored a hat-trick in an ultimately emphatic 5–0 victory. Thereafter Leeds' highest-profile victims were Derby County, as Revie's men swept smoothly towards their third Final in four years. The semi-final draw paired Leeds with Bill McGarry's Wolves, who were attempting to reach their first Final since 1960. The clash gave Revie's team the perfect opportunity to gain revenge for the trauma of blowing the double at Molineux eleven months previously. A photograph of Revie's players punching the air as the draw came out of the hat suggested they would relish the opportunity. Wolves had yet to concede a goal in their FA Cup campaign, and the match, held at Maine Road, was a predictably defensive encounter. The single goal, which Revie had correctly predicted would prove decisive, was lashed in from close range by Billy Bremner on 68 minutes. His furious celebrations in front of the Leeds supporters suggested their fiery talisman had exorcised the Molineux demons.

Leeds' FA Cup Final opponents were Second Division Sunderland, whose manager Bob Stokoe was an even more virulent critic of Revie than Clough. It was the definitive David versus Goliath encounter. A team from the Second had not won the FA Cup since 1931 and, understandably, the media consensus was that Sunderland did not have a prayer against probably the finest club side in Europe. 'No way Leeds can lose it,' asserted the *Daily Mail* on the morning of the match. While Revie made his routine noises about respecting his opponents, in private he was less equivocal. 'Before the game I could not see any way we could lose,' he later admitted. 'We had the players, the experience, the firepower and the team spirit.' Ever-cautious, however, he would not countenance any public display of confidence, and once again this would contribute to his team's undoing. As his squad set off for London, he explained how the 'quiet route to success' meant treating this game 'as just another match'.

It was a catastrophic misjudgement. A carefree Sunderland had been grandstanding in London for days, determined to extract every last ounce of enjoyment from an occasion they can never have expected to grace. Moreover, with United in purdah Bob Stokoe had free rein to begin an unsubtle but effective bout of psychological warfare against his opposite number. His first outburst was the usual nonsense about the allocation of 'England's dressing room', which had gone to United, and the matter of having the Leeds fans at the tunnel end, where the teams would enter the stadium. The latter complaint was especially meretricious. Stokoe knew full well that 81,000 of the 100,000 crowd – the Sunderland supporters and 62,000 'neutrals' – would be rooting for his team.

Rather than dismissing or simply ignoring Stokoe's absurd gripe, Revie unwittingly revealed that it had fed his neurosis, commenting wearily that, 'We get blamed for practically all it is possible to get blamed for these days.' Wolves manager Bill McGarry's attack of sour grapes gave Stokoe more ammunition, as he declared himself 'staggered' in the aftermath of his side's semi-final defeat, 'at the way Bremner went the whole 90 minutes disputing every decision that went against his team'. 'I am not trying to knock Leeds in any way,' agreed a disingenuous Stokoe, 'but we are playing a real professional side and, let's face it, the word professionalism can embrace a multitude of sins as well as virtues. The case about Bremner is the only comment I want to make about Leeds. My message is simple. I want Mr [Ken] Burns, the Cup Final referee, to make the decisions and not Mr Bremner.' Holed up in the team's hotel, Bremner declined to get drawn into a slanging match. 'It's like Wilfred Pickles' "Have a go" week,' was the Leeds captain's gnomic response.

It is impossible to prove that Stokoe's bid to prejudice Burns had an effect on the outcome of the match, but when the game came around, the Leeds captain would be uncharacteristically out of sorts. We also know that Burns' relations with Leeds had been strained since the

1967 semi-final. Certainly the Sunderland boss had no doubts: 'They [the media] did a marvellous job for me,' confirmed Stokoe, proving himself a master of the gamesmanship he had so hypocritically condemned to some credulous journalists. 'I'm not saying the referee was influenced, but he didn't allow Bremner to get at him.'

By the morning of the match the Leeds players were unsettled, their manager's innate anxieties heightening their own. A team used to snapping and scrapping and battling against the odds was acutely uncomfortable in the role of overwhelming favourites. One photographer in the team hotel who was rash enough to take a picture of the team had his camera torn from his hands. Revie did not like the team being photographed before games – another daft superstition.

Dave Watson, the craggy Sunderland centre-half who would later play under Revie for England, recalled watching the Leeds players being interviewed at their hotel. 'They were very subdued,' he observed. 'No one was cracking any jokes. The answers were very clipped, as if they were afraid to give something away. We thought: "What's wrong with them?"' Sunderland's mood could not have been more different. 'Our lot were the complete opposite, clowning around,' said Watson. 'We all fell about. Bob Stokoe was there, with one of the directors, and everyone was splitting their sides... everyone except [ITV's match commentator] Brian Moore.' Stokoe even allowed the cameras on to the team coach, something then unprecedented. In the tunnel Sunderland wore their cares as lightly as Leeds were tense and preoccupied. 'When we came out the noise was like being hit in the face by a sledgehammer,' Dave Watson remembered. 'All the neutrals seemed to be backing us. Again, that seemed to get to Leeds.'

This time United could not blame injuries for the nightmare about to unfold. Cherry, deputizing for Cooper, was the only member of the team not to have played at Wembley before. Otherwise Leeds were at full-strength, with Jack Charlton the only player missing from the victorious team of 1972. As in 1970, Eddie Gray was touted as the probable match-winner, particularly as he would be running at Dickie Malone, supposedly Sunderland's 'weak link' at right-back.

Gray, however, who rarely disappointed in high-profile games, would eventually be substituted. With the rain falling steadily, both sides began uncertainly on a slippery pitch, but Sunderland's non-stop running and chasing stopped Leeds from settling into their rhythm.

Watson, later capped sixty-five times for his country, was the unsung hero of the occasion, though it is not his name that is remembered. Yet he was lucky on 10 minutes when a foul on Bremner in the penalty area went unpunished. Had referee Ken Burns taken Stokoe's entreaties on board? Watson, too, had a hand in Sunderland's goal, which came on 31 minutes, taking three United players with him as Billy Hughes curled in a corner from the right, beyond Leeds' defensive cover. Watson's run caused the sort of carnage that Jack Charlton had patented for United. If any team should not have been distracted by it, that team should have been Leeds, who'd been using the trick for almost a decade. Over-preparation and Revie's obsession with Watson's aerial potency in those assiduously devoured dossiers was their undoing, as the defence was left open to a sucker punch by Watson's clever dummy. Midfielder Ian Porterfield cushioned the ball on his thigh before crashing a right volley into the roof of the net.

With an hour to go, and regular chances coming their way at frequent intervals, Leeds should not have been unduly concerned; but something was patently wrong. As the teams emerged for the second half, the red and white striped shirts galloped past those in white, eager to return to the fray. 'United players appear to know their fate' was the caption to a newspaper photograph published the next day, of the Leeds players ambling back on to the field. Of the eight men in shot, only Peter Lorimer is not staring fixedly at the ground.

Leeds did start the second half far better than they had finished the first, but for the umpteenth time their luck was out when it really mattered. Cherry had the ball in the net on 50 minutes but the goal was ruled out, quite rightly, for a foul on Sunderland's goalkeeper Montgomery. The pivotal moment of the game came with a quarter of the match remaining. Trevor Cherry, linking up with the attack, hurled himself at a Paul Reaney cross to power in a diving header. Montgomery parried the ball to Lorimer, who drilled in the ball from close range. 'And Lorimer makes it one each!' bellowed BBC commentator David Coleman. Except that he had not. Montgomery, twisting in mid-air, had somehow managed to push the ball on to the crossbar, from where it bounced back past a prone and despairing Cherry. The Sunderland goalkeeper had pulled off Wembley's most memorable save, but he knew little about it. 'I just threw myself where I thought the shot would go, and it hit my hand,' he recalled. The moment might have been manufactured to fuel the fatalism with which Revie imbued his team. 'I think we knew then that we were never going to score,' said Billy Bremner. 'We didn't stop trying, but I think we all felt that it wasn't going to be our day.' Despite Cherry and Madeley being thrown into the attack and Yorath replacing the ineffective Gray, there was no way back for Leeds. Paul Madeley came closest to equalizing, with an angled shot that was stopped on the line, but it was Sunderland who finished the stronger.

At the final whistle Revie stood rigid in the rain, pain etched into his face. Stokoe, who had flouted Cup Final protocol by wearing a red tracksuit, came skipping and jumping onto the pitch to hug his match-winning goalkeeper. Grace in victory was not in the script. 'I hadn't a lucky suit like Don Revie,' he jibed, 'so I just came as one of the lads.'

In the war of words whipped up by Fleet Street in Cup Final week Revie had been hopelessly outgunned and, although the result might have embarrassed the pundits, it delighted his numerous detractors. Artistic license was freely issued, the *Daily Mail*'s Vincent Mulchrone being among the more fanciful observers. 'In Sunderland,' he wrote, 'there is one job for every forty boys and the thirty-nine stepping straight from school to the dole queue wrote a sign on the wall begging the lads to put Sunderland on the map. The lads obliged.' One Sunderland supporter was so overcome with delight that he hurled an armchair through his front window. When Stokoe's team returned to Sunderland to parade the cup, bed-ridden patients at the local hospital demanded to be wheeled outside so they could salute their heroes. 'Leeds, a paradox of arch-professionalism and high superstition,' wrote another scribe, 'wilted like men crushed by divine intervention.' 'My main memory is the journey after the game to our hotel for our banquet in the evening,' recalled Allan Clarke, United's Wembley hero twelve months before. 'I've never seen so many fans crying after a defeat – it was so obvious they felt we'd let them down, and that hurt more than not winning the cup.'

Commendably, Revie declined the opportunity to vent his spleen at Stokoe after the game: 'The better team won on the day,' he admitted. However, he would later acknowledge that the result was the most shattering experience of his career – and by now he had a raft of them to choose from. In an unaccustomed speech at the post-match banquet he struck that note of plaintive defiance he habitually adopted under siege. 'It's a bit unusual for me to stand up,' he began, 'but I feel our players have done enough in ten years to walk in to your applause, even without the FA Cup. We never tried to cheat, we tried to be honest, and I would be less than honest if I did not ask you to salute the most consistent side that ever lived.'

For some Leeds supporters, however, defeat by Sunderland was another signal that the long-serving backbone of Revie's team had reached its sell-by date. Debate raged on the letters page of the local paper, where several self-consciously heretical correspondents started to lambaste the manager and his team. 'The unpalatable truth is that Leeds had only themselves to blame...' declared one of them, 'but were betrayed by a malady which seems unforgivable. Giles, the midfield mainspring, is no longer the effortless general and is too easily caught in possession... United must hope the much-missed Cooper recaptures his England form and Don Revie must also consider the claims of Jordan and the promising Frank Gray.'

United would soon have the opportunity to prove such gloomy prognostication wrong in the Final of the European Cup Winners' Cup, but there was to be a rather significant hiccup in their preparations. Just three days after declaring that the obituaries being written for his side were premature, Revie sensationally gave them substance. A day before the Final in Salonika, northern Greece, the Leeds manager held a breakfast meeting with the Everton chairman, John Moores. He was heading for Elland Road's exit door.

Bill McGarry, Bobby Robson of Ipswich and Jimmy Armfield, then of Bolton, had all turned the Everton job down. Quite why Revie was Moores' fourth choice is unclear. The episode reflects particularly poorly on Revie, who set such store by meticulous preparation for important games. Once again, the prospect of more money had given him itchy feet. Everton were offering an annual salary of £20,000 – £3,000 more than he was earning at Leeds. At forty-six the Leeds manager was perfectly entitled to seek a better-paid job, but his timing stank. His players admitted talk of his departure unsettled them, as their minds turned to the onerous task of defeating Italian giants AC Milan, and if Revie's strategy was to blackmail the United Board into giving him a rise, it hardly endeared him to the supporters.

Amid feverish rumours of his imminent departure, the affair descended into farce. On 14 May, as his team prepared to board their plane for Greece, Revie drove to Moores' Merseyside home to discuss terms. By the time he'd reached the outskirts of Liverpool the United manager was completely lost. He pulled over at a set of traffic lights and asked for directions to Freshfields, the suburb in which Moores lived. 'There was no doubt the driver was Revie,' said the Everton supporter who ended up giving him directions. 'He was driving a yellow Mercedes [Revie's new club car] and, unless he had a twin, it simply had to be him.' The rumour was given further credibility when Revie joined his players at Manchester Airport for the flight to Greece – normally he would have joined them at Elland Road for the coach trip there. Furthermore, the previous Saturday, Revie had been in the BBC team of commentators for England's game with Northern Ireland at Goodison – another opportunity for Everton's directors to sound him out.

Revie himself did nothing to quash the speculation, refusing to confirm or deny the rumours. The *Yorkshire Evening Post* drew its own conclusion. 'Unless he has a change of mind, or United persuade him to stay,' it mused, 'Revie seems likely to sever his connection with the club that gave him his chance of management 12 years ago, and which he in turn steered from the depths of the Second Division to a place of prominence in Europe.'

He had indeed turned Elland Road from a scrapyard into a shrine, transformed a team that, back in the late 1950s, even the club's own supporters had disdainfully nicknamed 'the clowns'. Yet it is surprising that Revie's disloyalty did not attract more criticism. In the valedictory pieces that were already being penned on his reign at Leeds, the tone is one of pathetic gratitude. Despite nearly a decade at the summit of British football, the city of Leeds still harboured the suspicion that the Revie era would prove a glorious aberration.

Revie brushed aside talk that AC Milan, a point ahead of Juventus and Lazio at the top of the Italian league, would be more concerned with winning the national championship than the Cup Winner's Cup: 'Milan will want to win this cup first and win the title afterwards.' For Leeds, Mick Bates, Joe Jordan, Frank Gray and Paul Madeley stood in for Bremner, Clarke, Giles and Eddie Gray. To add to Revie's problems, Giles failed a fitness test on a hamstring strain.

A minor source of encouragement was the raucous support of a 45,000-strong crowd at the new Kaftatzoglio Stadium. Jack Mansell, a former Rotherham United manager then in charge of one of Salonika's three Greek First Division sides, told the press that the locals were 'Leeds United daft. There was tremendous disappointment here when they lost the FA Cup Final,' he added, rather improbably. 'All my players are Leeds fans and three of my players actually cried.' A thunderous deluge greeted the teams as they took the field. It provided a fitting backcloth to a tempestuous match, remembered now mainly for the scandalous performance of referee Christos Michas. The Greek's name was to be forever added to the Elland Road roll-call of infamy, to sit alongside those of Burns, Hardaker, Tinkler and Stokoe.

Milan gained the benefit of Michas' first dubious decision after just four minutes, when Paul Madeley was mysteriously penalized for a foul on Milan striker Bigon, despite it being obvious that Madeley had won the ball cleanly, barely touching his opponent. Chiarugi took full advantage of Michas' generosity. He rifled the free-kick into the net off the base of a post, aided by a slight deflection from a United defender. A chorus of booing greeted his celebrations. United might have buckled, but as nine Italians retreated to their own penalty area, they fought back.

It was soon clear, however, that Leeds had more to contend with than their illustrious opponents. After both Lorimer and Hunter had gone close, Jones was scythed down in the box as he followed in a Jordan shot. Michas waved play on. Early in the second half United were denied a second clear penalty when Romeo Benetti blatantly handled a Paul Reaney shot from the right; to trump it all, Michas ignored a third spot-kick appeal when Lorimer was hacked down as he surged in from the right wing. United could not contain their frustration. Minutes from time, Hunter was mangled from behind by Rivera and, in the mêlée that followed, was sent off along with Sogliano of Milan.

It was a bitterly deflating end to another season of 'if onlys'. Milan's lap of honour was virtually ignored by the Greeks, who considered Revie's team the real winners. They had good reason. Immediately after the game, UEFA and his own federation suspended Michas, yet United were not offered the replay they deserved and no inquiry followed.

The Italian game has ever been tainted by the stench of corruption, and that May evening in Salonika was certainly not the first or last time that doubt has been cast on a Serie A club's success. In that very same year, 1973, an honest Portuguese referee, Francisco Marques Lobo, thwarted an attempt to bribe him to bend Derby County's European Cup semi-final in favour of Juventus. It inspired Brian Glanville and Keith Botsford's forensic examination of Italian clubs' corruption of European referees, *The Golden Fix*. For Don Revie, United's failure to win anything and the clear signs that his team's star was on the wane seem to have resolved his dilemma over his future. It was the perfect opportunity to call time on the great Leeds experiment and to get the hell out while he still could.

THIRTEEN

SECOND COMING

I n May 1973 Don Revie jetted off to Greece for a family holiday, his future undecided while, back in Leeds, the self-flagellation continued. United just didn't deserve him. The club's average league attendance in a season which had seen Leeds finish third and contest two Cup Finals, was under 36,000. Goodison Park had attracted 35,000 a game, despite the fact that Everton had finished seventeenth and been knocked out of the FA Cup in the fourth round. Furthermore, in 1969 when Leeds had won the title, the average gate at Elland Road was 37,000. The following year, when Everton triumphed, the champions had pulled in 49,000. The raw statistics were depressing enough, but an atypically trenchant comment piece in the *Yorkshire Evening Post* got to the real heart of the matter: 'The city has carped and cribbed, grumbled about admission charges and generally shown itself quick to criticise and slow to praise. Perhaps thoughts like this are passing through Don Revie's mind as he basks in sunny Greece. If so, who can blame him?'

The supporters' gloom was heightened by reports that pools tycoon John Moores had raised the ante. Everton were now said to be offering a £50,000 signing-on fee and an eight-year contract – an astonishing £250,000 before tax. How could anyone – and especially Revie, with his own family to support as well as the elderly relatives he had insisted on moving in with them – possibly turn down that kind of money? Football's best-known stars were less extravagantly remunerated in 1973, but a 'present' of £50,000 needs to be set in context. That very same week the annual conference of the National

Union of Mineworkers was calling for members working at the coal-face to be paid £2,000 a year.

The outlook appeared bleak for Leeds. Yet two days later at 9 a.m. club secretary Keith Archer received a phone call. It was Don Revie calling from his hotel room, and he informed the bemused Archer that he wanted to stay. Revie's reasons remained unclear: 'I have no further comment to make,' he told the press, 'and my only wish is that I be allowed to spend the remainder of my holiday in peace.' One theory suggested that Everton had been pulled up by the Government's pay and prices board for offering their quarry a £25,000 salary and a tax-free 'golden hello' of £50,000. In the early 1970s, a time of acute industrial strife, it was not so simple for an employer to pay an employee his perceived market value. A paragraph in the relevant legislation stated that recruits to existing jobs should not be paid more than the people they replaced.

Whatever the truth of the matter, the Leeds players were under-standably delighted. '[Don] has built up a family spirit at Elland and no doubt that will continue as before,' said Billy Bremner. It was now confidently assumed that Revie would finish his managerial career at Leeds, in around 1980. The forty-six-year-old had repeatedly stated that he did not want to continue in management beyond the age of fifty-five. The sighs of relief, however, were premature; the saga was not finished. A week later Revie casually revealed that he had been approached with lucrative offers to take up coaching and managerial jobs in Greece, and announced that in light of these new develop-ments he would be discussing his future with the Leeds board on his return from holiday.

Only a month before, Don Revie had been driving aimlessly around Liverpool trying to find John Moores. Now he was cruising the Aegean on a yacht owned by the president of Olympiakos, Nicos Goulandras. When he got ashore, the president of the Greek Football Association was waiting for him, dangling a bait of £20,000 a year tax-free, plus bonuses, as an inducement to take over the Greek national side. As if that were not enough to conquer the charms of West

Yorkshire, Panathinaikos were ready to top the offer, willing to go as high as £28,000 p.a., also tax-free. Leeds' new chairman, Manny Cussins, was as weary of the affair as the supporters. 'There's a Board meeting on Tuesday. Beyond that you know as much as I do,' he said. That meeting must have been an expensive one, for Revie ended up staying, but the Greek interlude had planted an idea in his mind. A few years later, when Revie's reign as England manager came to its ignominious end, the prospect of warmer climes and a huge tax-exempt salary would prove too good to turn down.

Most newspapers wrote off Leeds' title chances for 1973, citing the teams' failure to beat Sunderland as evidence of their physical decline. Yet, with the exception of Bremner and Giles, most of the key players were still under thirty. Moreover, some of the changes forced on Revie gave his team a little more efficiency and a lot more zap. Sprake, now in the shadow of the less extravagantly gifted but far more reliable Harvey, left for Birmingham, affronted at failing to be awarded a testimonial. Jack Charlton had also gone, though his farewell had been marked by a memorable goodbye clash against Leeds' European Cup nemesis, Celtic.

Although Revie had offered Charlton a further two-year contract that would have extended his career until the age of forty, Leeds' longest-serving player left the club in the summer of 1973 to become manager of Middlesborough. He had arrived for his job interview there armed with a list of demands provided by Revie – a kind of crib-sheet on how to run a club – and, typically unorthodox, turned the tables to grill his bemused interviewers. Charlton read out his terms and gave the panel ten minutes to 'take them or leave them' before they could even ask him any questions – but he was offered the position all the same. He made a great start in his new profession, winning promotion at his first attempt, and subsequently started Sheffield Wednesday's revival after more than a decade's decline before his well-chronicled success with the Republic of Ireland national side. The only mystery of Charlton's managerial career is why he was never offered the chance to save Leeds during the club's long decline when he had a far better track record than anyone else. It seems that the Leeds Board were apprehensive about just how much freedom he would have demanded. List or no list, it's doubtful that they would have willingly surrendered total control a second time.

Gordon McQueen was primed to step into Charlton's shoes; his best mate, Joe Jordan was also fast maturing and would provide top-class cover in attack. Otherwise it was a case of 'as you were' – there were to be no forays into the transfer market, despite funds being available. Revie gave a testy reply when quizzed once again about his conservatism. 'I am well aware there's been a lot of talk about the team breaking up,' he said. 'But what people have forgotten is that we have introduced a number of younger players in the last few years – Jordan, McQueen, Frank Gray, Cherry, Bates and Gary Liddell. These are young players who will only get better as time goes on.' Hindsight shows that Revie was broadly correct, but even Leeds fans will raise a quizzical eyebrow at the name of Gary 'who he?' Liddell. Teenage full-back Peter Hampton, an England youth player, would also break through into the first-team squad – but this youngster was no Terry Cooper.

Revie's puzzling failure to replenish his squad is partly explained by the dim view he took of the raw talent brought to his attention. 'The standard of youngsters coming into English soccer has dropped alarmingly in recent years,' he lamented. 'One of the reasons [is] the type of coaching lads get at schoolboy level. I appreciate that many teachers give up a lot of their spare time to the game without extra payment. But it would help enormously if ALL concentrated a bit more on developing the basic skills of their lads, instead of making them conform to 4–4–2 or 4–3–3 systems.' He added: 'It's staggering the number of hours we at Leeds have to spend teaching junior play-ers the fundamentals of the game... kicking, dribbling and passing, etc. Not so long ago, it was rare to come across any lad who needed intensive coaching in these skills.' Revie's observation that English players were falling behind their continental counterparts in techni-cal ability would be borne out in future years. He blamed the

Football Association for banning players from being paid for their coaching services. 'If Billy Bremner went into a school in Leeds and asked boys to practise ball control, I'm sure they would do it,' he observed. Here he was being a bit too mercenary on his players' behalf. The FA expected players to hone their coaching prowess in the schools for free, to show their commitment as both Revie and Jack Charlton had done. Called 'putting something back', it was something very few professionals objected to.

Revie's options were, of course, already circumscribed by his insistence that newcomers conform to the club's notoriously insular and defiantly unsophisticated culture. In the freewheeling 1970s such players were becoming harder to find. Revie's explanation to the gifted Scot 'Slim' Jim Baxter on why he would not be signing him is a good example. 'I'm told you drink everything that is brewed and distilled up here, that there aren't enough girls for you to chase, and that you're not averse to the odd brawl.' An unfazed Baxter sighed, before replying, 'You're remarkably well-informed.'

Having decided to stay at Leeds, Revie was determined to atone for the embarrassment of the previous season. He could now admit the extent of his disappointment at losing to Sunderland. 'It only really hit me at the post-match banquet,' he said. 'As our guests were leaving, I slumped into my chair and cried like a child.' The scale of Revie's ambition in what was to be his final season only became clear at the team talk preceding the opening league match. In *Sniffer*, his latest autobiography, Allan Clarke recalls the gauntlet thrown down by Revie before his bemused team: 'The gaffer said, "Right lads, we've been the best team for the last decade. I know we haven't won as much as we should have, but that's in the past. Now I've had a thought in the close season – can we go through the whole campaign unbeaten?" We all looked at each other in silence and then, after a while we said…. "Yes it's possible." It was certainly a different pep talk to most seasons. Of course you start off aiming to win all your games, but to actually set it as a target – this was different.'

As ever, Revie not only wanted to win, he also wanted to be lauded for winning. In early 1972 the nation had been forced to acknowledge his players' brilliance as they adopted a more expansive brand of football, but the season just past had seen a deterioration in discipline. Norman Hunter and Trevor Cherry were the worst offenders, each collecting eight bookings by March. After two years' grace from the press, 'Dirty Leeds' had been reborn in style. At the season's end the Football Association slapped a suspended £3,000 fine on Leeds, again warning the club to put its house in order. Revie responded with a charm offensive, calling a press conference at which he promised an improvement in the players' behaviour. The club had also appointed its own spin-doctor to woo its detractors, a man in his twenties called Peter Fay. For home games the practice of kicking cheap plastic footballs into the crowd would continue.

Some of Revie's critics would never be convinced. A 1974 issue of the groundbreakingly tongue-in-cheek *Foul* magazine praised Leeds for their 'high-level chess' and 'intellectual sophistication'. If Revie had stopped reading there, he would have been elated, but author Peter Ball had more to say. 'Away from home, Leeds display as much sense of adventure as the average Women's Institute. They can still clog with the best. Norman "Bites yer Legs" Hunter is the main culprit, [but] Bremner and Giles both contribute mightily to the cause on occasions.' The article was titled 'Leeds, the Ultimate Defence'. Once again, Revie had been damned by faint praise.

To say that Leeds still lacked adventure is a view not borne out by the facts. In each of the previous three seasons Leeds had been among the two highest scoring sides in the First Division, and in one of those seasons were top. In 1972/73 only champions Liverpool, who finished with 72, bettered their total of 71 league goals. The two other clubs involved in the title shake-up, Arsenal and Ipswich Town, had finished up in the mid-50s. The new season would see Revie loosen the shackles still further. Training sessions now emphasized shooting practice; his players were instructed to let fly within sight of goal. His captain, who had always had an eye for goal, would play further upfield, driving into the penalty area to support the strikers. The tactic worked – Billy Bremner would score four in the first four games.

It must almost have seemed as if Revie, the arch-pragmatist, had undergone some sort of Damascene conversion. But the man's craving for success would never be subordinated to the desire to entertain and impress. What had happened was that just days after their humbling by Sunderland, Leeds had signed off the previous season with a 6–1 drubbing of Arsenal at Elland Road. Though only 25,000 turned up to see it, it was one of the most significant results of Revie's reign. 'It is impossible to minimize the effect which that result had on the Leeds players,' he commented. 'I look upon it as one of the most important wins this club has achieved since I became manager.' If a policy of all-out attack could wreak such havoc, he reasoned, perhaps he should relax a bit more and trust his players to deliver. This new offensive mindset was trialled in a close season practice match behind closed doors. Bradford Park Avenue were swept aside 5–0, with Mick Jones grabbing a hat-trick. The die was cast.

In the early weeks of the season Leeds would play some of the most fluid, precise and penetrative football the First Division had ever seen. Nineteen goals were scored in seven successive victories, leaving the press purring. John Arlott, more famous as the lyrical chronicler of a different sport, cricket, joined in the plaudits. In the wake of Leeds' seventh win, a 2–1 defeat of Southampton, he wrote in the *Guardian*: 'Wearing the white strip of a blameless life, Leeds moved in a ceaseless flow, back in packed in defence, competing for the midfield, sweeping forward with backs overlapping. Yet it was all so controlled, almost amiable... so free from the aura of violence they used to generate.'

The run began with a 3–1 win over Everton, with Leeds virtually at full strength. Eddie Gray had returned to the team after missing most of the previous season. However, it was two early victories in North London that really caught the eye. The capital, where his team were most reviled, had not been a happy hunting ground for Revie in recent years. His team had not won there in the league for two and a half years – they had not beaten Arsenal at Highbury since 1969. The game against Arsenal on 28 August was also expected to test Revie's commitment to good conduct. The opening game had passed by without a hint of a booking or stern lecture for either side, but clashes with the Gunners were always fraught affairs. In the corresponding fixture the previous season the referee assigned to the fixture, the Welsh martinet Clive Thomas, had booked six players – five of them from Leeds.

Arsenal came into the match brimful of confidence following a 3–0 drubbing of Manchester United on the opening day, and went in front after just 90 seconds. For half an hour, it seemed that Revie's hopes of a season without defeat were to be dashed at a humiliatingly early stage. Arsenal besieged the Leeds penalty area and a second goal seemed inevitable. In the second half, however, the midfield duo of Giles and Bremner, together with a rejuvenated Eddie Gray, took a stranglehold on the midfield. Arsenal, fluid, swift and sure of themselves in the first period, were suddenly run ragged. On 50 minutes Peter Lorimer unleashed a 30-yard thunderbolt, which left Bob Wilson clutching at the air as it ripped into the net. The balance of power had shifted. Six minutes later a Paul Madeley strike put United in front after a sweeping move begun by Clarke in his own half, which then involved Giles and Gray. For the rest of the match Leeds assumed a dominance of Arsenal they had rarely, if ever, enjoyed at Highbury.

The thin-skinned Revie was overjoyed, not only with the victory, but also with the muted appreciation of the home fans. 'Hearing the London supporters applaud us for our second-half football was like music in my ears,' he exulted. 'I have been saying for years we have players in our side with world-class footballing skills. People have refused to believe me.' At Tottenham four days later, ripples of spontaneous applause could again be heard as the home crowd marvelled at Leeds' speed of thought and movement. Billy Bremner scored twice in the first 14 minutes, Allan Clarke adding a third before the half-hour. As a contest, the match was over soon after it had begun.

For the second time in five days Revie's team had achieved a notable feat: winning rare praise from two sets of hitherto hostile supporters while displaying exemplary behaviour on the field. The manager revelled in his fleeting popularity. Even the referee, Roger Kirkpatrick, had buttonholed him in a White Hart Lane corridor to pass on his compliments. 'He told me it had been a pleasure to be on the same field as Leeds United,' Revie boasted. 'Mr Kirkpatrick also said that he had never had any trouble with us but wanted to point out that he thought my players had been the model of good behaviour and were a credit to the game.' Hamming it up, Revie claimed to be so impressed that he asked Kirkpatrick to repeat his little homily to the players. The official obliged, adding, 'I had to say something. If this is what Leeds intend to do in every game, on behalf of my fellow referees I had to say thank you in advance. I wish all matches were played in the same spirit.'

In the wake of their seventh straight win United's dressing room was honoured by a visit from Vernon Stokes, chairman of the FA Disciplinary Commission. The man who had hung the £3,000 fine around Leeds' neck also wanted to add his compliments. According to Revie, Stokes told the players they were setting a 'wonderful example for everyone connected with English football'. For the newly PR-savvy Leeds manager, that one comment was as important as the seven wins. Or so he claimed: 'By not disputing referees' decisions, or becoming involved in feuds with opposing players, our lads have been able to devote 100% attention to their football.'

Revie was relishing his new incarnation as the scourge of negativity. In his programme notes for the game against Wolves on 5 September, he railed at managers who were constantly traducing the game's image. 'Stop this constant bickering and sniping,' he implored. 'It serves no constructive purpose whatsoever... I am slowly sinking in a surfeit of bad publicity. All I seem to read in the back pages is how bad the game is.' If Revie detected any irony in such sentiments, he didn't let it show. He did, however, issue a rather defensive explanation of why the aesthetic appeal of the 1974 Leeds team contrasted so sharply with the 1964 vintage, as ever calling his favourite witness in his defence: 'Bill Shankly once made an apt summing up of what Division Two football is all about when he said: "You can't play your way out.

You've got to claw your way out." It hurts me to admit now, but Leeds certainly clawed their way out of Division Two.

'Our championship success that season was due to a rather defensive, physical style which made us probably the hardest team to beat in the League... Once we got a goal I would light a cigar, sit back on the trainers' bench and enjoy the rest of the game, secure in the knowledge that it would need a minor miracle for the other side to equalise. Maybe we did not exactly endear ourselves to the soccer purists in those days, but we had to be realistic. Had we attempted to produce the uninhibited, constructive football which is a hallmark of today's Leeds team, we would probably still be languishing in Division Two.'

A reasonable hypothesis, one supposes, but what Revie omitted to explain is why he had persisted with that reductive approach for so long after promotion had been won. Had it been jettisoned earlier, even his own players maintained, his side might have won more. Now, however, Revie was displaying the missionary zeal of the true convert. 'It's essential that more [league managers] put the emphasis on open, attacking football,' he insisted, 'creating a situation whereby players are given the chance to express themselves and therefore develop their basic skills.'

By mid-September 1974 the Sunderland manager Bob Stokoe was among those proclaiming – perhaps mischievously – that the title race was already over. Billy Bremner dismissed the suggestion as 'silly talk' and, indeed, a week later United would drop their first point. A crowd of 47,000 packed in to Elland Road to see Tommy Docherty's Manchester United, the last side to beat Leeds in a home league match, scuffle their way to a goal-less draw. The Manager of the Month award for August tempered Revie's disappointment, all the more so since it was presented to him before the game by Eric Morecambe, then a director of Luton Town.

Ipswich Town ejected a weakened Leeds team from the League Cup a week later. This was of negligible interest to Revie, preoccupied as he was with the idea of remaining unbeaten in the league, an achievement that he calculated would secure his place in the pantheon of great post-war managers. It was beginning to seem possible, though an injury to Eddie Gray in the Manchester United game did not aid his cause. The winger would play just once more that season. Injuries, the bane of his last three seasons, threatened to ruin a fourth when United suffered a further blow before the home match against Liverpool with the loss of Johnny Giles to a long-term calf problem. Fortunately, Mick Bates proved a capable deputy, and a Mick Jones header secured a narrow victory. Giles, too, would be absent for most of the season.

On 15 December a 2–1 win at Chelsea saw Leeds overhaul Liverpool's record of nineteen games unbeaten from the start of the season, but their play was becoming less fluent, victories no longer seemed effortless, and they were being punctuated with draws. One particularly lacklustre display provoked the manager's wrath: 'The boss read the riot act,' recalled Peter Lorimer, '...tore into us. The lads were a bit shocked he came on so strong.'

One source of satisfaction for Revie was the dramatic improvement in attendances at Elland Road. Not even the Leeds public could cavil at the entertainment on offer that particular year. In the early months of the season the average gate topped 40,000, something Revie thought he would never see. Away from home his team were the top attraction, notwithstanding George Best's short-lived return to Manchester United. For once Leeds were bucking the trend – the gradual decline in football attendances, which would reach its peak in the 1980s, was already well underway. By the end of November fourteen of the twenty-two First Division clubs were reporting a decline on the previous season. Chelsea and Everton had suffered falls of 8000 and 7000 respectively.

High gates alone did not generate big profits to invest in new players. Then – as now – the Leeds manager stressed that a lengthy run in Europe was essential to generate much-needed funds. The Leeds public's appetite for the UEFA Cup was less keen, a partial reflection perhaps of Revie's waning interest in a competition the club had already won twice. After a crushing aggregate win over the Norwegian amateurs of Stromsgodset Drammen, some 27,000 turned up for the second-round tie with Hibernian. Both legs ended in stalemate, with United eventually prevailing in a penalty shoot-out in Edinburgh. The home leg of the third round, against the Portuguese side Vitoria Setubal, attracted only 14,000. Leeds won by a single goal while Revie watched from the stand – he had been banished from the dugout by UEFA after remaining on the pitch while the penalties were being taken at Easter Road. 'I think we'll manage to get through, though we'll miss the look of anxiety which the boss always has on his face when sitting in the trainers' dugout,' said Billy Bremner. 'He shows so much emotion during a game, I think he must die a thousand deaths every match.' Revie's team selection for the away leg, however, suggested he was saving his players' energy for more significant battles ahead. Bremner, Hunter and Jones were all missing for the game in Portugal, along with the injured Giles and Eddie Gray. To no one's great surprise, United went down 3–1.

Just after Christmas, Leeds' unbeaten league run came within seconds of being ended at St Andrews, Birmingham. A Joe Jordan goal rescued a point three minutes from time. Over the next few weeks the murmurings that Revie's men had run out of steam would rise to a crescendo. The New Year would begin with a glut of draws, though an impressive 3–1 home win over Arsenal steadied fraying nerves. The sparseness of the crowd – just 26,000 – was partly explained by the energy crisis then gripping the nation: a ban on floodlighting dictated that the match had to be played on a Tuesday afternoon. Before the game, Revie had interrogated his players on the reasons for their declining form, which had seen them draw four of the previous five league games. Billy Bremner's account of the meeting suggested the manager had reverted to type – the team was not performing 'professionally' enough. 'At our chat we agreed we were a little slack at throw-ins and free-kicks and we were not challenging strongly enough when the opposition were in possession.'

Revie's local newspaper column betrayed his growing anxiety. Its theme was the nervous tension to which players – and managers – were increasingly subject to in a game where money was talking ever more loudly. Liverpool's Steve Heighway, apparently, had been troubled by excessive blinking in matches, and complained of 'huge emotional ups and downs'. Revie empathized with the stricken winger. Many Leeds players took sleeping pills the night before a match, he revealed, while the highly-strung Bremner would disappear to his hotel bedroom on away days and not be sighted until the following morning. 'Fans and critics annoy me sometimes,' he declared, 'because they just don't appreciate how easy it can be to make mistakes when there's so much at stake financially and there's an audience of thousands, occasionally millions.'

A comfortable 2–0 win at Old Trafford against a Manchester United team battling relegation took Leeds' unbeaten run to twenty-nine matches. Revie's men were nine points clear of a Liverpool side that had finally hit form, though Bill Shankly's men had a game in hand. The gulf was huge but bridgeable. Leeds still had to play seven other top ten sides, among them Liverpool at Anfield. Once again Revie had transmitted his doubts to his players, and once again his neurosis would inhibit his team. The first hint of imminent implosion came at Elland Road on 19 February in a fifth-round FA Cup replay against Second Division Bristol City. In front of an incredulous Bill Shankly, Leeds lost by the only goal, their first home defeat of the season.

After an absence of almost two years, Terry Cooper finally returned to duty the following Saturday on the substitute's bench for the league game at Stoke. For a while it appeared that normal service had been resumed, despite the absence of Jones, McQueen and Reaney. Goals from Bremner and Clarke within the first 20 minutes saw Leeds establish a two-goal lead. However, the loss of Giles before the restart with a hamstring strain proved a bridge too far for Revie. Too many players were injured or carrying injuries, and too many more were playing out of position. Suddenly Leeds looked disjointed. Stoke stormed back into the match, drawing level before half-time.

The onslaught continued after the break, and as Leeds went 3–2 down in the 68th minute, tempers began to fray. Clarke and Cooper were booked for disputing a goal kick decision with referee John Homewood, Revie's early-season 'good behaviour' injunction conveniently forgotten.

Revie had burdened his thin squad with a task that no top division side has ever achieved and his reaction to defeat was hardly constructive. All his players remember that his response was his usual threat to 'get the chequebook out' if they didn't come back properly from this defeat. It was an astounding ploy, not least because they'd only lost one game. In any case, he'd used it so often it had clearly lost its impact. The players didn't respond, or at least not as their manager would have wished. Draws against Leicester City and Newcastle United followed, before a scrabbled 1–0 victory over Manchester City.

The 16 March clash with Liverpool was billed as a potential title decider, and the gates were locked at Anfield 75 minutes before kick-off. Enigmatic as ever, Revie said he had named a squad of thirteen for the game because he was superstitious. It proved an unlucky decision. A goal from an unblinking Steve Heighway eight minutes from time gave Liverpool the points. It was the eighth time that season that a goal in the last 10 minutes had clinched a draw or a point for Liverpool, a habit they would sustain for years to come. 'We planned to attack, but Liverpool's pressure was so great we just could not get going,' said Bremner. 'In short we were cuffed and we deserved to be.'

Leeds' lead at the top was now cut to six points, while Shankly's men also had two games in hand. The title was still in United's hands, but its destination was no longer a foregone conclusion. Bremner set a target of 12 points from the last 14, but it was to prove too optimistic. A week later Leeds plunged to a 4–1 defeat at home to Burnley, who were then seventh in the table. Burnley's manager Jimmy Adamson had once claimed he would make them the team of the 1970s. A few years later he would fail to make Leeds the team of the 1980s. 'Leeds were haunted by doubt, undermined by misunderstandings... their reputation was on the verge of destruction,' wrote Brian

James in the *Sunday Times*. The shock result followed an astonishing snub by the Burnley directors and their autocratic chairman, Bob Lord, in response to Manny Cussins' warning that if Lord had appeared in the boardroom or director's box at Elland Road, he would walk out. Lord's offence had been his well-publicized anti-Semitic remark the previous year during the negotiation of a TV rights deal, that 'We have to stand up against a move to get soccer on the cheap by the Jews who run television.' The Burnley Board had countered by boycotting the game en masse.

In an attempt to arrest the decline, Revie dropped Peter Lorimer for the next game at West Ham and restored a partially fit Giles to the midfield. The slump continued. United were beaten 3–1 after taking the lead. At 1–1 Clarke had seen a perfectly good goal disallowed for offside, and his bad day was compounded when he was booked for haranguing the referee. For the first time Liverpool were now in a position to overhaul Leeds, but Revie remained optimistic. 'I had the feeling that we turned the corner at Upton Park. We gave one of our best performances of the season, particularly in the first half, and we had only ourselves to blame for the goals we conceded.' It was a shrewd observation, but Revie was taking no chances. Paul Madeley and Norman Hunter were withdrawn from an England international against Portugal, much to the chagrin of Alf Ramsey. The FA claimed they had not been notified in time that the players were injured. Suspiciously, both men returned for the visit of Derby.

The Rams had a grim record at Elland Road, but Dave Mackay, who had replaced Brian Clough as manager, was confident. 'Derby are playing better than at any time since 1972,' he said. 'Leeds have something of an inferiority complex because of missing out on so many trophies in the final weeks of the season, and I think we can win.' The match saw a welcome return to form for Peter Lorimer and put Leeds firmly back on the title trail. It was Lorimer who lobbed home the first goal in a 2–0 victory, his first from open play since 8 September. There was to be no return to the imperious form of the early weeks of the season, however. Jittery draws followed away to Coventry and at home to Sheffield United in a run of three matches in four days. As usual, Leeds had not been spared the traditional Easter fixture pile-up, and United travelled to Bramall Lane just twenty-four hours later for the return game. At half-time the match was goal-less and Liverpool had already scored four against Manchester City. Disaster beckoned.

Ironically, it was to be the recently pilloried Lorimer who would prove the hero, together with a limping but always game Mick Jones. Lorimer scored twice in the second half to give Leeds a crucial victory. Lorimer scored again in a 3–2 win over Ipswich the following Saturday as the Liverpool derby at Anfield ended 0–0. Clarke, Cherry and Bremner were all booked for time-wasting, though this particular manifestation of gamesmanship could surely be excused. Liverpool could only win it now were they to win each of their remaining three games against Arsenal, West Ham and Tottenham. Bill Shankly, who doggedly refused to concede the crown, also needed Leeds to lose at Queens Park Rangers.

To their immense relief United were spared the prospect of another last-gasp calamity. A Ray Kennedy goal gave Arsenal victory at Anfield and took the championship to Leeds for the second time. 'The players were secretly praying that Arsenal would do it,' said Lorimer. 'The tension at QPR on the Saturday would have been unbearable.' As he sifted through the greeting telegrams on his desk the next day, Revie ventured the opinion that Leeds' second title win was a greater achievement than the first. In 1968/69 the side had kept to a settled formation, but this year had had to do without as many as five inter-nationals at a time. 'I feel as though someone has come along and lifted six tons of coal off my back,' the manager added. 'I feel as though I am walking on air.'

It had been a great week for Revie, said a jubilant Les Cocker – 'the championship, *This is Your Life* and he even beat Val Doonican at golf'. Shankly, his 'double' hopes dashed, was dignified in defeat. 'My congratulations. I know Leeds care about everyone from the cleaning ladies right through, and that's how it should be.' One of those laundry women to whom the Liverpool manager was referring was Kathleen Smith: 'We must wash about 200 shirts a week,' she exulted, 'but this has made it all worthwhile.'

FOURTEEN

SUSPICIOUS MINDS

Mrs Smith never had to wash Don Revie's training kit again.

Most summers for the past five years he had flirted with the idea of leaving, but had always allowed himself to be persuaded to stay. As early as 1971, he'd been preparing for a life away from the game, negotiating a ten-year consultancy deal with the United board to commence on New Year's Day 1980 as part of an inducement not to walk out when suitors came calling. In 1974, he knew that in six years time, he could happily retire to a life of golf and punditry and still pick up £10,000 a year for turning up to a few board meetings. To get to that point, however, he was going to have to leave or else start the dismantling process forthwith. It became increasingly obvious which proposition he preferred.

For most of May and June 1974, while Bremner, Harvey, Jordan and Lorimer were starring for Scotland at the World Cup in West Germany, press speculation in England was still focused on the identity of Sir Alf Ramsey's successor as England manager. Initially, at least, Revie's name was not prominent in the predictions, which ludicrously favoured such luminaries as Leicester's Jimmy Bloomfield, Coventry's Gordon Milne and QPR's Gordon Jago. In public Revie continued to express no interest, vowing that he had waited five long years for another crack at the European Cup and professing his distaste at how the FA had ditched Ramsey. But in private he was busy responding to feelers put out by Ted Croker, the secretary of the FA.

The go-between was the *Sunday People's* Tom Holley, United's former centre-half who had been a stalwart of the team on either side of the war and had covered the Elland Road beat throughout Revie's tenure.

He was summoned by Revie and told to approach Dick Wragg, the chairman of the FA's international committee, to stress that the Leeds manager wanted the England job offered by Croker despite his public hints that his loyalty to his employers was too robust to break. It was the start of much clandestine to-ing and fro-ing, so reminiscent of his dalliances with Birmingham City, Sheffield United, Everton and Panathinaikos, but this time Revie did not pull back from the brink and, after four previous aborted threats to leave, finally tendered his resignation at the beginning of July. The prospect of abandoning his professional family and enduring long, lonely spells in White's Hotel, Lancaster Gate, away from Elsie and his children, who would stay in Leeds, did not dissuade him.

At first the Leeds board attempted to wangle a payment of almost £500,000 from the FA in compensation for the poaching of their manager, but in the end, after Revie strenuously but inaccurately insisted that he had made the first move and much press disquiet over their mercenary posturing, they reluctantly let him go for only a token contribution. 'This must be any manager's dream,' Revie said, beaming blissfully alongside Croker at the press conference. He then came over like a Teesside Don Corleone with the jowls to match: 'I also have a feeling of sadness. I have tried to build the club into a family and there must be sadness when anyone leaves a family. [With England I will] try to develop the same family spirit that we have had at Leeds.'

Before clearing his desk, however, he still had one outstanding duty to perform – to fix the succession. Unlike Liverpool, where Bill Shankly, who resigned twelve days after Revie left Leeds, was replaced by his trusted lieutenant Bob Paisley, there was never any possibility that one of Revie's backroom boys would inherit his office. They all had their qualities, Syd Owen and Les Cocker in particular, but none had the leadership skills to take full control of a squad that took their status as Revie's subordinates for granted. In any case, Revie had already earmarked Cocker as his England assistant.

Instead Revie recalled the manner of his own appointment and looked to the dressing room to fill the vacancy. The outstanding candidate there was John Giles, whose wit, intelligence and fibre were respected by all his peers. He was also the only one with any experience of management, having been in charge of the Republic of Ireland for the past year as player-coach. He was persuaded by Revie to let the board know that he would be willing to take over and drove to Elland Road to meet them. It went so well that, according to Peter Lorimer, afterwards the chairman, Manny Cussins, phoned Giles with the news they had accepted Revie's advice and that he would be given the job the next day.

By no coincidence, Revie was at Elland Road the following morning along with the players and, having formally said his goodbyes, asked the club secretary, Keith Archer, to fetch Cussins to announce Giles's promotion. But Archer was sent back with the message that a development had occurred: the press conference was cancelled and a coronation would not be immediately forthcoming. The delay, it transpires, was caused by Billy Bremner protesting that his credentials for Revie's job should also be put to the board.

Although the captain had his supporters in the dressing room, most notably his best friend and room-mate Allan Clarke, the majority of the squad felt that Giles, with his remorselessly logical outlook, possessed a steel and clout the instinctive and passionate Bremner lacked. 'To me,' says Eddie Gray, 'the characteristic that made John the more influential of the two as a player – his calculating, dispassionate streak – set him apart from Billy even more as a potential Leeds manager.' Despite the fact that Giles was the best man for the job, a man who knew the club inside-out and had the rigour and savvy to make a success of it, Cussins and his directors took fright at the prospect of alienating Bremner and potentially losing one half of the team's fulcrum. They asked for more time to consider their predicament and during this hiatus Giles withdrew, saying he would not be the cause of a split and would stay in the ranks.

Two months later, when the club was still looking for a new manager, the *Guardian* asked United director Bob Roberts if there was any truth to the rumours that he had argued with Revie before his resignation and had consequently wanted to put him in his place. Indeed there had been an incident at White Hart Lane the previous season when two directors had been left behind in London on Revie's orders after failing to meet his 5.30pm departure time for the coach. Roberts, however, denied allegations of animosity towards the former manager. But the players' testimonies, published during the last decade, reveal that Bremner learned of Giles's impending appointment after a leak from a boardroom mole. Whether by accident or design, Revie's last bequest to the club had been sabotaged from within.

The board responded to Giles's tactful retreat by claiming they had always been looking for a man with 'European experience' and the former chairman, Percy Woodward, trotted out the party line when asked why Revie's wishes had been ignored. 'It's not for the manager who is leaving to invite his successor,' he pontificated, revealing how much had changed since the days when Harry Reynolds doted on his manager's every word. For a board that had lingered long in its manager's shadow, there seemed to be a determination in their pronouncements to reclaim their prerogative. Advertising the job was a gesture that proved their authority, at least to them, and emphasised that for all his achievements it was to them and not the man who had brought them wealth and prestige that the club actually belonged.

By July 10, two days after Revie's failed coup on behalf of Giles, Cussins claimed to have received almost one hundred and fifty applications for the post. Within a week he had a shortlist of four, not all of whom had actually applied: Ipswich Town's Bobby Robson, Bolton Wanderers' Jimmy Armfield, Motherwell's Ian St John and, most intriguingly of all, Brighton's Brian Clough. The Ipswich chairman made it clear that Robson would honour his contract at Portman Road, forcing Leeds to back off, and they did not get round to talking to Armfield until two months later. They did, however, interview St John. After his meeting with the board at the service station at Scotch Corner, the former Liverpool striker was informed by Jock Stein, who had rung up a Leeds director to recommend him, that 'my man says everything went great and the job will be yours'.

St John, however, knew that the recruitment panel still had Clough to meet. Thanks to the *Yorkshire Evening Post*, the Leeds public did too and one supporter was determined to stop Revie's biggest bugbear from getting his job. George Hindle organised an anti-Clough petition and got 400 signatures on only his first night canvassing in the Merrion Centre. The paper's weekly postbag also measured the scale of the opposition and was divided six letters to one against the former Derby manager's appointment. 'I would have thought that Clough's dislike of Leeds United and particularly the present players has been made pretty obvious,' wrote Mr H. Adams, 'and the Leeds board must have very short memories if they can overlook this fact.' Tellingly, though, in the same edition came Bob Roberts' opinion that the naysayers could go and hang. 'There are times when you can wipe the slate clean,' he said. The board's bloody-mindedness in the face of the outrage they had provoked and their desire openly to demonstrate their independence would cost them a fortune, not to mention their dignity.

When Manny Cussins telephoned Brian Clough in his Mallorca retreat at Cala Millor and asked him about his availability, the chairman knew he was speaking to the club's biggest critic. During the past two years Clough had said United's poor disciplinary record warranted automatic relegation, accused Bremner of tyrannising referees and provoked a walk-out at the Queen's Hotel's Yorksport annual dinner by beginning his toast to the guest of honour with the self-satisfied smile and rudeness of the self-styled iconoclast. 'In spite of the fact that Peter Lorimer falls when he hasn't been kicked and protests when he has nothing to protest about . . . ' was as far as he got before being deluged by boos.

Revie's friend Shankly had a better way of handling Clough's bombast. 'You've got more chance with the rain,' the Liverpool manager wryly said of him. 'At least it stops now and again.' But Clough's needling about Leeds got under Revie's skin and his response to the allegations emanating from Clough's office at the Baseball Ground was uncharacteristically sarcastic for someone who was normally so guarded in his public pronouncements. 'We all know that Clough can walk on water,' he snapped. 'I think it is time he shut his mouth.' One of Revie's later superstitions was standing in his overcoat in front of the dressing room mirror manically combing his hair to ward off bad luck. It left him impeccably groomed but could not prevent his bitter adversary from occupying his own office within eighteen months of demanding Leeds's demotion.

Clough and his assistant, Peter Taylor, had resigned from Derby in October 1973 and joined Brighton after a month-long campaign for their reinstatement had petered out when his successor and former captain, Dave Mackay, refused to be browbeaten into clearing the way for their return. They spent eight months at the Goldstone Ground, endured humiliation in the FA Cup when thrashed by non-League Walton and Hersham 4-0 and ended the season in nineteenth place precisely two years after winning the title. The Leeds board wanted a manager who would not be intimidated by the challenge of handling the league champions nor by the precedent Revie had set. It is also fair to say they thought they were being clever and were chuffed with themselves that they had caught everyone off guard with their unorthodox choice. In Clough and Taylor they felt they had found a pair with the pedigree to win the European Cup, charm the media, gradually overhaul the squad and build attendances. It would also help to establish the club, their property, in its own right and stop the perception that they were the somewhat jammy benefactors of Revie's genius.

Clough's desire for the job was obvious. He felt isolated on the south coast and had lost the patience to work with journeymen players. In January 1974 he had missed matches to go to Madison Square Garden for the second Ali-Frazier fight and had spent most of February in Derbyshire knocking on doors for his friend, the Labour MP Philip Whitehead, before the year's first general election. When Cussins offered him the possibility of escaping the Third Division and the south of England for good, he took the first available flight out of Mallorca to meet him.

The talks in a Hove hotel went well save for one major stumbling block – Taylor, whose insecurity about his status had sparked the conflict that cost them their jobs at Derby, was going to stay and manage Brighton, the position he'd been filling in all but name ever since they got there. Cussins and Roberts, who were expecting to recruit a management partnership that had only ever operated together in the professional game, were never given the chance to air their concerns that the deal had changed. Clough pre-empted any wavering by marching out of the room at 2 am and, on the basis of a verbal offer to him and his erstwhile No 2, announced to the journalists, who he had already tipped-off to turn up: 'Gentlemen. I've just been appointed the manager of Leeds United.' He may well have got the job anyway, but he stitched them up, daring them to contradict him in front of the press, rather than taking the chance.

If Cussins smiled for the cameras more ruefully than joyfully after being mugged by Clough's smart manoeuvre, he masked his unease well in extravagant endorsements. 'Despite the unfortunate publicity he gets, he is a first-class manager,' the chairman said. 'I'm certain United's players and fans will soon take to him. Although his contract is for four years, I hope he will stay with us for life.' Clough's elation was evident from his face and he struck the perfect tone, even offering a disingenuous but diplomatic tribute to the man he had enjoyed baiting for the past four years as well as an olive branch to the fans. 'I regard supporters as the backbone of any club,' he said. 'My aim will be to win the friendship and respect of all those who backed United under my predecessor – a man I regard as a first-class bloke by the way – and to attract more recruits.' Mike Bamber, the Brighton chairman, was furious with the way Leeds had enticed away his manager and seemingly announced his defection without agreeing a settlement. He immediately threatened to sue. His former employer's recompense, quipped Clough as he left the press conference, came in the form of Taylor, who was staying behind. It was a compensation package that proved too dear for both Clough and Cussins.

Although the Leeds players had been back in pre-season training for almost a fortnight on the day of his appointment, Clough drove from Hove to Heathrow to catch a flight back to Mallorca to rejoin his family for the last week of their summer holiday. When he finally turned up at Elland Road, nine days after accepting the job, he was too late to attend the annual pre-season party for the players, their partners, the board and the entire staff. Lateness was to become the norm and, though he cited the traffic on the M1 between his home near Derby and United's training ground in Fullerton Park as the reason, directors and journalists turned a blind eye to the blatantly false excuse, knowing full well he spent most nights in the Dragonara hotel, a mere three miles from his office.

On his first day Clough turned up with his two sons, Simon and Nigel, following his own advice to former Derby midfielder Alan Durban on how to deal with hostile situations. 'When you're in trouble,' he said, 'bring your children along to the meeting.' Even his most implacable opponents, he surmised, would be intimidated by the thought of upsetting such charming and bonny 'bairns'. He need not have bothered – the Leeds players were never going to garland him as he stepped out of his Mercedes on Monday 31 July 1974 but they were not naïve enough to confront him or, indeed, not to give him a chance.

He kept his distance for the first few days, letting Jimmy Gordon, the Scot he had brought from Derby to replace Les Cocker, take the training. He also gave the impression in his pronouncements that his departure from Derby had profoundly changed him. The abrasive and witty Clough of old was replaced, at least in public, by a humble and wary figure. 'How do you improve on Don Revie's record?' he pondered. 'This is the nightmare I am living with. I will try to do better, try to win the League again, try to win a cup.' Asked if he envisaged a change of style, he said: 'Leeds have been restricted by their intense approach in the past, I feel. If a flower has nothing but water it dies, if it has only sunshine, it withers. It has got to have a combination of both to bring it to full bloom.' So far, so good and the United players responded in kind with Hunter saying the club had pulled together with the players giving 100 per cent to Clough while Lorimer emphasised, 'there is no doubt he is a very good manager'.

During the first week a few grumbles were heard about the lack of focus and discipline at training but it didn't show in their first friendly, a 3-1 victory over Huddersfield at Leeds Road on the Thursday. However, the following day, Clough, who had limited himself to the odd word on the Fullerton Park pitch, decided it was time to address the squad en masse. His behaviour that morning and conduct over the following forty days were so extraordinary, several theories on his 44-day reign have since emerged. To his admirers he is an honest man whose fearless character forced him to speak the truth about a cynical and morally corrupt organisation despite the risk of redundancy. Many others think it was just a simple culture clash between a bumptious outsider and some rather precious players. To those less enamoured of him, however, it looks at times like an elaborate joke, the work of a kamikaze manager embarked on a demented project of self-driven constructive dismissal.

Of all the psychological weapons in Clough's armoury, rudeness was the most overworked. At times he perfectly fitted the stereotype of the 'I say what I like and like what I bloody well say' strident Yorkshire-man delivering impertinent tripe with self-congratulation plastered across his face. His speech to his assembled squad on the fifth day of his tenure combined the diplomacy of Harvey Smith and Chubby Brown with the unassuming traits of Naseem Hamed and Jeremy Clarkson. Until this point the players' grievances might have been shrugged off as essentially trivial. There had been murmurings about his timekeeping and the odd suggestion that the pace of training had slackened. The insults that had been tossed their way over the past four years could be excused as the new manager's famous chutzpah, and even Clough's insistence on throwing away Revie's office furniture was greeted with more bemusement than annoyance. They may even have been prepared to forgive him for the things he had said, but now they found that he was unwilling to forgive them for the things they had done. On the Friday morning Clough called a team meeting where, without Peter Taylor's discretion and diplomacy to restrain him, he committed professional suicide.

'You might have been wondering why I haven't said a lot this week,' was his opening remark. 'The reason is that I have been forming my own opinions.' He then proceeded to rattle a few of these 'opinions' off. To Norman Hunter, he said: 'You've got a terrible reputation in the game and I know you'd like to be liked.' Hunter looked him square in the eye and responded in kind: 'I couldn't give a fuck.' He then moved on to Lorimer, the king of 'making a meal' of tackles and Giles, 'another with a bad reputation'. Following Hunter's lead, they robustly stood up for themselves, pointing out the amount of fouls Clough's Derby players had committed against them.

He then paused to praise Gordon McQueen and Allan Clarke before rounding on his final target, the popular Eddie Gray. The winger's long-standing thigh injury had restricted him to only sixty-seven league appearances over the past four seasons, which prompted Clough to say: 'If you were a racehorse you would have been shot years ago.' Instead of crediting him for his tenacity in fighting back so many times, Clough, a man whose own career had been truncated by injury, waded in with a flippant quip on a sensitive subject and consequently offended Gray and most of his team-mates.

He saved his catch-all condemnation till the end. 'I might as well tell you now,' he said, as if there had been much room for misinterpretation. 'You may have won all the domestic honours and some European honours, but as far as I am concerned you can all throw every one of your medals in the bin. You never won any of them fairly.' With that he was gone, back up to his office with the brand new furniture and new secretary, Maureen Holdsworth, he had insisted on. It was to become his haven for the next five weeks even if, somewhat ominously, his nameplate kept falling off the door despite several attempts by the club's handyman to glue it back in place.

Clough had a week after his outburst to prepare the team for the Charity Shield against Liverpool, a week that passed without further explosions. However, his lack of punctuality and habit of making the players wait around until he was ready to train continued to rankle and probably inspired more of the kicks he received during training than the memory of the previous Friday's tirade. Discussions about squad strengthening continued with Cussins, but the price of his principal target, Leicester's Peter Shilton, frightened the board, who were aware of the popularity of the incumbent, David Harvey, and were still labouring under the traditional English prejudice that goalkeepers were not worth huge fees. Shilton moved to Stoke instead for £325,000 and Clough had to settle with the £250,000 the board gave board gave him to spend on Nottingham Forest's mercurial forward Duncan McKenzie.

After a meeting at a Sheffield hotel where McKenzie was greeted by the sight of his new manager walking towards him with a cigar clenched between his teeth and a bottle of champagne under each arm, the enigmatic striker became Leeds' record purchase. A few days after signing his contract, Clough made contact again, this time asking him to be his eyes and ears in the dressing room. McKenzie, only the club's second ever six-figure signing and faced with the prospect of trying to become the first outsider immediately to make it as a first-team regular since Allan Clarke four years previously, thought his mission already daunting enough and turned Clough down.

Previewing the Wembley match, Hugh McIlvanney interpreted the significance of the signing of McKenzie for those who were new to Clough's approach. 'His opening flourish of spending,' he wrote, 'has not surprised those who know him well, for it was obvious he could not come in behind Don Revie without announcing by the most tangible means that the firm was very definitely under new management.' Striding out of the tunnel two paces respectfully behind the departing Bill Shankly, leading the team he had denounced for 'violent behaviour, both physical and verbal', symbolised, Clough hoped, that decisive break with the past. The match itself, however, usually the season's prologue with little to recommend it, became synonymous with what the *Observer's* Julie Welch called 'a horrifying sustained period of aggression'. Leeds having hauled themselves back into the game with Trevor Cherry's equaliser in the second half, the scoreline was overshadowed by a fight between Billy Bremner and Kevin Keegan which only ended when both were sent off.

It had been a niggly game throughout, with both Liverpool's Tommy Smith and United's Giles being booked. When Keegan obstructed Bremner, who was trying to take a quick free-kick, the Leeds captain kicked him and subsequently found himself on the receiving end of the Liverpool forward's fist. Their team-mates soon piled in, with Lorimer grabbing Bremner and pulling him away, but both protagonists continued to argue while the referee was in the process of booking them and he lost his patience and instead sent the pair off. They were the first British players ever to be dismissed at Wembley and if that was not disgrace enough they stripped off their shirts on the walk to the tunnel and threw them on the ground. Liverpool went on to win on penalties, but both sides lost by having their best players suspended for a mandatory three games, which was extended by eight more when the disciplinary panel met. Consequently, it was one of only two matches that Bremner, Revie's talisman, played for his successor and far from signalling a new dawn, in Clough's mind it epitomised the team's spiteful nature. Two years earlier he had said he 'despised what they stood for'; now it was his job to transform them and rebuild Leeds to reflect his own ideals. The only way he could do this was by changing the way they were perceived while they continued to win things. Without results, though, he did not stand a chance.

The League champions began their season against Stoke, the team that had ended their 29-match unbeaten run back in February, and again Leeds were smashed in the Potteries, this time 3-0. It was the first of six League games for Clough, a run that left them with only one win and two draws. Considering they had won the opening seven games of the previous season, the contrast was pretty stark. It was fair to say that Leeds had probably declined in a year but even those who thought Revie had left the team at the right time had to take into account that he had won four and drawn two of his last six games in charge, only three months before Clough took over.

Bremner's absence through suspension did not help and neither did Clough's failure to persuade the Peter Taylor to jack in his job at Brighton and come to his rescue. With only Allan Clarke, whom he continued to praise to the hilt, as his ally he was desperate for familiar faces and made a successful £130,000 bid to Derby for John McGovern and John O'Hare, two mainstays of his 1971-72 title-winning side. According to legend the two were thought sub-standard and ostracised on their arrival in the dressing room, but not according to Duncan McKenzie's account. 'No one ever thought for a moment that Brian Clough had bought two scrubbers,' he said. 'They were accepted and recognised as top-class professionals.' Clough, however, had spent

£380,000 in 10 days, more than Revie had spent in his last ten years at the club, and needed his signings to have an immediate impact.

He got his first victory in his third League match, a 1-0 victory against Birmingham with O'Hare and McGovern in the starting XI, but it was earned in front of a crowd of only 30,820. A defeat and a draw followed and by the time they played Luton on 7 September, they were in 18th place and the attendance had dwindled to 26,450. Sadly, the match took place only three days after the co-architect of Leeds's rise, Harry Reynolds, had collapsed and died during a reserve game and, though the players wore black armbands in his memory, they couldn't pay tribute by winning. The game, a 1-1 draw, was marred by the fans' barracking of McGovern, who was unfortunate to be wearing the suspended Bremner's shirt. The Scot would go on to have the last laugh by winning the European Cup twice with Nottingham Forest but his style as the ultimate unobtrusive link-player, or 'water carrier' as they subsequently became known, contrasted so conspicuously with Bremner's all-round dynamism that he became a convenient crowd scapegoat. Afterwards Clough, himself a recipient of the bird, said: 'It was the first time I had felt ashamed to be a Yorkshireman.'

He still claimed to have the full backing of the players, saying 'I have never been so convinced of anything in my life as that', but he said the spectre of Don Revie still loomed large over his squad. 'Every time I go through the dressing room door the players are expecting him to walk in not me,' he lamented. 'He is certainly not going to be forgotten in four or five weeks. It will take months and months to forget him.' Clough couldn't quite see that the club and its players were so entwined with his predecessor, his values and achievements, that forgetting him was inconceivable.

Getting rid of a few of Revie's players might have given him greater scope to impose his thinking on them but so many of them had come into the first team at roughly the same time back in the mid-sixties that the club had lumbered itself with a huge backlog of forthcoming testimonials. Offloading them before their payday was proving tricky to engineer. Twice he thought Giles might leave, either as Huddersfield's assistant manager or as Tottenham's manager, but the midfielder was enjoying playing too much to abandon Leeds's quest for the European Cup and wanted the benefit game to which he was entitled. Shortly after the Luton draw Clough struck a deal with Forest to sell Terry Cooper, the England left-back who had played only four games in more than two years after breaking his leg. 'I have little choice but to leave,' Cooper said. 'Brian Clough has declared his hand in my case. What is the point in staying at a club when it is apparent you are not wanted.' Unfortunately for Clough, Cooper was still wanted, at least by the board, who used the fact that they had not been informed that his sale had been agreed as a catalyst to address United's travails. At a board meeting on the Monday night, panicked by low crowds, the hostility of the fans and by the club's lack of direction, they decided to act. But they wanted someone else to do their dirty work for them.

Cussins and his vice-chairman called a meeting with the players and Clough, ostensibly to get to the bottom of why the champions had fallen so far. 'Why are things going wrong?' he asked. After some debate, the taciturn Paul Madeley, the least likely of assassins, stood up and said to Clough: 'I just don't think you can manage.' It gave Sam Bolton, the vice-chairman, who had opposed hiring Clough, the ammunition he was looking for. 'I told you we should have never hired this man,' he said to Cussins as the meeting broke up. That night Leeds drew with Third Division Huddersfield Town in the League Cup, a draw only achieved by an 89th minute goal from Peter Lorimer, and on the bus home the chairman invited the manager back to his house for a drink. What was discussed in Alwoodley that night has never been revealed but the following afternoon the *Yorkshire Evening Post* reported that a 'vote of no confidence' from the players had left Clough's job 'hanging by a thread'. He was sacked the next day.

Speculation about the cause of his dismissal was rife but the most cited reasons were his semi-detached approach to training, his failure to explain coherently what he expected tactically and keeping his transfer business secret from the board. When Clough left Elland Road on September 12, with a pay-off of £100,000 and his club Mercedes, he grinned for the photographers and let Cussins hang himself with his words. 'What has been done is for the good of the club,' the chairman said. 'The club and the happiness of the players must come first. Nothing can be successful unless the staff is happy.' Clough walked away with the reflection that what had happened 'was a very sad day for Leeds and for football', hinting that player power had caused his demise. Cussins refused to elaborate further and made for his Rolls Royce, saying: 'We've been spoilt by Don Revie.'

Pinpointing the blame is easy in this case. It rests on the one hand with the board, for hiring him in the first place and then professing shock when he acted entirely predictably, at least according to his own previous actions and pronouncements, and on the other with Clough himself, for his graceless impetuosity and lack of commonsense. The one person who can be exonerated is Don Revie, the ghost who bedevilled Clough's mind. He intervened with neither players nor directors to sack the man who was now steering the club he had built off the edge of a cliff. Not that Clough was going to let him off the hook.

Austin Mitchell, the co-host with Richard Whiteley of Yorkshire Television's local news programme Calendar and a self-professed Leeds fan, invited Clough and Revie on to the show to discuss the 'Elland Road crisis'. In a tour de force performance, Clough rattled Revie, forcing the England manager to look brooding and saturnine while his successor sparkled. In the allotted time they argued over the tiniest details – Terry Yorath's 'enteritis', how many players contracts were up for renewal and whether Frankie Gray could play up front, for example – but Clough kept scoring points with well-aimed barbs at Revie's record. They even got into a strange bout of one-upmanship over who was, literally, the most hands-on with the players after Revie ridiculed Clough's decision not to have a team meeting on his first day in charge.

Clough: 'Talk to them? I took the shirts off their backs after they'd finished training.'
Revie: 'I used to do that and massage them on Thursday.'
Clough: 'Well that was my approach too, of course.'

Revie looked increasingly uncomfortable the more Clough relaxed into his old self, and was made to look rather silly when saying 'no, no, no' to counter Clough's statement that his ambition had been to win the League 'better' than Revie, by losing only three games instead of four. 'There is no way to win it better,' Revie glowered. It is a remarkable piece of television but one that should never have happened. Whatever possessed the England manager to parade his hyper-sensitivity to criticism and allow his greatest detractor to expose his vulnerability is beyond comprehension. He had maintained all along that what happened at Leeds now was nothing to do with him but, it seems, he could not resist fighting an old enemy one more time. Whatever Revie had won in the past, even his greatest admirers would concede that Clough, who was far more nimble with words, gave him a pasting on television. It wasn't the last time that Revie would look mournful in a camera's glare.

Even when he sacked him Cussins had declared that Clough was 'the best manager in the League outside Don Revie'. Now, presumably, as Clough quipped, that left Leeds chasing the third-best manager in the country. It wasn't to be Johnny Giles, who was offered the job by a board split three votes to two in his favour. Learning of the opposition of Bob Roberts and Percy Woodward, he said: 'The board do not appear to be united and I don't want any bad feeling to spread.' Meanwhile United won two and drew two with the caretaker Maurice Lindley in charge before settling on a successor, Bolton's Jimmy Armfield. The former England captain said the Leeds panel who came to offer him the job 'were four men in a flap', and that he was in two minds whether to accept until he received an invitation from Don Revie to go for a chat.

'All you have to do with those players,' Revie said, 'is send them out on the field. They'll do the rest. You'll be able to sit in the stand and pick up your bonus. They're the best players in the country.' His endorsement worked and Armfield took the job, thrillingly almost proving that the players were still capable of a glorious swan song, not just by being the best players in the country, but in Europe as well. In the League Armfield's light touch and Bremner's return on November 9 after injury and suspension galvanised them and they won five of the captain's first seven games back to take them well clear of relegation danger. The skipper had missed the first round of the European Cup, a 5-3 aggregate victory over FC Zurich, when Lindley was minding the shop. He was also absent for Armfield's debut in the competition, the second-round first leg 2-1 defeat of Ujpesti Dozsa in Budapest, but he made a scoring return in the 3-0 home leg victory and proceeded to stamp his mark on the tournament with a series of inspirational performances full of industry and brio.

With Clough gone and Bremner back, Leeds rallied to such an extent that they finished in ninth place in the League, only eight points behind the champions Derby County. Instructively for those who say the side was on its last legs when Revie left and saved themselves for Europe, they had been seven points behind the leaders after six games when Clough was sacked. Had they started the season better, back-to-back titles were not out of the question. They survived humiliation in the FA Cup after drawing with non-League Wimbledon when Dickie Guy saved Peter Lorimer's penalty, Richard Stilgoe celebrating the feat in a song on Nationwide which mildly took the piss out of Leeds' decline. But they won the replay and were only knocked out in the quarter-finals after enduring three replays with Ipswich Town. By that point they were already in the European Cup semi-final, having beaten Anderlecht home and away in the preceding round.

The first leg against the Belgians took place at Elland Road in swirling fog. It was was thick enough to leave the South Stand fans imploring the Kop to tell them what was happening whenever Leeds attacked at that end, and at several points visibility was so low the match could and probably should have been abandoned. Even the press box lost sight of the players – like 'ancient armies lost in cannon smoke,' wrote David Lacey. The clearest picture came on television and there it was plain to see how Bremner and Giles combined magnificently to open up Anderlecht's flanks and provide a series of centres for Joe Jordan and Gordon McQueen to exploit. Both Scots scored, as did Lorimer, and Bremner went on to win the away leg 1-0 with an impudent chip. Small wonder Leeds fans often supported Scotland and that the club attracted so many supporters from north of the border.

Before United's European Cup semi-final against Barcelona, the League and FA fell back on their established practices and refused to help the club's preparations, forcing them to play six matches in twelve days. For once, however, this didn't have its customary effect. The Catalans had not conceded a goal in the competition to date but Bremner soon rectified that, scoring with a forceful drive in the ninth minute. Paul Madeley, playing at the heart of defence in the absence of Hunter, matched Johan Cruyff stride for stride around Elland Road and Leeds created several decent chances in the first half for McQueen and Allan Clarke but could not extend their lead. When Juan Manuel Asensi equalised with twenty-five minutes to go, Leeds looked spent but then Paul Reaney, of all people, grabbed the game by the scruff of its neck, went on a marauding run and crossed for Jordan to tee-up Clarke to score the winner.

Another early goal in the return leg at the Camp Nou, this time from Lorimer after eight minutes, gave Leeds a two-goal cushion which they fought skilfully and doggedly to protect for more than an hour. There was some alarm when Barcelona got one back, multiplied almost immediately by a foul from McQueen who was sent off after whacking the home side's scorer, Clares so forcibly that he was knocked out cold for almost a minute. Once again Leeds had Billy Bremner to thank for delivering them from danger when he ran behind the reserve goalkeeper David Stewart to kick a shot from Johan Neeskens off the line with only two minutes of the game to go. The reward for his tireless endeavour was to lead the team he had so relentlessly driven on into their first and only European Cup final.

Oddly Leeds had twenty-eight days rest between their sixty-fourth match of the season, the last of the League campaign and the sixty-fifth, the European Cup final in Paris. Armfield, whom David Lacey praised for 'his calming influence on the disturbed Leeds psyche following the Clough cataclysm', arranged four friendlies over the month to keep the players in shape. Ten years on from their European bow in 1965, more than half the team from their first ever tie against Torino a decade ago – Reaney, Bremner, Madeley, Hunter, Lorimer and Giles – walked out at the Parc des Princes for the biggest game in the club's history. The man leading Leeds and the reigning champions, Bayern Munich, out on to the pitch that evening was also a familiar face. The French official Michel Kitabdjian, who had refereed the Elland Road European Cup semi-final leg against Celtic in 1970, escorted Bremner and Franz Beckenbauer to the touchline by the dignitaries' box. His presence was not a happy omen.

Leeds, cheered on by Revie who was alongside David Coleman in the BBC's commentary box, dominated the match for an hour, putting on a performance full of aggressive, fluent and incisive football that put Bayern Munich, who finished only tenth in the Bundesliga, on the back foot. The only favour Kitabdjian did Leeds was to allow Terry Yorath to stay on the field after his brutal foul on Bjorn Andersson which saw the Swede stretchered off. In the first-half alone Kitabdjian turned down two penalty appeals, the first for a Beckenbauer hand-ball, the second when the Bayern captain slid in, missed the ball and wrapped both legs around Allan Clarke. In his autobiography even Beckenbauer concedes that the tackle should have been a penalty but he applauded the referee on the night.

In the second-half, with Leeds having had six attempts on goal to Bayern Munich's none, United put the ball into the net for what appeared to be the opening goal. The free-kick, quickly taken by Giles found the unmarked Madeley who headed it back into the centre of the penalty box where it was cleared to Peter Lorimer who blasted the volley past Sepp Maier. The Leeds players all ran off to celebrate and Bayern, apart from Beckenbauer, trudged off for the restart. The Bayern captain stood at the back and put his right arm up almost as an afterthought which prompted Kitabdjian to consult the linesman, already back at the half-way line for the kick-off. He then blew his whistle and awarded a free-kick against Bremner for offside.

If Bremner was offside it was marginal and it is debatable whether he was interfering with play. The decision only added to the fury of the Leeds players and supporters. Even before Bayern had picked Leeds off on the counter-attack to score twice to win the match a section of the United support behind Maier's goal had begun to tear out the plastic seats and rain them down on the French riot police mustered below.

One Leeds fan managed to get over the moat at the bottom of the terraces and scaled the wire fence to get a run at the pitch. He was swiftly tackled by stewards, and in the charged atmosphere their kicking of him only riled the Leeds fans further. The rioting escalated beyond the final whistle and got so out of hand that Bobby Collins, the club's former captain, was head-butted outside the ground by a Leeds fan fooled by his vaguely Teutonic appearance.

The feeling that Leeds were robbed persists to this day and the club's fans can still be heard to sing 'We are the champions, champions of Europe!' at every match, in recognition of what had been denied to them. Even the mild-mannered Armfield said afterwards: 'I felt exactly as I did when our home was burgled.' Two years after losing the FA Cup to Sunderland the press wrote the team's epitaph: 'let down by their old failings of missing chances and losing their nerve when it really mattered, this was a re-run of all the bold failures.' It was a harsh assessment given the referee's handling of the game but they were right in a sense. This was the end of Revie's team – Giles would leave that summer, Bremner and Hunter a year later. And, with a four-year European ban imposed on them for their fans' behaviour, it was the end of Leeds as a European force, a spectacular Champions League run under David O'Leary notwithstanding.

After the match Revie left the BBC commentary box to offer words of consolation to his former charges, knowing full well that the revolution he had initiated at the Vetch Field in September 1962, when he gave Gary Sprake, Paul Reaney, Norman Hunter and Rod Johnson their debuts, had finally run its course. The family was about to leave home.

Don Revie had yet to make his debut as England manager by the time Brian Clough was sacked by Leeds and he got off to a pretty decent start, winning six and drawing three of the nine matches of his first year in charge. He tried to impose his influence on the squad – in came the dossiers and bingo games – and also on the fans by encouraging them to sing 'Land of Hope and Glory' before internationals, however both initiatives failed. The 'family spirit' did not translate to the national team and many of the players found themselves sniggering at the manager's hopelessly naff and anachronistic attempts to replicate the bonding he had orchestrated at Elland Road.

The predominant features of his reign were his thin skin whenever criticised and a selection policy that was recklessly catholic. 'With Alf Ramsey it was more difficult to get out of his side than in, but it was completely different with Don Revie,' his first captain, Alan Ball said. One of his biggest problems was his relationship with Sir Harold Thompson, the pompous vice-chairman of the Football Association who took over as chairman in 1976. At an official dinner, when Revie and Elsie were sat next to Thompson, the England manager objected to Sir Harold's habit of referring to him by his surname. 'When I get to know you better Revie, I shall call you Don,' the Oxford professor snottily said. Revie, in a brilliant but career-damaging reply, said: 'When I get to know you better Thompson, I shall call you Sir Harold.' Revie was England manager for three years, a job he quickly came to hate. Feeling the heat of public opinion following the defeat to Italy in 1976 which made qualification for the 1978 World Cup look remote, he began looking for a way out and found it when he was approached by the United Arab Emirates Football Association to take over as national coach. Initially he turned it down but when Italy beat Finland and made England's chances of World Cup qualification even more unlikely, he boarded a plane to Dubai to discuss the matter further. After flying out to South America to finish England's summer tour, he asked the FA to pay up his contract on the grounds that they had been lining up Bobby Robson to replace him. When they refused he contacted the *Daily Mail*, sold them the story of his resignation and boarded a plane to the Middle East.

'The day I took the job,' he wrote, 'I was excited by the prospect of having the pick of the country. But I'd been spoiled for choice at Leeds and I realised there are no more around like Billy Bremner and Johnny Giles. As soon as it dawned on me that we were short of players who combined skill and commitment I should have forgotten all about trying to play more controlled attractive football and settled for a real bastard of a team.' In his parting shot he could not resist mentioning the two players closest to his heart and mourn how the whole of

England could not match his favoured sons.

His escape from Lancaster Gate, and decision to fight the ten-year ban from English football a vengeful Thompson had imposed upon him, gave the green light to his detractors, and they soon began to rake over all the stories about match-fixing. Stories from the title-decider against Wolverhampton Wanderers in 1972 when he and Bremner were accused of trying to bribe the Wolves players were aired and, though Bremner won £100,000 in libel damages from the Sunday People in 1982 when they were reprinted, the smear continued to tarnish both men's reputations. Others, including Frank McLintock, have echoed the allegations that Revie made them an offer 'to take it easy' when playing against Leeds, but to date, even in the wake of Revie's death, irrefutable evidence is still yet to emerge

In November 1979 Don Revie returned to Britain to fight his ban from English football in the High Court. His barrister, Gilbert Gray QC, easily demolished Sir Harold Thompson's case. 'Sir Harold, he said, 'in his own court was effectively prosecutor, witness, judge and jury.' Calling the FA's punishment of Revie a restraint of trade, Gray damned the governing body's in-house disciplinary tribunal as 'a more tightly closed shop than a trade union could devise.' Mr Justice Cantley upheld Revie's appeal under the Right to Work Act and cited legal precedent to dismiss the FA's penalty as unfair. Revie's victory, however, had a hollow ring and the judge took the opportunity after announcing his verdict to condemn the former England manager's behaviour. 'He presented to the public a sensational and notorious example of disloyalty, breach of duty, discourtesy and selfishness,' Mr Cantley said. Revie had won in principle but the stigma dogged him for the rest of his life. He never worked in English football again. Don Revie's Middle Eastern exile continued until 1984 when he returned to Britain and embraced retirement.

The decision to take the England job had proven an ignominious move for all parties, Don Revie, the Football Association and, above all, Leeds United – hardly a fitting end to such an exceptional project.More and more as Revie returned to Elland Road in the mid-80s in his consultancy role, it might have seemed as if he had never been there. The club, once again, teetering towards insolvency with a team of has-beens and never-would-bes in a half-empty, dilapidated stadium, had come full circle – back to the brink of relegation to the Third Division. Only he had had the drive to get them out of it the first time. Ultimately, it would take decades, sixteen managers and hundreds of millions of pounds to leave the club in a lower division than the one he found it in and with only one more major trophy in the Elland Road display case than on the day he left – the truest measure of the man and what he had achieved.

POSTSCRIPT

IN THE END

I n the midst of a happy retirement, in 1987 at the age of fifty-nine, far away from the stress of the press vilification that had dogged him for ten years, Don Revie was diagnosed with Motor Neurone Disease. Boldly, he re-emerged from his exile in Scotland to campaign for funds to promote research into his terminal condition. He elicited much help, sympathy and respect from a host of former colleagues, from a handful of his international players (most notably Kevin Keegan), from his remaining allies in the press and even from those who had been his most disparaging critics. Naturally enough, however, he found the greatest support from those who had never abandoned him – from the players, staff and fans of Leeds United.

In 1988, now shockingly frail and confined to a wheelchair, Don Revie made his final appearance at Elland Road. Received onto the pitch by a guard of honour comprising every one of his 'sons' (save for the uninvited pariah, Gary Sprake), he watched the testimonial match arranged by the club to raise funds for research into the disease with a fierce pride and, he admitted, not a few tears. As he took his leave of them, his players seemed upbeat if a little mannered, and, once he had left the ground, the whole day took on an elegiac tone, with each of his 'boys', one by one, giving the media the soundbites they so craved. It wasn't a day for profound reflection: everyone said essentially the same thing – he was a great manager and, more importantly, a great man.

Unsurprisingly, it was left to Billy Bremner to come up with the phrase to sum up his mentor. 'He is Leeds United,' he said simply. The words may sound a little glib now, but that tribute remains the most apt epitaph. Moreover, even more than ten years since his death it's still correct to employ the present tense. The whole club is built on and continues to reflect Don Revie's personality and career. That sustained success, tantalizingly elusive on so many occasions, never definitively achieved, has given the club and its supporters, these authors included, a certain manic edge, not lacking in confidence as such, but distinctly prone to chippy cynicism and bouts of despair. It is also, of course, a reflection of how far the club travelled so quickly, from nothing to glory and back again in twenty years, from clogs to clogs in three generations, as the Yorkshire analogy succinctly puts it. Similarly, the true Revie dilemma – does bad luck cause insecurity and pessimism, or is it the other way round? – has turned most Leeds fans into magnificently obsessive conspiracy theorists. To this day they are distrustful of the FA and always quick to decipher any hint of anti-Leeds bias in the media, a bias that many are convinced stems from a lingering distaste of Revie and his team.

So just how good were Revie's Leeds? The best club side to have emerged up to that point in English football history? It is possible to make such a case, based on their sheer resilience and the consistency of their performances and results for ten years. Perhaps the last word should go to David Miller, so often one of their most scornful critics. In March 1988 Liverpool's dominance of the domestic game was at its zenith. They had equalled United's record of twenty-nine matches unbeaten from the start of the season, and would have beaten it with a victory over Everton. To the immense satisfaction of Leeds supporters, they failed. That Allan Clarke's brother scored the goal that defeated them would have put an ironic smile on Revie's face, too. In the run-up to that Merseyside derby Miller pondered on which was the better side – and he chose Leeds. 'Leeds were a far better team than they allowed themselves to appear,' he wrote. 'This was at least partially because of the marvellous efficiency of their game, comparable to Liverpool's, was undermined by that undercurrent of almost neurotic caution emanating from their manager. If the two teams were to meet, Leeds would win – but that's what most people said before they played Sunderland.' As ever with Miller, there is a back-handed compliment to go with the garland, but it's one which still grants Revie and his team their hard-fought place at the pinnacle of the domestic game.

Don Revie died on 26 May 1989, a victim of his terrible disease. His funeral service at Warriston Crematorium, on the outskirts of Edinburgh, was a simple affair at which both his families were present. Their former boss had ordered them 'to have a few drinks on me'. Thousands had lined the route of the funeral procession of his great friend Bill Shankly. At Warriston just a few hundred were present. No one attended from English football's governing bodies.

ACKNOWLEDGEMENTS

ithout the contribution of so many people, it is doubtful that this book would ever have reached publication. First and foremost we must thank Graham Coster, our editor, for his patience, guidance and expertise.

Secondly, Malcolm Rogerson's many hours of research in Leeds Central Library proved invaluable, as was Andrew Bagchi's fervent grasp of Leeds United's history.

David Luxton's enthusiasm for the project not only contributed the title but also spurred the authors on when stuck down numerous cul-de-sacs. Heartfelt thanks must also go to John Gaustad, without whom the whole idea might never have left the pub, and to James Brown and Neil Jeffries at IFG, who helped get the book moving in its earliest days.

We are extremely grateful to Ben Clissitt, who asked the difficult questions and managed to put us in touch with the right people, and to Richard Lewis, Matt Mankelow, Liam Doyle and Chris Bradshaw for their intelligent and often provocative suggestions.

Thanks to Eddie Gray (and his remarkable secretary Karen Bouldy) for agreeing to speak to us and for ironing out several flights of fancy.

Finally, thanks to the families: to Sue Rogerson, Angela and Saral Bagchi for tireless support, to Joseph Rogerson, the next generation of Leeds supporter, to Lindsey Rogerson for enduring many lost weekends and to Alison Kirby for her encouragement, optimism and the sound advice given in her role as the first critical audience for the early parts of the book.

BIBLIOGRAPHY

Bale, Bernard, *Bremner! The Legend of Billy Bremner*, André Deutsch, 1998

Brears, Peter, *Images of Leeds 1850–1960*, Breedon Books, 1992

Bremner, Billy, *You Get Nowt for Being Second*, Souvenir Press, 1969

Burt, Steven & Grady, Kevin, *The Illustrated History of Leeds*, Breedon Books, 1994

Charles, John, *The Gentle Giant*, Stanley Paul, 1962

Charlton, Jack with Byrne, Peter, *Jack Charlton: The Autobiography*, Partridge Press, 1996

Charlton, Jack, *For Leeds and England*, Stanley Paul, 1967

Clarke, Allan with Richards, Steve, *Goals Are My Business*, Pelham, 1970

Clough, Brian with Sadler, John, *Clough – The Autobiography*, Partridge Press, 1994

Dunphy, Eamonn, *A Strange Kind of Glory: Sir Matt Busby and Manchester United*, William Heinemann, 1991

Giles, Johnny, as told to Tomas, Jason, *Forward with Leeds*, Stanley Paul, 1970

Gray, Eddie & Tomas, Eddie, *Marching on Together – My Life with Leeds United*, Headline, 2001

Jarred, Martin & Macdonald, Malcolm, *Leeds United: A Complete Record 1919–1989*, Breedon Books, 1989

Leeds United Book of Football No. 1, Souvenir Press, 1969

Leeds United Book of Football No. 2, Souvenir Press, 1970

Macdonald, Malcolm & Jarred, Martin, *The Leeds United Story*, Breedon Books, 1992

Mourant, Andrew, *Don Revie – Portrait of a Footballing Enigma*, Mainstream, 1990

Mourant, Andrew, *Leeds United Player by Player*, Guinness 1992

Revie, Don, *Soccer's Happy Wanderer*, Museum Press 1955

Saffer, David, *Sniffer! The Life and Times of Allan Clarke*, Tempus, 2001

Warters, Don, *Leeds United: The Official History of the Club*, Wensum, 1979

INDEX

Science & Technology Library
Trafford College
Talbot Road
Stretford
Manchester
M32 0XH